THE EUROZONE CRISIS A
TRANSFORMATION OF EU GO ᴠ ᴇʀɴ ANCE

The EU is once again in transformation, experimenting with reforms of its internal and external governance in response to the Euro crisis. No one knows yet how this reform process will play out, but its consequences are sure to be momentous, not only for the EU itself, but also for the wider global order. To analyse these developments, Rodrigues and Xiarchogiannopoulou have assembled a stellar group of scholars, whose kaleidoscopic reflections will be of compelling interest to anyone concerned with the future of European governance.

Jonathan Zeitlin, University of Amsterdam, The Netherlands

Connecting the Euro crisis and EU governance issues, this book is as timely as social science volumes get!

Gerda Falkner, University of Vienna, Austria

There could be no better moment for the publication of a book like this. Europe is in deep transformation and this edited volume presents a collection of outstanding assessments of the different transformation processes that are currently on their way. The authors present a fascinating mix between the analysis of current policy debates in the context of the recent crisis and theoretical considerations related to scholarship on the European multi-level governance. The chapter selection is impressive: the strength of the volume is that it brings together scholarship at the border between politics, economics, social politics, welfare analysis, and international relations.

Henrik Enderlein, Professor of Political Economy,
Director of Jacques Delors Institut, Hertie School of Governance, Berlin

University of Edinburgh

30150   027386686

Globalisation, Europe, Multilateralism

Institutionally supported by the Institute for European Studies at the
Université libre de Bruxelles

Mario TELÒ, Series editor (mtelo@ulb.ac.be)

The Institut d'Etudes Européennes de l'Université Libre de Bruxelles (IEE-ULB) is a leading research institution, with a large global collaborative university network. As part of successful research consortia, the IEE-ULB was awarded two EU funded programmes. The first is an international multidisciplinary doctoral programme in Globalisation, Europe, Multilateralism funded by the DG Culture and Education EU Commission. Over a seven year period, this programme will fund up to 50 PhD students as well as hosting PhD school seminars on every continent. The second programme is GR:EEN (Global Reordering: Evolving European Networks), funded by DG research EU Commission. This is an integrated research project including 16 universities on five continents. The remarkable quality of these senior and junior scholars included in the project allows extensive research both in EU studies and in global governance. Volumes in this series share innovative research objectives around Globalisation, the EU's evolution within it, the changing Multilateral cooperation, and the role of transnational networks; emergent multipolarity and international order; comparative regionalism and interregionalism; EU's foreign policy and external relations.

The series includes collaborative volumes, research based monographs and textbooks with the aim of contributing to the innovation of European Integration and International studies. Every book is reviewed by an international referees process, scientific workshops discussing the first drafts, anonymous referees and advice by the International editorial board members. Other titles in the series can be found at the back of this book.

The Eurozone Crisis and the Transformation of EU Governance
Internal and External Implications

Edited by

MARIA JOÃO RODRIGUES
Université Libre de Bruxelles, Belgium

ELENI XIARCHOGIANNOPOULOU
Université Libre de Bruxelles, Belgium

Published by
Ashgate Publishing Limited
Wey Court East
Union Road
Farnham
Surrey, GU9 7PT
England

Ashgate Publishing Company
110 Cherry Street
Suite 3-1
Burlington, VT 05401-3818
USA

www.ashgate.com

British Library Cataloguing in Publication Data
A catalogue record for this book is available from the British Library

The Library of Congress has cataloged the printed edition as follows:
The Eurozone crisis and the transformation of EU governance : internal and external implications / edited by Maria João Rodrigues and Eleni Xiarchogiannopoulou.
       pages cm.—(Globalisation, Europe, multilateralism series)
   Includes bibliographical references and index.
   ISBN 978-1-4724-3307-7 (hardback)—ISBN 978-1-4724-3310-7 (pbk)—ISBN 978-1-4724-3308-4 (ebook)—978-1-4724-3309-1 (epub) 1. European Union countries—Economic conditions—21st century. 2. European Union countries—Politics and government—21st century. 3. Global Financial Crisis, 2008–2009—Political aspects—European Union countries. 4. European Union countries—Economic policy.
5. Financial crises—European Union countries. I. Rodrigues, Maria João, author, editor of compilation. II. Xiarchogiannopoulou, Eleni, author, editor of compilation.
   HC240.E895 2014
   337.1'42—dc23
                                                                                    2013045819

ISBN 9781472433077 (hbk)
ISBN 9781472433107 (pbk)
ISBN 9781472433084 (ebk – PDF)
ISBN 9781472433091 (ebk – ePUB)

Printed in the United Kingdom by Henry Ling Limited, at the Dorset Press, Dorchester, DT1 1HD

Contents

List of Figures and Tables

Figures

Tables

List of Contributors

Susana Borrás is a professor on innovation and governance. She conducts research on the interaction between governments and innovation. As a social scientist expert on public policy, two of her leading questions concern what governments can do to foster and to improve socio-technical innovation in the economy, and what makes some decisions regarding socio-technical and innovation change democratically legitimate and others not. Her comparative analyses show the importance that socially and governmentally defined institutions have on innovation performance and on democratic legitimacy of science and technology. Her main attention is in the European Union, both at the supra-national level as well as national and local (cluster) levels. In particular she studies the complex interactions between public and private realms, which have been called 'new modes of governance'.

Susana Borrás has a part-time affiliation at CIRCLE, Lund University, Sweden, as Visiting Professor. She is a serving member of the Danish Research Policy Council and is the advisor to the Danish Minister. She is a board member of the EU-Spri Forum academic association, and a board member on the Danish European Community Studies Association (ECSA-DK), and the FORFI programme at the Norwegian Research Council. She was previously Director of the Jean Monnet Centre of Excellence at the Copenhagen Business School (2010–13).

Michelle Cini is Professor of European Politics in the School of Sociology, Politics and International Studies at the University of Bristol. She is co-editor of the *Journal of Common Market Studies*, and co-edits the Oxford University Press textbook, *European Union Politics*. Her research has focused, among other things, on the politics of the European Commission and EU competition and state aid policy. Her current research is on public ethics and institutional change in EU institutions.

Stefan Collignon has been Ordinary Professor of Political Economy at Sant'Anna School of Advanced Studies, Pisa, since October 2007, and International Chief Economist of the Centro Europa Ricerche (CER), Roma, since July 2007. He is the founder of the Euro Asia Forum at Sant'Anna School of Advanced Studies.

Previously, he was Centennial Professor of European Political Economy at the London School of Economics and Political Science (LSE) from January 2001 to 2005. During 2005 to 2007 he was Visiting Professor at Harvard University, Faculty of Arts and Sciences, Government Department, and an associate of the Minda de Gunzburg Centre for European Studies at Harvard. He has also taught at the University of Hamburg, the Institut d'Etudes Politiques in Paris and Lille, the College of Europe in Bruges and at the Free University of Berlin (1997–2000).

Stefan Collignon has served as Deputy Director General for Europe in the Federal Ministry of Finance in Berlin for 1999–2000. He was also member of the Supervisory Board Glunz AG (1999–2010).

Stefan Collignon was born in 1951 and received his PhD and Habilitation from the Free University of Berlin. He also studied at the Institut d'Etudes Politiques (Paris), the University of Dar es Salaam, Queen Elizabeth House in Oxford and the London School of Economics. Since 1990 he has been president of the Association France-Birmanie.

He joined First National Bank in Dallas in 1975, worked with the German Volunteer Service in Tanzania (1977–1979) and was Chairman and Managing Director of Dorcas Ltd., London (1980–1989). From 1989 to 1998 Dr Collignon was Director of Research and Communication at the Association for the Monetary Union of Europe (Paris).

Professor Collignon is the author of numerous books on monetary economics, and the political economy of regional integration. His articles are available on his website: www.stefancollignon.eu.

Caroline de la Porte is Associate Professor at the Political Science Department of the Centre for Welfare State Studies, University of Southern Denmark and coordinates the Euro-politics network of the department. She teaches sociology, comparative welfare state theories and EU and welfare state reform. Her research interests are the Europeanization of employment and social policy, EU governance of policy coordination and the Lisbon Strategy, the EES, the OMC in social policy, new modes of governance in the EU, and labour market and social policy reform in the central and eastern European countries.

Rainer Eising is Professor of Comparative Politics at the Ruhr-University Bochum. He has published widely on EU policy-making, interest representation and governance.

Sergio Fabbrini is Director of the LUISS School of Government and Professor of Political Science and International Relations at LUISS Guido Carli, where he holds the Jean Monnet Chair in European Institutions and Politics. He co-founded and then directed the School of International Studies at the University of Trento from 2006 to 2009. Since 1996, he has been Recurrent Professor of Comparative Politics at the Department of Political Science and Institute of Governmental Studies, University of California at Berkeley.

In 2004 he succeeded Giovanni Sartori as Editor of *Rivista Italiana di Scienza Politica*, which he directed until 2009. In 2006 he was the first Italian scholar to be awarded the European Amalfi Prize for Sociology and Social Sciences, and in 2009 he won the Filippo Burzio Prize for the Political Sciences. In 2011, he was the winner of the Capalbio Prize for Europe. He was Jemolo Fellow at Nuffield

College, Oxford University and Jean Monnet Chair Professor at the Robert Schuman Centre for Advanced Studies, European University Institute, Florence. He was Fulbright Professor at the Department of Government and the Kennedy School of Government at Harvard University. He has lectured and taught in many countries of Europe, North and South America and Asia and he is a referee for several international academic journals. He has directed several international and Italian research groups.

By the end of 2012, Sergio Fabbrini had published fourteen books, two co-authored books and fourteen edited or co-edited books, and hundreds of articles and essays in seven languages on comparative and European government and politics, American government and politics, international and transatlantic relations and foreign policy, Italian politics and political theory.

Janine Goetschy is both a political scientist and sociologist. She has been Senior Research Fellow at CNRS (France) since 1976, attached to IDHE-Cachan and University of Nanterre, and has been teaching 'EU social policy' at the Institute for European Studies (ULB, Belgium) for the last 12 years. She has been working on comparative industrial relations and EU-level social, economic and institutional matters, and is the author of about hundred publications. She sits on various editorial boards of international scientific journals.

Elke Heins is Lecturer in Social Policy at the University of Edinburgh, UK. Her research and teaching focuses on social policy and welfare reform in Europe from a comparative perspective, with a particular interest in labour market policy as well as health policy. Recent publications have dealt with the concept of flexicurity and reforms of the National Health Service (NHS) in the UK.

Anton Hemerijck is Dean of the Faculty of Social Sciences at the VU University Amsterdam, and Vice-Rector. Between 2001 and 2009 he was director of the Netherlands Council for Government Policy (WRR). In that period he also held a chair in Comparative European Social Policy in the Department of Public Administration at Erasmus University Rotterdam. He studied economics at Tilburg University (1979–1986) and obtained his doctorate from Oxford University in 1993.

He publishes widely on issues of comparative social and economic policy and institutional policy analysis. Between 1997 and 2000 he was Senior Researcher at the Max-Planck-Institute for the Study of Societies, working on the large comparative project on Welfare and Work in the Open Economy, directed by Fritz W. Scharpf and Vivien A. Schmidt. He has also been involved in drafting reports on social policy for Portuguese (2000), Belgian (2001), Greek (2003), Finnish (2006), German (2007) and Portuguese (2007) presidencies of the EU.

Important publications include *A Dutch Miracle* with Jelle Visser (Amsterdam University Press, 1997), *Why We Need a New Welfare State* with Gosta Esping

Andersen, Duncan Gallie and John Myles (Oxford University Press, 2002) and *Changing Welfare States* (Oxford University Press, 2013).

Zoe Lefkofridi is the Max Weber Post-doctoral Research Fellow at the European University Institute. Prior to joining the EUI, she was Post-doctoral Fellow at the University of Vienna and a Visiting Scholar at Stanford University. She studies democracy, representation and European integration, with a focus on political inequalities (gender, migration) and extremism.

Daniel Mügge is a political economist and works as Assistant Professor at the Political Science Department of the University of Amsterdam. His research concentrates on financial markets and their governance. In 2009, his dissertation on European financial markets was honoured with the ECPR Jean Blondel prize as best European political science dissertation of the year. Daniel spent the first half of 2012 as a Visiting Scholar at the Center for European Studies at Harvard University. He is also co-editor of the *Review of International Political Economy*.

In the GR:EEN project, Daniel coordinates the work on financial markets. In that context he is editing a book for Oxford University Press as well as a special issue of the *Journal for European Public Policy*.

Claudio Radaelli is Professor of Political Science at the University of Exeter, where he directs the Jean Monnet Centre for European Governance. At Exeter, he teaches modules on regulatory impact assessment, European integration, Europeanization and the politics of nonviolence. His research interests lie in theoretical policy analysis, policy learning theories, bureaucratic politics, research design, and Europeanization. Empirically, over the last three years Claudio has worked in the fields of comparative regulatory reforms, policy narratives in Europe and the USA, experiments with policy-makers, policy appraisal instruments in different European countries, and the politics of nonviolence in Italy. He has published *Designing Research in the Social Sciences* (Sage, 2012) with Fabrizio Gilardi and Martino Maggetti; *Research Design in European Studies* (Palgrave, 2012), co-edited with Theofanis Exadaktylos; and *Politics in Italy 2013* (Berghahn Books) co-edited with Aldo di Virgilio. He is carrying out a four-year project on Analysis of Learning in Regulatory Governance funded by the European Research Council, Advanced Grants Section.

Daniel Rasch is a PhD candidate at the Ruhr-University Bochum. He has a MA degree in Social Science (focus on international relations) and works as a researcher on interest group participation in the European Union. His main areas of research are comparative politics, political economy and research methods.

Maria João Rodrigues is Professor of European Economic Policies at the Institute for European Studies, Université Libre de Bruxelles (IEE-ULB) and the Lisbon University Institute (ISCTE-IUL). She was minister of employment in

Portugal (1995–1997) and has developed a European career since then. Known as the 'mother of the Lisbon Strategy', she has been special adviser to the European Commission, several EU Presidencies and national governments. By chairing several EU high-level groups and preparing European Council meetings over the last 15 years, she has been involved in the design and implementation of several EU policies: the strategy for growth and jobs and economic and social policies; the Lisbon Treaty negotiation; the Erasmus Programme and the New Skills for New Jobs Initiative; the strategic partnerships with China, Brazil, South Africa and USA; and the Eurozone crisis. She was the chair of the Advisory Group for socio-economic sciences in the European Commission in charge of preparing the 7th Framework Research Programme, has had many publications including ten books and delivered many conferences in and outside Europe. She is also a Member of the Advisory Board of the European Policy Centre (Brussels) and of the Governing Board of Notre Europe (Paris). Maria holds three Master's degrees and a PhD in economics from the University of Paris 1 Pantheon-Sorbonne, as well as a Degree in Sociology from the University of Lisbon. Among several national awards, she was awarded the Légion d'Honneur at Officier grade in France.

Patrycja Rozbicka is a post-doctoral researcher at the Ruhr University Bochum. Previously, she was a PhD researcher in the Department of Social and Political Science at the European University Institute in Florence, Italy. Her main areas of interest and publications are: participation of interest groups in the EU political system and policy-making, EU environmental policy, and coalitions and networks studies.

Born in 1936, **Philippe C. Schmitter** is a graduate of the Graduate Institute for International Studies of the University of Geneva, and took his doctorate at the University of California at Berkeley. Since 1967 he has been successively Assistant Professor, Associate Professor and Professor in the Politics Department of the University of Chicago, then at the European University Institute (1982–86) and at Stanford (1986–96). He has been visiting professor at the Universities of Paris-I, Geneva, Mannheim and Zürich, and Fellow of the Humboldt Foundation, Guggenheim Foundation and the Palo Alto Centre for Advanced Studies in the Behavioral Sciences.

   He has published books and articles on comparative politics, on regional integration in Western Europe and Latin America, on the transition from authoritarian rule in Southern Europe and Latin America, and on the intermediation of class, sectoral and professional interests. His current work is on the political characteristics of the emerging Euro-polity, on the consolidation of democracy in Southern and Eastern countries, and on the possibility of post-liberal democracy in Western Europe and North America.

   Philippe Schmitter was Professor of Political Science at the European University Institute in Florence, Department of Political and Social Sciences until September 2004. He was then nominated Professorial Fellow at the same

Institution. He is now Professor Emeritus at the Department of Political and Social Sciences at the European University Institute.

After having held positions in various departments in charge of industrial policy in the French Ministry of Industry, **Christian Stoffaës** was at Electricité de France, director successively of strategy, audit and control, and international relations. He is Professor of International Economy at the University Paris 2 Panthéon Assas, Honorary Chairman of the Centre d'Etudes Prospectives et d'Informations Internationales, the Institute of International Economy, attached to the Prime Minister's office.

Eleni Xiarchogiannopoulou is a GR:EEN Post-doctoral Research Fellow at the Institute for European Studies, Université Libre de Bruxelles, Belgium. She is working on the external dimension of Europeanization and the European Modes of Governance in the area of 'social' trade policy. Previously she worked at the European Institute, London School of Economics where she participated in many research projects including those on the Europeanization of Greek public policy and the Greek Core Executive. Her research interests include policy discourse analysis within the context of discursive institutionalism, external/internal Europeanization, multi-dimensional EU policies, and EU governance.

List of Abbreviations

AGS	Annual Growth Survey
AIFM	Alternative Investment Fund Managers
BBA	British Bankers Association
BdB	Bundesverband deutscher Banken
BEPG	Broad Economic Policy Guidelines
CFSP	Common Foreign and Security Policies
CIS	Commonwealth of Independent States
CME	Coordinated Market Economies
CRAs	Credit rating agencies
CRBP	Capital Requirements and Bonuses Package
DSG	Deposit Schemes Guarantees
EBA	European Banking Authority
EBA	Everything but the Arms
ECB	European Central Bank
ECI	European Citizens' Initiative
ECJ	European Court of Justice
ECN	European Competition Network
ECSC	European Coal and Steel Community
EDA	European Debt Agency
EDP	Excessive Deficit Procedure
EEAS	European External Action Service
EEC	European Economic Community
EES	European Employment Strategy
EFSF	European Financial Stability Facility
EFSM	European Financial Stability Mechanism
EIOPA	European Insurance and Occupational Pensions Authority
EMU	Economic and Monetary Union
EP	European Parliament
EPAs	Economic Partnership Agreements
ESA	European Securities Authority
ESFS	European System of Financial Supervisors
ESM	European Stability Mechanism
ESRB	European Systemic Risk Board
EU	European Union
FC	Fiscal Compact
FSB	Financial Stability Board
FTAs	Free Trade Agreements

GATT	General Agreement on Tariffs and Trade
GDP	Gross Domestic Product
GNP	Gross National Product
GSP	Generalised System of Preferences
ICN	International Competition Network
ICS	Investor Compensation Scheme
IFRS	International Financial Reporting Standards
IGCs	Inter-Governmental Conferences
ILO	International Labour Organisation
IMF	International Monetary Fund
IPS	Investors Protection Scheme
LDC	Least Developed Countries
LME	Liberal Market Economies
LS	Lisbon Strategy
MCR	Merger Control Regulation
MFN	Most Favoured Nation
MiFI	Markets in Financial Instruments
MIP	Macroeconomic Imbalance Procedure
MS	Member State(s)
MTOs	Medium-Term Objectives
NAFTA	North American Free Trade Agreement
NAPs	National Action Plans
NCB	National Central Banks
NIFA	New International Financial Architecture
NPM	New Public Management
NRPs	National Reform Programmes
OCA	Optimal Currency Area
OECD	Organisation for Economic Co-operation and Development
OMC	Open Method of Coordination
OMCs	Open Methods of Coordination
OMT	Outright Monetary Transactions
OTC	Over-The-Country
PES	Public Employment Services
PTAs	Preferential Trade Agreements
QMV	Qualified Majority Vote
RQMV	Reverse Qualified Majority Vote
SC	Social Conditionality
SGP	Stability and Growth Pact
TARP	Troubled Assets Relief Programme
TFEU	Treaty on the Functioning of the European Union
TINA	There is No Alternative
TSCG	Treaty on Stability Coordination and Governance
TUE	Treaty on the European Union
UCITS	Undertakings for Collective Investment in Transferable Securities

UK	United Kingdom
UN	United Nations
UNCTAD	United Nations Conference on Trade and Development
US	United States
USA	United States of America
WB	World Bank
WTO	World Trade Organisation

Introduction

Maria João Rodrigues and Eleni Xiarchogiannopoulou

Research on European governance is central to an understanding of both the process of European integration and its external role as a laboratory for multilevel governance. A range of diverse issues is addressed by this research field, notably the specificities of the European Union (EU) polity, the international experience of federalisms, the diversity of the EU modes of governance, the Europeanization of national policies, the interplay between European convergence and national diversity, the policy coherence and consistency in a multilevel governance system, and the modalities of differentiated integration.

This transformation of EU governance can also have marked consequences for its external outreach and for its role as an inspiration to other examples of regional integration. EU governance has been transformed by the combined effects of a sequence of different crises:

- the limits of a growth model which is no longer sustainable in the present context of globalisation;
- the financial crisis starting in 2008 and the economic and social crisis which have followed;
- the Eurozone crisis combining sovereign debt with bank debt and exposing the imbalances in the Eurozone and the flaws of the European Monetary Union (EMU) architecture;
- the crisis of EU integration triggered by the need for major reforms in the EMU.

These central policy and theoretical challenges are being addressed by an increasing number of researchers on European governance. This book aims to present recent findings of some of the most renowned of these researchers, based on a thorough personal and collective elaboration. Following a preparatory workshop which took place in April 2013, these authors have decided to put a particular emphasis on the impact of the recent Eurozone crisis which is having far-reaching implications for European governance.

The transformations of European governance and the implications of the Eurozone crisis are analysed in this book in the following sequence:

I. European modes of governance: concepts, recent trends and international implications

II. The transformation of European economic governance
III. The transformation of European social policy governance
IV. The international dimension of the transformation of EU governance

Part I focuses on the broader conceptual and empirical implications of the Eurozone crisis for the different modes of EU governance. Zoe Lefkofridi and Philippe C. Schmitter consider that the EU is at a make-or-break moment. The crisis could be beneficial or detrimental to its future. They revisit Schmitter's model of crisis-induced decision-making cycles (1970) and critically discuss why the crisis might not be as benign as originally thought. This intriguing question will overshadow the rest of the book, including its conclusion, where some contrasting scenarios for the unfolding of this crisis are sketched.

Michelle Cini begins with the premise that the euro crisis is likely to have had a dramatic effect on a wide range of EU policies, particularly in the sphere of economic affairs. In the case of competition policy – a central and classic EU mode of governance – there are some obvious effects for the EU's state aid policy. However, in other aspects of the policy, the impact has been less extensive, with the Commission promoting a 'business as usual' line in its treatment of competition cases. In terms of the internationalisation of EU competition policy, a shift in the EU's position was witnessed prior to the onset of the economic crisis, but there has been no dramatic policy change since the mid-2000s. Rather, the focus has been placed on the incremental adaptation (convergence?) of transatlantic policy, which some have labelled as evidence of an Americanisation of EU competition policy. However, here is no evidence to suggest that this has been affected by the euro crisis.

Susana Borrás and Claudio Radaelli appraise the contribution of the Open Method of Coordination (OMC) in the responses to the crisis of the Eurozone and the consolidation of EU governance. To answer this research question, they establish the conditions for different usages of OMC – a less conventional mode of governance – in various policy fields. The latter can be used to explore, to learn or to converge towards pre-determined solutions. They then discuss how these usages are combined with the emerging governance architecture of the Eurozone, taking into account the consequences of the asymmetries, especially in terms of divergence among Member States. They argue that the re-definition of national budgetary discipline and macro-economic surveillance calls the meaning of coordination into question: is the OMC a governance mode used to promote learning, exploration or surveillance? They show that OMC usages are bent towards surveillance, monitoring and compliance with pre-determined solutions. This choice is risky, given conditions of high uncertainty. To bend the OMC towards surveillance can work only if the solution can be defined in advance by the strong players of the Eurozone. If, instead, structural reforms require learning and exploration at the domestic level, it is a mistake to reduce the variety of OMC to a single dimension of usage. There are few in-built mechanisms to learn lessons and adjust (or even change) on the basis of exploration and learning.

Part II focuses on the implications of the Eurozone crisis for economic governance. Sergio Fabbrini considers that the Eurozone crisis has called into question the dual constitutional structure of the Lisbon Treaty: supranational for the single market and intergovernmental for the EMU, *inter alia*. The intergovernmental EU has not been able to guarantee an effective decision-making process, nor legitimacy to the EMU outcome. The basis of the intergovernmental institutional framework, constituted by a centralised monetary policy (in the Frankfurt-based European Central Bank) and decentralised financial, fiscal and budgetary policies (in the Member States), has been challenged by the Eurozone crisis. Under the financial threat of the euro's collapse, the heads of state and governments of the EU Member States eventually ended up in dramatically redefining the intergovernmental system of economic governance in Europe (and the Eurozone in particular). The new measures and treaties have unevenly centralised economic and financial policies, with some Member States being less autonomous than others. Moreover, these measures were considered ineffective by the financial markets and illegitimate by the affected citizens. After the analysis of the intergovernmental EU and its difficulty in dealing with the crucial dilemmas of collective action, the chapter identifies three basic strategies for dealing with the limits of the intergovernmental logic of the EMU, discussing the pros and cons of each of them.

Christian Stoffaës addresses the controversial issue of the debt burden in Europe. In 2014 its level has reached 100 per cent of Gross Domestic Product (GDP), equalling the historical level of post-war debt. Debt from the First World War in Europe was solved by deflation, the Depression and the rise of political extremism, and that of World War Two by hyperinflation. In both periods, the spoliation of creditors resulted from the restructuring/cancellation of a significant part of the debt. There is the same dilemma in 2013: national governments' debts should be recognised officially as being non-reimbursable, argues Stoffaës: better an orderly process than a disorderly spoliation.

A historical precedent deserves to be considered: the federal assumption of state debts mark the founding moment of the American nation. The true founding act of the Union was the resounding success of the Hamilton Plan: it rooted the legitimacy of the federal government. This was a new departure for America: government credit restored the abundance of available funds and brought general prosperity and the Treasury Department was created to administer the public debt and raise taxes. For Hamilton, a permanent federal debt of a reasonable size was 'the powerful cement of our nation'. The parallel with our great euro-debate is tempting, while the weight of cumulative debt stifles the South, exacerbates divisions and raises populist extremism. Accumulated public debts appear to be non-reimbursable when to reduce the debt from 100 per cent to 60 per cent of Gross National Product (GNP) will require not simply balanced budgets but budgets in excess for at least a decade, pensions and civil servants reduced by 10 to 20 per cent austerity and deflation. Some fear that Eurobond issuance generates a huge 'moral hazard' from the impecunious nations when they have not (yet) proven that they have cured their addiction to debt without risk. Choosing the right path will be the key to success.

Stefan Collignon addresses key issues of the road map to complete the EMU. While the global crisis originated in policy mistakes in the United States, the Eurozone crisis was home-made because the economic management of the Eurozone was institutionally unable to respond in a coherent, unified and cooperative fashion. It is evident that the economic policies of an early exit from the post-global crisis were mistaken and that the Eurozone has no democratic mechanism to correct such policy mistakes. This chapter also discusses the policy innovations made during the crisis, notably the European Semester, the European Stability Mechanism (ESM) set up by governments, the excessive imbalance procedure controlled by the Commission, and the Outright Monetary Transactions (OMT) programme of the European Central Bank (ECB). It will also discuss the missing aspects, namely a weak banking union and lack of democratic control of the policies decided by the Council. Finally, this chapter traces some alternative policy options for a left agenda to revive Europe. It deals with public debt sustainability, and policies to stimulate investment and growth. In this context, it will suggest better wage coordination, improving financial integration and surveillance, and raise the issue of a transfer union.

Rainer Eising, Daniel Rasch and Patrycja Rozbicka address new policies for the regulation of the financial markets in the EU that are meant to raise financial market stability and increase consumer protection. They analyse the three directive proposals on Alternative Investment Fund Managers, Deposit Guarantee Schemes and Investor Compensation Schemes as case studies to study the agenda-setting processes, political mobilisation, media coverage, and the policy frames of the actors. They do so by scrutinising EU level and national level consultations and by using a content analysis of official documents of the political institutions, as well as examining the media coverage and the individual stakeholders' position papers. The findings indicate that the different legislative state of affairs on the Commission's proposals is best accounted for by different issue characteristics of the proposals.

Part III focuses on the implications of the Eurozone crisis for social policy governance. Janine Goetschy analyses EU social policy and its complex relationship with European integration. Her contribution aims for a better insight into the EU's social policy developments which were shaped over time by EU economic integration (spill-over effects) and member state interests. Its major fragilities lie in its complex and subordinate relationship with EU economic policies and the growing diversity of social systems it had to face within the EU, due to its successive enlargements on the one hand and the crisis impact since 2008 on the other. However, the increasing variety of its regulatory paths and governance processes has been reflecting its adaptation capacity in a global economy. With successive crises since 2008 and the subsequent setting-up of a series of EU level economic reforms, Social Europe has not yet found its appropriate place and cruising speed to render those economic reforms legitimate and provide sufficient trust and assets to EU citizens in the face of the ongoing changes in their national economic, social and employment systems.

Anton Hemerijck considers that the Eurozone crisis clearly marks a serious 'stress test' for twenty-first-century European cooperation and national welfare provision. Will its aftermath, like that of the Great Depression and 'great inflation' predecessors, mark a new opportunity to reconfigure and perhaps re-legitimise social policy and the European project? Or are the European welfare states, and the Single Market and EMU, in danger of becoming 'crisis casualties' in the cascade of violent economic, social and political aftershocks across Europe, unleashed by the global financial crisis? Protracted failures to resolve the Eurozone crisis at the supranational level are increasingly mirrored by domestic political pressures to water down ruling governments' commitment to European solutions. In spring 2013, the financial markets seemed to have calmed down somewhat, but in the expectation of a long slump with levels of unemployment not seen since the 1930s, 2013's capital market acquiescence could be deceptive. This chapter argues for room for a more realistic and slower pace of fiscal adjustment coupled with long-term productivity-enhancing domestic social (investment) reforms and informed by readily available evidence about the new efficiency–equity frontier. Effectively, the chapter wishes to challenge, on economic, institutional and political grounds, the false 'necessity' of the prevailing *pensée unique* of social austerity.

Caroline de la Porte and Elke Heins analyse how various policy coordination instruments affect social and labour market policy directly or indirectly. To capture these dynamics, they develop a typology of 'intrusiveness' along three dimensions: the degree of interference in sensitive policy areas, the degree of surveillance and, last but not least, the degree of coercion. On this basis, they then investigate whether, and if so, how, the intrusiveness of selected monetary and social policy instruments has altered pre- and post-crisis. They argue that with the onset of the crisis, the dominance of soft coordination instruments at EU level has been replaced by an era of harder conditionality. At the same time, recalibrating social policies supporting a social investment strategy have been sidelined by retrenchment policies. Consequently, the voluntary aspects of the Open Method of Coordination (OMC), which had occasional recalibrating effects in the 2000s, have been transformed into more coercive policy coordination processes with strong and direct welfare retrenchment effects. In the context of the sovereign debt crisis, various old and new OMC-like instruments, coupled with an austerity agenda, seem necessary to prevent default and the collapse of the common currency. However, far-reaching structural reforms may have lasting policy and institutional repercussions, undermining the solidarity principle on which European welfare states are built.

Finally, Part IV focuses on the international dimension of this transformation of European governance. Eleni Xiarchogiannopoulou looks at the EU's 'social' trade policy and specifically at the Generalised System of Preferences (GSP).

The GSP is a trade policy programme that allows the exemption of developing countries from export tariffs, as a way of assisting their growth and development. One of its characteristics is that the EU also uses it to promote the ratification and application of basic human rights, and labour, sustainable development and good governance standards in developing countries. It does so through 'social' conditionality. Developing countries that ratify and apply basic human rights, and labour, sustainable development and good governance standards qualify for additional trade preferences (carrots), while failure of compliance results in the withdrawal of the preferences (sticks). This chapter also assesses the progress the EU has made in this policy area and the limitations put on its efforts to project its rules of governance externally. It will do so by reflecting on the theory of the external dimension of Europeanization. The chapter will also discuss the issues of internal policy coherence and of the European crisis, and their implications on the EU's external action.

Daniel Mügge recalls that in light of the still-ongoing financial crisis, the EU has overhauled both the rules that govern its financial markets and the institutional structures through which these rules are devised and enforced. This chapter explores the international implications of these transformations of EU financial governance and asks to what degree they have affected the logic of global financial governance. *Ex ante*, strong and binding global re-regulatory efforts, for example in the G20, could both be a complement to EU reforms and a constraint on them. More specifically, this chapter establishes how strong the case for a European commitment to global rule harmonisation remains, in light of the EU-internal transformations of recent years. It examines a broad range of policy domains, but only in two of them – capital adequacy rules and derivatives trading – is there a strong rationale for globally harmonised rules, even in the face of substantive disagreement, in particular with the USA. In all other domains, the EU is well-equipped to enhance financial stability through unilateral reforms, because the costs of internationally divergent rules are much lower than commonly assumed. In spite of the widespread lip-service given to united global action through the G20, the reshuffling of policy goals within the EU in favour of financial stability means that a solid commitment to global financial governance is often more a constraint than a complement for EU efforts to make its financial markets and economy more stable.

Maria João Rodrigues directs this discussion in a broader international dimension, first of all by making an international comparison between the Eurozone's experience with other monetary zones. All of them are complemented with fiscal unions, which have a basic set of similar features: common principles of fiscal discipline in the sub-central governments, but also a central government with a relevant budget based on own tax resources and a Treasury responsible to issue common debt. It is also important to analyse the sequence of steps needed to build this combination between monetary union, fiscal union and political union, according to the available international experience. This sequence started with a political union first, a fiscal union next and a monetary union only afterwards. This international comparison highlights the specificity of the EU, with an uncompleted EMU and with a very different sequencing in its construction. This also enables a detailed assessment of the governance reforms which have been triggered by the Eurozone crisis: these new instruments have been mainly designed in an intergovernmental direction. So far, the paradigm of 'mutual insurance' has been preferred to a more federal or 'Community' paradigm.

The interplay between the Eurozone crisis and EU external action is also analysed. Two different questions should be addressed for policy assessment: How has the EU's external action responded to this crisis? How has this crisis shaped the EU's external action? From this viewpoint it is possible to identify two quite different periods: the first, during the financial and economic crisis between 2008 and 2010, when the EU was a key-player; the second, during the Eurozone crisis after 2010, when the EU also became a source of global problems. This chapter concludes with suggestions to overcome the major flaws which were identified.

Hence, the transformations of European governance and the particular implications of the Eurozone crisis are analysed in this book with the aim not only of testing and developing new theoretical approaches and concepts, but also of exploring and inspiring new possible solutions. Europe once again needs a period of intensive scientific and political creativity.

This book develops a deeper analysis of the recent transformations of EU governance and its international implications. It places particular emphasis on the important transformations that EU economic governance has undergone due to the impact of globalisation, the need to move to a new growth model and the Eurozone crisis. The book also contributes to the growing debate on the international implications of the Eurozone crisis, the risks of global recession and the weakening of European international influence. It develops a useful deeper analysis of the recent transformation of the EU governance in order to better assess its international impacts. The contributions of this edited volume are motivated by the observation that, in spite of its internal problems, the EU remains the most advanced regional laboratory of multilateralism and the most advanced experience of a new growth model.

The volume is part of the new GR:EEN-GEM book series and the direct product of the GR:EEN multidisciplinary research programme on multilateral global governance. Accordingly we would like to acknowledge the support of the FP7 large-scale integrated research project GR:EEN – Global Reordering: Evolution through European Networks (European Commission Project Number 266809).

PART I
European Modes of Governance:
Concepts, Recent Trends and
International Implications

Chapter 1

A Good or a Bad Crisis for the European Union?

Zoe Lefkofridi and Philippe C. Schmitter

1. Introduction[1]

Europe is facing three crises: the crisis of its national 'real-existing' democracies; the crisis of the regional institutions of the European Union and the crisis of the common European currency. Each has its independent origins and characteristics. National, liberal, representative democracy existed before the initiation of the European integration process – at least, in Western Europe – and only subsequently became a prerequisite for membership in it. The European Union existed for some time and was functioning reasonably well without a common currency. The Euro was thrust upon its member-states mainly due to German re-unification and only 17 of 27 of them eventually decided to join it.

However spaced out in time or differently motivated in function, the three crises have become simultaneous and begun to interact with each other creating unexpected and threatening consequences. It is even conceivable that they could cascade downwards – that the demise of the Euro could lead to the collapse of the European Union that could trigger a major change of regime in EU member-states. Originally, the fear was that shifts in the composition of national governments could threaten the viability of supra-national governance arrangements. Now, it is the inverse.

In this essay, we re-examine the role of crisis and crisis-management at the European level – without penetrating further down to their eventual implications for national politics at either the governmental or regime level. We ask first what is peculiar to this crisis compared to the many others that have characterised the integration process since its initiation in the early 1950s. Compared to them, this one has attracted unprecedented and widespread public attention. Very few party politicians, interest group spokesmen, international financial analysts, journalists or television pundits could remain indifferent to what EU officials were saying. EU jargon moved beyond university lecture halls and parliaments and penetrated the national media and personal discussions around the continent. Citizens in all 27 EU MS found themselves sharing anxieties and reflecting on the same issues. For some, more regional integration seemed an opportunity – even a necessary part of

---

1 This chapter draws on Schmitter (2012) and Lefkofridi and Schmitter (2014).

the solution; for others (and there were far more of them), it was perceived as a serious threat to its very existence.

Is the crisis going to be a 'good' or 'bad' one for the process of European integration? Whether the Eurozone breaks up or advances further – even more whether the EU as a whole survives or perishes – is of concern to the approximately 500 million Europeans that are directly affected by the uncertainty of the outcome. This, in turn, feeds back to the global economic and political order. Given that the crisis is far from over and that the European project is still at a make-or-break moment, attempting to answer this question is a fundamental obligation for the social sciences. To date, economists and financial experts, who disagree about the root of the problem and, consequently, about the appropriate remedy, have almost completely dominated the debate – despite the fact that the problem Europe has been facing since the beginning of the crisis is political.

Approaching the question from this perspective, we revisit Schmitter's model of crisis-induced decision-making cycles (1970) in Section 2. Based on this theory, the present crisis seems to have the anticipated characteristics of a 'good' one. It might even be the *transcending* one; whereby, economic union would transform itself into political union. Observing the developments with this model in mind (Section 3), we see that, as expected, the EU has been forced out of its entropic 'zone of indifference' and compelled to consider major extensions of its scope and authority in favour of fiscal and banking unity – which in turn would seem to imply taking steps towards political union. But 'political' union remains the least overtly debated outcome and the one that, at least for the moment, both rulers and citizens find the hardest to imagine. We will discuss critically whether and why this crisis might be a 'good' one for transcending the EU's existing limitations or a very 'bad' one that could even threaten its very existence (Section 4). In conclusion, we make some final reflections regarding potential future developments (Section 5).

2. The Role of Crisis in the Process of Integration

Crises have been an integral part of the process of European integration and, by and large, they have had a positive effect. The collective reaction to them by national actors has led to an increase in the authority and an expansion of the tasks of the institutions of the EU and its predecessors.

The underlying reason for this is obvious. It begins with the unprecedented nature of the process of integrating sovereign national states peacefully into a regional organisation. The actors involved have an intrinsic difficulty in acting rationally because it is so difficult to assess the costs and benefits of possible courses of action: first, because the range of alternatives (especially given the presumption of peaceful negotiation among relative equals rather than violent imposition by the strongest) is so different from analogous choices made during their respective processes of national integration; second, because however well-considered their policies and well-intentioned their implementation, they are bound to generate unexpected and, often, undesired consequences. The crisis of the Euro and the public finances of several MS is a near perfect example of how causal complexity and unanticipated consequences can impact the process of regional integration.

In an article written four decades ago, Schmitter (1970) incorporated this notion of intrinsic crisis into a revised understanding of the basic neo-functionalist paradigm developed by Ernst Haas (1968). Schmitter's argument rested on the assumption that treaty-based international organisations, whether regional or global, were especially prone to entropy. They would settle into a self-encapsulating 'zone of indifference' based on their initial task endowment and resources, and simply continue to perform the circumscribed tasks assigned to them by treaty with as little impact as possible upon either their MS or other international organisations – until a crisis would force them to revise their practices.

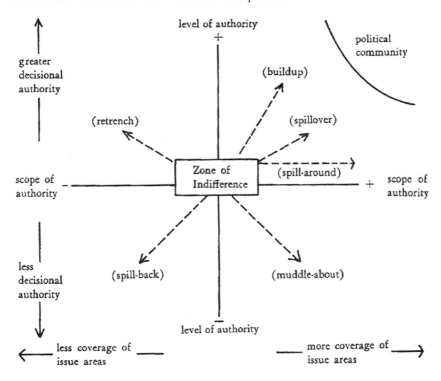

Figure 1.1   Alternative actor strategies

In times of crisis, there are alternative strategies that actors (national states, supra-national functionaries, regional political parties, cross-national interest associations and social movements) can adopt (Figure 1.1). The resulting outcome of their conflicts, if the crisis is sufficient, forces the regional organisation out of

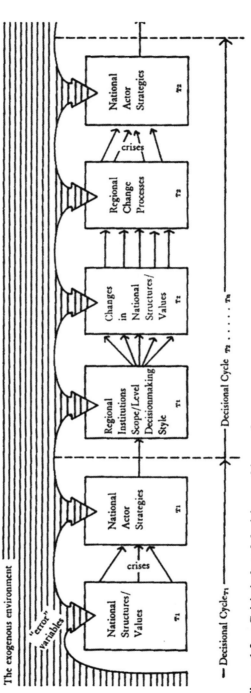

Figure 1.2   Crisis-induced decision-making cycles

its zone of indifference. Given favourable conditions, this will enhance either the scope of its tasks or the level of its authority. And, under especially favourable conditions, a package deal can emerge that accomplishes both, an outcome labelled as 'spill-over'.

The argument has an implicit temporal structure and consists of decision cycles induced by successive crises. These cycles first change the strategies of national actors – governments and non-governmental organisations – that, in turn, place pressure on the scope and level of regional institutions (Figure 1.2).[2] If the response is expansive, this changes the perception of national and sectoral interests (and eventually, their very identities) that then triggers further changes at the regional level which, as the result of a subsequent crisis, transform the basic expectations and strategies of national actors *et ainsi de suite*. For what a 'good' crisis should do is to fail to meet established member expectations and/or to raise the prospect of new opportunities and, thereby, to compel actors to redefine either the tasks or the level of authority (or both) of regional organisations by making their collective agreement 'spill-over' into previously untreated or ignored areas.

In the almost 50-year process of integration, the original European Economic Community has changed its overriding goal from regional security to trade promotion to agricultural subsidisation and fishing regulation to encouraging cross-investment and financial liberalisation, to coping with the competitive pressures of globalisation – not to mention the more recent goals of police cooperation, immigration, energy, transport and foreign and security policy. Each time the EU has expanded its competences, the stakes in the game have involved ever more complex packages of policies whose interactive effects and emergent properties have proven more difficult to predict.

What has made the EU unique is precisely this capacity to exploit successive crises positively by repeatedly breaking out of its momentary zone of indifference. At least until 2014, no other regional organisation has acquired this dynamic characteristic. The key hypothesis was (and still is) that this has been due to three distinctive factors:

1. The high level of supranationality that was initially given to the Secretariat of the European Coal and Steel Community and then passed on to its successor, the European Economic Community – combined with the unusually 'collegial' nature of decision making within its Commission

---

2   On a glossary of outcomes other than spill-over: (a) 'spill-around': the proliferation of functionally specialised independent, but strictly intergovernmental, institutions; (b) 'build-up', the concession by MS of greater authority to the supranational organisation without expanding the scope of its mandate; (c) 'muddle-about', when national actors try to maintain regional cooperation without changing/adjusting institutions; and (d) 'spill-back', which denotes withdrawal from previous commitments by MSs. See also Niemann and Schmitter (2009).

whose members were chosen by member governments but were not supposed to represent their national interests.

2. The existence of a rapidly expanding number and variety of non-state organisations – interest associations and social movements – that formed at the regional level and became capable of exerting influence on EU policy-making across the borders of MS and independently of their governments.

3. Needless to say, both of these features rested on the fact that all of the MS were liberal democracies that tolerated both the relative autonomy of supra-national organisations and the formation of cross-national associations.

3. The Transcending Cycle?

In theory, the present Euro-crisis would seem to conform almost perfectly to what Schmitter (1970) modelled as 'the Transcending Cycle' (Figure 1.3). This cycle of decision-making should have compelled actors in MS to:

1. engage in more comprehensive policy coordination across sectors and policy arenas, thereby institutionalising at the supra-national level the central governing mechanisms of planning, budgeting and taxation characteristics of a federal polity;

2. break out of predominantly national alliance patterns and form more salient cross-national ones, thereby laying the foundation for the establishment of the most important missing element in the emerging EU polity, namely, a distinctively European party system. Once this was accomplished, the five-year cycle of elections to the European Parliament (EP) would become much more significant to citizens and eventually result in the formation of an EU government transparently dependent upon their results and not upon the opaque calculations of member governments as at present.

In short, this was supposed to be the crisis that would drive the EU from economic to political integration.

In practice, however, we are not (yet) there. EU decision making during the Euro-crisis has been reluctant and disappointing. MS since the outbreak of the global financial crisis have retreated to more exclusive and state-centric calculations of interest and often undermined decisions they themselves took at EU Summits (Barroso 2012a). In general, developments have fallen – at least so far – short of the second expectation, while evidence regarding the realisation of the first one is mixed.

To be sure, the crisis was sufficient to force the Union to break free from its 'zone of indifference'. Predictably, the Commission tried to exploit the opportunity by advancing several proposals for reinforcing its authority in fiscal, budgetary and banking decision making and even raised the prospect of a 'quantum leap'

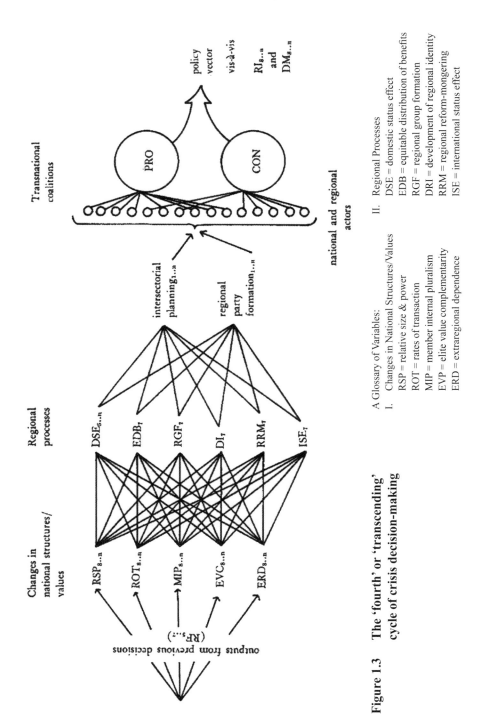

Figure 1.3   The 'fourth' or 'transcending' cycle of crisis decision-making

A Glossary of Variables:

I. Changes in National Structures/Values
    RSP = relative size & power
    ROT = rates of transaction
    MIP = member internal pluralism
    EVP = elite value complementarity
    ERD = extraregional dependence

II. Regional Processes
    DSE = domestic status effect
    EDB = equitable distribution of benefits
    RGF = regional group formation
    DRI = development of regional identity
    RRM = regional reform-mongering
    ISE = international status effect

towards political union (Barroso 2012a, b, c; Reding 2012 a, b, c; European Commission 2012a).

Moreover, and without EP involvement, the Presidents of the European Council, the Commission, the Eurogroup and the European Central Bank (ECB) made joint proposals for integrated frameworks of financial, budgetary, and economic policy (Van Rompuy 2012). If ratified and implemented, these would transfer a very substantial set of new competences to the EU level, thereby enhancing the role for EU institutions in such sensitive policy areas as public expenditure, revenue and borrowing.

Given their political sensitivity, their proponents recognised that such initiatives would require 'strong mechanisms for legitimate and accountable joint decision making', that is, a strengthening and extension of democracy (Van Rompuy 2012; see also European Commission 2012a). Their joint proposal did not specify how this would be achieved. But in his 'State of the Union Address' to the EP, Barroso (2012c) spoke of strengthening EU democracy through the reinforcement of Europarties by enhancing their role in the nomination of candidates for the Presidency of the Commission – a competence that has been previously based on intergovernmental consensus. *Inter alia*, Barroso committed himself to tabling ideas for treaty change before the 2014 EP elections, so as 'to move towards a federation of nation-states' (Barroso 2012c). His choice of the dreaded F-word caused vivid debates among MEPs and was widely commented on in the national media of MS.

'More Europe' – even 'more political and democratic Europe' – has crept onto the agenda as a result of the crisis and there is gradual acknowledgment of the need for a 'European public space' (Barroso 2012b; Draghi 2012) or a 'European political space' (Future of Europe Group 2012: 8), but the objective remains ambiguous – even among its proponents. Whether and how the aforementioned ideas will become fully fledged proposals and whether representatives from other, more reluctant, MS (for example, the UK, Denmark or Finland) would endorse them remains highly uncertain, especially since ratification of any treaty containing these new rules would require the unanimous approval of all 27 MS.

Last, but definitely not least, mass publics – rather than favouring more integration in gratitude for the benefits it has given them – have by and large expressed hostility to the prospect of political union. According to recent polls, citizens in the core countries of France and Germany have only weak (and declining) faith in Europe (*Die Welt* 2012; *Le Figaro* 2012). EU-wide public opinion surveys show that, on the aggregate, fewer citizens throughout the EU trust national *and* EU institutions[3] than in the past, although they do tend to trust

---

3   Rates of trust in national and EU institutions are inter-related. Arnold et al. (2012) study the determinants of trust in the EU and find that at the individual level, what matters are the utilities people perceive to gain from EU membership, their ideology, and their satisfaction with life as well as with the way democracy functions. Moreover, EU citizens living in MSs with high levels of (perceived) corruption, high public expenses on welfare and low decision-making power in the EU are more likely to trust EU institutions.

the latter more than the former with solving the crisis. This downward trend has accelerated since the crisis began in the autumn of 2009, but it had started even earlier (Standard Eurobarometer 2011: 19–21).

4. A 'Bad' Crisis?

Could it just be that the 'good' crisis that Schmitter imagined 40 years ago has turned out to be a 'bad' one? This would not be just a miscalculation, but a serious one – in both theoretical and practical terms. Not only would it invalidate a major element in neo-functionalism, but it might even threaten the famous *acquis communitaire* reversing much, if not all, of what has been accomplished at the regional level since the early 1950s. It could even return Europe to its previous status as a squabbling set of antagonistic national states prone to using violence to settle their disputes or to aggressively expanding their respective domains.[4] In what follows, we reflect on whether and why this might not be as 'benign' a transcending cycle as Schmitter originally thought.

Endogenous and Exogenous Factors

The neo-functionalist approach underlying the cyclical model is essentially endogenous. It presumes that the crises that emerge are produced by the very functioning of the integration process itself and, hence, that their resolution can be internalised, that is, handled by apposite changes in regional institutions and their policies.

At first glance, the Euro-crisis seems to fit this specification. Given the EMU's deficient design at its origins, it was generated by the unregulated 'sovereign' behaviour of its MS in response to lower rates of interest and apparently unlimited opportunities for public and private borrowing. This, however, ignores two aberrant factors.

First, the timing of the crisis was triggered by a financial collapse that began, not in Europe, but in the United States and its resolution remains critically dependent on exogenous responses, especially on the reactions of international rating agencies and capital markets. No one imagined that, as a result, sovereign public debt would be treated the same as commercial private debt – even when it seemed to be protected by the umbrella of a common supra-national currency. Hence, it is worth contemplating whether, if the crisis of the Euro and of public finance in the weaker MS had occurred in a more settled (even an expansive) global financial context, it would have been a much better one for the process of European integration.

---

4 Hardcore neo-realist theorists of international relations have been predicting this long before the financial crisis, ever since the collapse of the Soviet Union removed what they considered to be the *raison d'être* of its existence (see Mearsheimer 1990).

Second, the 'spill-over' into monetary integration had little to do with immediate functional pressures and almost everything to do with the 'high politics' surrounding German unification. It was the product of an 'intergovernmental' (and very 'high politics') deal whereby Western Germany was allowed to reunify with Eastern Germany in exchange for ensuring its partners that it would remain firmly anchored in the EU. And that meant giving up the Deutsche Mark in exchange for a common European currency.[5] No doubt its deficient design would have eventually generated the sort of functionalist pressures envisaged by the theory, but that would have been much later, in more endogenous circumstances and, perhaps, at a different stage of the global business cycle.

Uneven vs Cumulative Impact of Crisis

One of the presumed causes of a 'good' crisis was supposed to be the unexpected and uneven functional distribution of costs and benefits of some regional policy across MS – and this has certainly occurred – but it implicitly assumed a fundamental underlying pluralism in the interest structures of the polities involved. In other words, the impact of the crisis should not have been cumulative – striking some distinct group of members in multiple dimensions with particular force and leaving the others relatively unaffected or even benefitted.

The Euro-crisis has definitely had such a cumulative impact. Moreover, it accentuated a North–South developmental and cultural cleavage within the EU that already existed with the result being that both sides have accused the other of immoral or overbearing behaviour, with neither side capable of expressing solidaristic or mutually sympathetic feelings.[6] For some populist politicians and media outlets, 'nation bashing' via recourse to cultural stereotypes has been used as a strategy for attracting frustrated citizens in both the North and South. This tactic has been especially damaging since it has long been presumed that the EU had succeeded in eliminating such nationalistic excesses and in promoting mutual trust across national borders.

The Role of an Epistemic Community

Both the early functionalism of David Mitrany and the neo-functionalism of Ernst Haas presumed a leading role for experts – whether in regional institutions or in the regional associations and movements surrounding them. They were expected to constitute what came to be known as an 'epistemic community' and, hence, were supposed to be capable of identifying the nature of the problem and agreeing upon the policies for its resolution. Needless to say, this theory also presumed

---

5   See Baun (1995). For a somewhat different account that emphasises the role of Jacques Delors and the Commission in 'cultivating' the spill-over, see Jabko (1999).

6   Compare with the bitter Greco-German exchange that has escalated to include the renewal of claims by Greeks for damages caused by Germany during World War II.

that such a consensus would include the need to expand the scope or enhance the authority of regional institutions as part of the problem-solving process.

During the last decades, a coherent and dedicated group of neo-liberal economists came to dominate both regional and global international financial institutions. This has resulted in policy choices becoming increasingly determined by their assumptions, models and policies (Chwieroth 2007) – which became immediately apparent during the Euro-crisis. All of the key players (the Commission, the ECB, the IMF – not to mention Germany and the other northern MS) advocated fiscal balance and budgetary austerity with the assumption that this would result in monetary stability and a shift of available investment from public institutions to private firms which in turn was supposed to have triggered a general expansion of both employment, production and prosperity. In the extreme version, elected governments were replaced by technocratic ones that were presumed to be more successful in pursuing these policies (*vide* Monti in Italy and Papademos in Greece).

Unfortunately, the result of these policies has been dramatically disappointing. Since May 2011, unemployment in the Eurozone increased by 1,820,000 persons and the aggregate unemployment rate reached 11.1 per cent (Eurostat 2012). Austerity policies and severe cuts in social protection have assumed tragic dimensions, leading to increased rates of homelessness, malnutrition and even so-called 'economic suicide' in the countries worse hit by the crisis. Worse for the process of integration, these developments have resulted in public opinion's increasingly associating the EU with declining incomes for most of the population and rising ones for the privileged few – exactly the opposite of its historical image (Standard Eurobarometer 2012). This anti-Europe trend has been reflected in popular protests and electoral results. Desperate and disappointed citizens look more and more for salvation from their national governments (who conveniently attempt to shift the blame to the EU).[7] And they increasingly do so by supporting populists on the left or right who proclaim their opposition to the Euro, EU policies and even to the EU itself. Unless an epistemological community of experts with different assumptions and norms emerges, the crisis is much more likely to be a 'bad' one for European integration.

Pro-integration Bias

The neo-functionalist approach was biased towards further integration – at least in the relatively favourable conditions initially present in Western Europe. Although the conditions that might lead to disintegration were not explicitly theorised, it was conceived as possible if groups sharing *short-run* negative expectations vis-à-vis the European project worked together in order to block a specific policy and were successful (Haas 1968). Groups with such negative expectations have

---

7　Which does not mean that they get away with avoiding the blame. Since 2008, incumbent governments have failed to be re-elected in 11 of the 27 MS.

not (yet) managed to halt or reverse the integration process as a whole, but they were successful in blocking the Constitutional Treaty at the national level (French and Dutch referenda 2005). As Europe is in deep crisis, and with public opinion increasingly associating the EU with negative outcomes, the prospect of disintegration has become openly discussed. Although relatively few groups (for example, *United Kingdom Independence Party*) advocate outright withdrawal from the EU, many other parties are overtly contrary to any further 'spill-overs' that would benefit European institutions and some even favour 'spill-backs' in specific policy areas (for example, *Freiheitliche Partei Österreichs, British National Party, le Front National*). The more radical proposals range from encouraging or compelling 'problematic' members to leave the Eurozone (for example, Strache 2010), to their own country's withdrawal from the Euro, to dramatically reducing their contribution to EU budget, to ending the common agricultural policy and, most, seriously, to reinstating the superiority of national over EU law.

Moreover, the momentary success of these anti-EU populist movements exerts pressure on mainstream parties to adopt some of these positions for immediate electoral purposes – if not to co-opt these extremists more securely into their ranks. The entire political spectrum has shifted away from the 'permissive consensus' that previously had prevailed and EU-related conflicts are threatening the internal unity of established parties. Despite this, most politicians remain aware that such proposals are not easy to implement without breaking up the entire project. What is particularly disturbing about monetary integration, as opposed to other EU policies, is the excessively high costs of defecting from it or allowing it to collapse altogether. It is one thing to revoke a tariff, to abandon a common fishing policy or to renege on an agreement for cooperation in police or foreign affairs, and quite another to abandon the Euro and return to national currencies. In short, once it has been implemented, a regional policy in this domain becomes virtually irrevocable and, even if it could be 'arranged' for one or two members of the Eurozone to leave, their removal would be bound to generate suspicion about others following suit in the future.

The Impact of Enlargement

The entire neo-functional approach completely ignored one of the EU's greatest successes, namely, its enlargement to include new MS. In the process of integration, the EEC/EC/EU has incorporated twenty-one MS in addition to the original six. But neo-functionalism lacked a theory of when or why this would occur and, most importantly for the present crisis, it had no understanding of how regional decision making might be affected by such an increase in the number of MS and the diversity of their socio-economic interests. To be sure, each time enlargement has occurred – thanks in large part to the sacred nature of the *acquis communitaire* – the effects on existing policy commitments and the likelihood of agreeing upon new ones has become less predictable.

Admittedly, only five of the new MS are so far in the Eurozone (Cyprus, Estonia, Malta, Slovakia and Slovenia), but all of them have been affected by its crisis. Moreover, the entire decision-making structure was designed since the beginning to over-represent these (and other) smaller MS. Whatever solution is found – for example, the much touted one of 'two-speed Europe', that is, of a core group going ahead to even further economic, monetary and even political integration, it will have to take into account the reactions (and voting weights) of these new MS in order to bring it about. And there is every indication that the more recent the membership, the more likely a given member is to be sensitive to being allotted second-class status. At the same time, the more rigorous the norms of economic governance become within the Eurozone, the more remote the prospect is for those on the outside to join it anytime soon.

La Finalité Politique

Neo-functionalists have been notoriously reluctant to speculate about the end-product of regional integration– its so-called *finalité politique.* The implicit assumption seems to have been that it would eventually approximate a supra-national federal state – perhaps one closer to the Swiss or Canadian model than the American one. At the core of this assumption was the idea that progressive spill-overs in tasks and authority (*compétences* in the EU jargon) would accumulatively contribute to the network of institutions in Brussels, especially the Commission, and that all national states would have the same rights and obligations.

Instead, the emerging EU polity has proven to be much more complex and unprecedented. Schmitter (1996) called this a '*condominio*' in that it has a fixed number of members at any given moment, but they have a variable set of rights and obligations. Moreover, the decision-making structure has become increasingly poly-centric with new institutions emerging that are not subordinated to the central administrative core in Brussels. And the ECB with its Eurozone and only 17 of the 27 EU members is a prime example of these two features. What this means is a built-in inability to know for sure which regional institutions are competent to make decisions alone or only in concert with others.

At various moments during the crisis, different and competing actors have emerged to declare their competence and respective responses: the ECB, the ECOFIN (Economic and Finance) Committee, the Commission, the President of the Eurogroup (not to be confused with the President of the Euro-Summit), the President of the Council of Ministers and the President of the European Council. It was the latter that produced two parallel agreements, the European Financial Stability Facility (EFSF) and the European Financial Stability Mechanism (EFSM) (note well that neither is a treaty) delegating unprecedented powers to the Commission to monitor its implementation and even to punish any transgressions of its terms. Needless to say, this type of poly-centrism (without an overriding constitutional mandate and without any increase in democratic accountability) greatly complicates the resolution of crises, confounds the comprehension of mass publics and, hence, jeopardises the legitimacy of whatever is eventually decided.

Politicisation

The original neo-functionalist assumption was that this had to happen eventually, but that when it happened, the crisis driven by it would generate higher levels of popular support based presumably on its 'output' legitimacy (that is, the positive material benefits the EU had generated for most Europeans in most MS). National politicians were expected to reject further extensions of regional competence because these increments would threaten their acquired status and undermine their historical importance.

But the empirical reality proved to be perverse. Over time, we have seen national political elites in MS prepared to sign away important aspects of sovereignty and national mass publics expressing suspicion or outright opposition to this – especially when they were given the chance to express themselves in referenda (for example, Draft Constitutional Treaty: France and Netherlands 2005, Treaty of Lisbon: Ireland 2008).

In fact, the referenda on treaty ratification conducted only in some MS constitute one of the few instances of direct public involvement in the integration process. But such referenda asked publics to approve or disapprove *faits accomplis*, that is, *after* decisions had been taken at the EU level. And, if they failed to vote 'correctly', they were given a second chance to change their minds. A different, input-oriented direct democratic tool was introduced and establishes a direct (albeit non-binding) link to the Commission: the European Citizen Initiative (ECI) (article 11.4 Lisbon Treaty). Since the ratification of the Treaty and its official launch in April 2012, there has emerged an ever longer list of prospective ECIs.[8] Although limited to matters involved in the implementation of existing Treaty provisions (that is, it cannot be used as an instrument for Treaty revision), the tool's success presupposes the presence of cross-national social movements or parties capable of mobilising one million citizens in seven MS – which probably means that it will be used in defence of more, rather than less, integration (as Schmitter had imagined).

Since its foundation by a restricted group of elite politicians and experts, the Union's legitimacy has relied on output, not input, democracy (Scharpf 1999; Bellamy 2010). Wider publics have not been afforded the opportunity to act either in defence of or in opposition to specific EU policies. This is because national political elites who structure the debate in both national and European electoral arenas and who, in turn, are supposed to constitute the exclusive institutional channels for regular citizens' expression about such matters have systematically

---

8   See official website: http://ec.europa.eu/citizens-initiative/public/initiatives/ongoing.

kept EU policies outside electoral politics (Pennings 2006).[9] Elections to the European Parliament have functioned as 'second-order elections' (Reif and Schmitt 1980) revolving either around national issues or around the 'wrong' EU issues (for example, constitutional design, see Lefkofridi and Kritzinger 2008; Mair 2000, 2007). In this way, national parties have suppressed their internal conflicts over EU policies and their limited capacity to act unilaterally on key public policy issues.[10] Even worse, instead of defending EU 'outputs' – even when faced with pro-EU publics, such as in Italy or Greece – mainstream political elites used 'Brussels' as an alibi when they had to promote unpopular reforms (Lefkofridi 2009; Smith 1997). This behaviour combined with low levels of EU-related knowledge among EU electorates has contributed to the EU's 'demonisation'.

As Mair (2007) observed, the crux of the problem was that the policies that got de-politicised at the national level did not get re-politicised at the EU level. For this to occur, likeminded national parties in different countries would have to integrate across national borders. But this requires a great deal of difficult programmatic coordination, not to mention change in internal organisation and sharing of leadership positions. This is because EU membership places party organisations in a multilevel policy arena where numerous other actors pursue their own policy objectives. National and sub-national parties have deliberately kept Europe on their organisational periphery (Poguntke et al. 2007; Ladrech 2009). Despite the transfer of sovereignty in so many policy areas, party elites did not transfer their organisations' 'loyalty' to the EU level. This is because they – even those momentarily involved at the EU level – have been deeply entrenched and professionalised in terms of career expectations in their respective national regimes (and this has been a crucial complication for EU democratisation, see Schmitter 2000).

As the public's 'permissive consensus' gradually transformed into 'constraining dissensus' (Hooghe and Marks 2009), extreme left – and right parties – took electoral advantage of the growing gap between citizens and mainstream elites

---

9   A key risk in organising contestation on the EU and its policies was that attitudes towards the EU and its policies 'could impel voters to political behaviour that (because of its degree of orthogonality with left/right orientations) undercuts the bases for contemporary party mobilisation' (Van der Eijk and Franklin 2004: 33). Scholars have thus portrayed the politicisation of European integration as a giant that is 'sleeping' (Van der Eijk and Franklin 2004: 33) or one that has been 'sedated' by the party cartel (Mair 2007).

10   According to Mair (2007) EU law, policies and institutions increasingly limit the policy space, the policy instruments and the policy repertoire at parties' disposal. In other words, integration 'ties' national parties' hands (Mair 2000): due to the supremacy of EU law, when incumbent national parties take EU-level policy decisions, subsequent government alternation at the national level cannot cancel these decisions. The Single Market and the Maastricht Treaty fundamentally changed national parties' policy arena and dampened important policy conflicts between left and right, especially regarding the management of the national economy (for example, Mair 2000, 2007; see also Johansson and Raunio 2001; Hix and Goetz 2000).

on European integration.[11] To be sure, it is difficult to discern whether support for fringe parties actually expresses opposition to the EU or opposition to domestic governmental policies – since supra-national and national policy-making are increasingly interwoven (Mair 2007).

It is precisely this (hidden) inter-relationship of regional and domestic policy that this crisis brought to light. Electoral outcomes in one member were increasingly recognised as affecting the governing coalitions' vulnerability in other MS and the EU as a whole. Thus, EU concerns penetrated deeply (and for the first time) in the conduct and results of recent French Presidential and Greek and Dutch parliamentary elections. In each of these, elites in office were called upon by their EU partners to commit to 'long-run' EU policy goals, at times when, due to widespread anti-EU sentiments, these policy positions were likely to have an obverse impact upon their parties' (short-run) vote optimisation strategies.

In sum, Europe's politicisation is here to stay, and this comes in an era of general public disenchantment with traditional parties.[12] New populist movements are constantly being formed,[13] while existing ones are gaining in support. Hence, pro-EU elites are under great pressure, not just to defend existing integration policies, but also to collectively articulate alternative ones in response to the crisis. And they may not be able to successfully accomplish the latter without admitting the necessity for political integration and, with it, the democratisation of their Union (see Schmitter 2000).

5. Conclusion

In response to the crisis, national representatives have shared a common short-run objective: to use EU institutions and resources to calm and dampen market fluctuations. In this, after some confusion and misdirection, they have been successful, at least for the moment. The Euro has survived. However, these same political elites must decide whether (and, if so, to what extent) they share longer-run objectives, not just to prevent a recurrence of the same crisis, but to ensure the legitimacy of the measures they have taken in response to the present one. Having devolved such substantial new competences upon EU institutions inevitably raises the sensitive issue of whether its citizens will tolerate being governed by a 'benevolent' technocracy without demanding more participation in it for themselves and accountability from their rulers for the policies they

---

11   In studies of congruence on European integration, elites systematically appear more supportive than publics (for example, Thomassen and Schmitt 1999; Mattila and Raunio 2012).

12   This, however, is a phenomenon observed long before the Euro-crisis (for example, Mair and van Biezen 2001).

13   For example: the Pirates (who even plan to run a common EP campaign); the Stronach party that advocates Austria's exit from the Eurozone (but not the EU).

have chosen. If not – if the motto 'no taxation (and budgeting and borrowing) without representation' still has any meaning – then the entire edifice of regional integration could be threatened and, with it, the security community Europeans have built around themselves during the past 60 years or so. As far as one can judge, no governing politician in Europe wants to bear responsibility for such a drastic 'spill-back', but how many are prepared to accept responsibility for political integration and supra-national democratisation has yet to be proven.

The crisis is not over and certainly its consequences will be felt for some time to come, which means that there is still an opportunity to turn an apparently bad crisis into a good one. Moreover, the instrument for doing so already exists in the form of that unprecedented delegation of competence to the Commission.[14] What will make the immediate difference will be the purpose to which it will exercise those powers. Two elements of change are likely to make the difference:

1. The emergence of agreement among a different epistemic community of economists – let us call them Keynesians or institutionalists; and
2. The cross-national formation of a political movement within a sufficient number of MS in favour of a set of expansionary as opposed to contractionary policies at the EU level (for example, Euro-bonds guaranteed by all MS; a programme of European-scale public works in energy and transport – even in research and development – financed by the European Investment Bank).

There does seem to be a critical mass of dissident economists (and plenty of social scientists) in favour of this, as well as an emerging coalition of national governments (of the Right in Spain and Portugal, of the left in France, of both in Greece and of Technocrats in Italy). It remains to be seen whether this will prove sufficient to nudge the European Council in such a new direction. If it is sufficient and (even more problematic) if it is successful, then the EU could re-acquire and greatly strengthen its association with economic prosperity and social justice – that famous 'European Model of Society' that Jacques Delors was so fond of invoking. What will still be missing is that, as yet to be defined and rarely invoked, 'European Model of Democracy' that will be necessary to legitimate such a massive 'spill-over' from the national to the supra-national level. Seen from this (admittedly improbable) perspective, the Euro-crisis could just be the detonator of that 'Transcending Cycle' that Schmitter imagined 40 years ago.

---

14   Guiliano Amato and Yves Mény (2012) have already baptised it as 'budgetary federalism'.

Chapter 2

Economic Crisis and the Internationalisation of EU Competition Policy

Michelle Cini

1. Introduction

The Euro-crisis not only risks discrediting the European integration process, but also all European Union (EU) policies, even where they have little to do with banking and sovereign debt. If this happens both the credibility of the policy within the EU and its external reach will be affected. The theoretical proposition that economic crisis limits a state's or a region's external influence might seem self-evident, and applied to the EU might even be said to be stating the obvious. Yet the claim deserves some empirical investigation if we are to better understand the way in which internal EU policies impinge on global governance. To address this question, the chapter discusses one policy case: competition policy. Competition provides an interesting research focus, as it is closely related to, but not at the core of, the debates regarding reforms to the EU's economic governance. From a governance perspective, the policy provides a fascinating case of institutional change, as it has been subject to a series of major reforms in the 2000s: a response both to challenges facing it and to criticisms levelled at it. According to Wilks these reforms institutionalised pre-existing neo-classical/neo-liberal economic and political principles within a new legal-cultural framework (Wilks 2009: 271–2) and they seek to present the competition regime as depoliticised and independent of the vagaries of political whim. As the key actor in both the making and enforcing of the policy, the European Commission (delegating a great deal of its work to the Directorate General for Competition) has decentralised much of the enforcement of the policy to national competition agencies (NCAs), while at the same time retaining control of its general direction. Meanwhile it has pursued an internationalisation agenda.

To examine the likelihood that the Euro-crisis will alter the EU's ability to influence the global governance of competition, this chapter draws on both secondary and primary sources. The chapter proceeds as follows: Section 2 examines the EU competition framework prior to 2008; Section 3, the European Commission response to the financial and later the Euro-crisis with regard to its competition policy; and finally Section 4 discusses the European Commission's external competition policy agenda. The conclusion argues that contrary to expectations the European Commission's external policy on competition has so far been little affected by the financial/Euro-crisis. This is because the policy has managed to retain its credibility internally within the EU during the crisis. This does not preclude a more subtle and longer-term effect on the capacity of the EU to pursue its preferred external approach in the future however.

2. The EU Competition Policy Framework

When the European Economic Community (EEC) set up its competition regime, competition policies were more the exception than the rule in Western Europe. Among the EEC's prospective member states only West Germany had fully fledged competition legislation (Cini and McGowan 2008: 18). Although the European Coal and Steel Community (ECSC) rules had set a precedent, the EEC entered largely uncharted territory as it worked to draft treaty provisions on competition. Ultimately a German-influenced model was chosen, which demanded the prior notification of all potentially anti-competitive agreements (or cartels) and potentially abusive dominant positions (or monopolies). Provisions for the control of domestic state aid (or subsidies) were also included though as yet, there was no reference to mergers and acquisitions.

The competition provisions of the Rome Treaty (excluding state aid policy) were implemented through a regulation known subsequently as 'Regulation 17' (European Council 1962). This became the pride of DG Competition, as it set out procedures to govern the day-to-day workings of the policy and gave the Commission substantial investigative powers. The model chosen for European competition regime was highly centralised and, as such, it endowed the Commission with a pre-eminent role in the enforcement of the policy. As an ally of the Commission for much of the policy's history, the European Court often confirmed the Commission's discretion in competition matters while at the same time establishing certain parameters for the policy and the Commission's role within it. However, over time, the Commission came under attack for failing to take high quality decisions based on robust economic theory.

The history of European-level merger control was very different from that of other forms of European competition policy as there was no explicit reference to mergers (or 'concentrations') in the Treaty of Rome. It was not until the Commission (supported by the Court) began to use the restrictive practices and monopoly provisions of the Treaty to deal with merger cases that member states felt forced to respond by agreeing on a long-promised regulation, which was designed to reduce uncertainty among the business community. This was initially agreed in 1989 with subsequent revision in 2004. State aid policy also followed its own trajectory. While the legal framework remained largely unchanged, there was a concerted push to implement the policy with greater rigour in the late 1980s given the subsidy pressures induced by the Single Market Programme. A far-reaching reform was proposed only at the end of 2012.

Launched in a White Paper in 1999 by former Commissioner, Karel van Miert, and his Director-General, Alexander Schaub (European Commission 1999), the reform of the EU's restrictive practices and monopoly policy was eventually put into effect in 2004. Although it had taken five years to translate the ideas in the White Paper into law, the Commission had been discussing the possibility of a reform of Regulation 17 for a much longer time. It had initially feared that initiating such a reform might open a 'Pandora's Box', which could allow national governments to claw back control over competition regulation. It is perhaps ironic then, that decentralisation was to become a defining feature of the reform.

On the cartel and monopoly side the modernisation package involved two main elements: the decentralisation of enforcement to the national level; and the reform of the Commission's decision-making and enforcement powers (European Council 2003). In a dramatic move, the reforms scrapped the Commission's centralised prior notification system. It also set up a European Competition Network (ECN) to iron out any differences of interpretation across the EU member states (Wilks 2005: 440–44). The detail of how the relationship between DG Competition, national competition agencies and the courts would work in practice was explained in a subsequent Commission Notice (European Commission 2004).

In pursuing this approach, DG Competition planned to free up resources to allow it to focus on the investigation of the most serious cases (hard-core cartels) that came to its attention either following complaints or on the basis of own-initiative investigations (Gauer et al. 2003). To that end, Regulation 1/2003, which introduced the reforms, gave DG Competition enhanced powers of investigation. It also increased the likelihood of a successful investigation and prosecution by adopting a 'leniency' programme which allowed immunity or reduced fines/penalties to be granted to whistle-blowers and compliant offenders. Moreover, the modernisation package included a reform of the EU's merger policy, in the form of a revision of the 1989 Merger Control Regulation (MCR). This introduced more explicit economic analysis into merger decision-making. It also altered the test of illegality, clarified some procedural issues, and introduced more flexibility into the sharing of cases with national authorities (Wilks 2005: 434).

These changes have to be understood in their political and institutional context (Akbar and Suder 2006). The approach not only involved softer decision-making instruments and the use of networks as a transmission belt for the Commission's competition culture (Lehmkuhl 2009), it also marked a sea-change in the extent and type of economic analysis used by DG Competition in its decisions on competition cases. This rested on market economy foundations and a view of economics which privileged the role of 'free competition, minimal government intervention, short-term economic efficiency, consumer welfare and a faith in market outcomes' (Wilks 2009: 272). This economic approach had implications for the kinds of anti-competitive exceptions to the general rule that would in future be allowed, raising problems of compatibility between the position of the Commission and that of the European Court (Witt 2012). It also implied a greater emphasis on private enforcement of the rules in national courts and increasingly on private arbitration

(Lehmkuhl 2009). This has been described as an 'Americanisation' of the existing policy (Wigger and Nölke 2007; see also Morgan and McGowan 2013).

Even if an Americanisation agenda is convincing in explaining certain aspects of the reform, Wilks (2005) focuses on a different set of arguments which supplement that line of argument. He makes a clear distinction between decentralisation presented as a way of tackling case overload and the imminent pressures of EU enlargement and the argument that the reforms constitute a further centralisation by subterfuge of the Commission's powers in this policy field, an explanation that he finds more convincing. In other words, he argues that the modernisation agenda was more about strengthening the hand of the Commission. It enhanced its control over the policy, over the NCAs and – indirectly – over national governments who might wish to pursue a policy different from that of the Commission, but who would find this increasingly difficult once the EU policy had been embedded in the domestic arena. The Commission pulled off an extraordinary coup (Wilks 2005: 437), in that the reforms institutionalised the Commission's approach to competition regulation across the EU. Seemingly, in recognition of this, the Commission began to talk of this aspect of the modernisation agenda as a way to enhance Europe-wide *cooperation* (Wilks 2005: 436).

3. The Crisis and the EU Competition Policy Response

In the first years of the financial and economic crisis, between 2007 and 2009, there was much speculation as to whether the crisis would undermine neoliberalism and whether this might mark a return to Keynesianism, or even to some form of Marxism, or whether some new model might emerge to substitute for the discredited old ways of doing things. This debate finds an echo in the commentary and academic literature on EU competition policy. Philip Lowe, Director-General of Competition in the Commission from 2002–09, remarked that the crisis ' … challenged current models of regulation and oversight in the financial sector, and raised questions about the role of the state in economic life' (Lowe 2009: 3), even though he did not claim that it dramatically affected competition policy. Wilks (2009: 436), by contrast, goes further, in questioning whether the core assumptions underpinning the competition model espoused by DG Competition might be undermined as a consequence of the crisis. Wigger and Buch-Hansen (2013) later argued that the policy had managed to survive more or less intact. They point to various reasons for this outcome: that the crisis was successfully construed as a crisis *within* and not *of* neoliberal capitalism; that the social power configuration within the neoliberal order remained unchallenged; that there were no clear counter-projects; that the Commission opposed radical change; and that there was no wider paradigm shift in the EU's regulatory architecture (Wigger and Buch-Hansen 2013). This does not mean that the policy did not have to adapt, only that it did not reach breaking point. More mundane reasons for this include the discursive and practical role played by the Competition Commissioner, Neelie Kroes, in the early stages of the crisis, and the distinctive character of EU competition policy (in that it includes a state aid control element).

From the start of the financial crisis, the European Commission came under immense pressure to relax its tough competition rules. At a time when many businesses were struggling for survival, competition policy seemed an unnecessary and potentially damaging luxury, one which was more suited to the good times pre-dating the crisis (Wilks 2009: 277). National governments took the lead in arguing for a relaxation of the rules (Kroes 2010: 3; Lowe 2009: 3) and to a degree in the early stages of the crisis, the Commission was 'on the back foot', reacting *post hoc* to decisions already taken by national government, rather than setting the agenda itself. Reynolds et al. (2009–10: 1673–4), for example, argue that DG Competition's response to the crisis evolved 'in real time' in September 2007 as the UK's bail-out of the Northern Rock bank was taking place.

The Competition Commissioner, Neelie Kroes, held her ground however and insisted that DG Competition be allowed to continue to enforce its competition rules. This was a daunting task, which meant an increasing workload for DG Competition, the learning of new skills and liaison with new institutions including central banks (Kroes 2010: 3). By the end of her term of office however, she could confidently claim that: 'Supporters of the view that competition breeds competitiveness, and that European consumers and businesses benefit from a level playing field, have effectively won the argument' (Kroes 2010: 3). This 'business as usual' (Kroes 2009) approach was intended to reinforce the view that the EU would not make the same mistakes as the US during the Great Depression in the relaxing of antitrust rules (Kroes 2010: 3; Tranholm-Schwarz et al. 2009: 3). Competition policy, the Commissioner argued, was part of the solution, not part of the problem (Kroes 2010: 4). Kroes's discourse was clear and consistent (for example, Kroes 2008 and 2009) and it continued under her successor Joaquín Almunia from 2010.

The aspect of competition policy most affected in the early stages of the crisis was state aid policy, as a consequence of the huge bank bail-outs in 2007 and 2008. The levels of aid being granted over this period were 'awe-inspiring' (Wilks 2009: 273) rising from 0.5 per cent of the EU's Gross Domestic Product (GDP) in 2007 to 3.6 per cent in 2009 (Aydin and Thomas 2012: 540). It was not until the collapse of Lehman Brothers in September 2008 however that the Commission agreed to exempt bail-outs under what was then Article 87 (3)(b) (now Article 107(3)(b)), which allowed aid to be exempt as a consequence of a 'serious disturbance in the economy'. Prior to this date, assessments had to be made using the less generous Article 87(3)(c) (now Article 107(3)(c)) (Lowe 2009: 4). The Lehman Brothers debâcle prompted the Commission to start developing its new framework (Kroes 2010: 4). This ultimately comprised four Commission Communications: covering state aid to the banking sector (European Commission 2008a); the recapitalisation of banks (European Commission 2008b); the treatment of impaired assets (European Commission 2009a); and bank restructuring (European Commission 2009b; Bomhoff et al. 2009). Each of these Communications adapted existing rules to the context allowing the Commissioner to argue that the competition framework remained intact in terms of the principles applied, while demonstrating flexibility in adjusting to the difficult circumstances of the crisis in the financial sector. For example, it allowed for flexibility in defining certain (borderline) support as state aid, thereby removing it from the EU's legal framework (Reynolds et al. 2009–10: 1676). This was often referred to as the 'balanced approach'.

It was not long before issues in the real economy also had to be dealt with, particularly with respect to the impact of the 'credit crunch'. The broader context for this was the European Economic Recovery Plan of 26 November 2008 (European Commission 2008c). The banks may have been 'saved' by huge injections of state aid; but they were not lending to each other, or to businesses and individuals. The economy was coming to a standstill as a consequence. In response, the Commission, among other initiatives outside the field of competition policy, introduced what became known as the Temporary Framework for State Aid, which 'would maximise what Member States could squeeze out of the system without fundamentally altering it' (Kroes 2010: 4).

In other areas of competition policy beyond state aid control, the Commission was on even more solid ground in claiming that they had withstood the crisis (Kroes 2010: 6). Here, too, a flexible approach was introduced. In merger policy, DG Competition acted more swiftly than usual, so that governments and firms would not have to wait for lengthy periods for a Commission decision (Reynolds et al. 2009–10: 1696), as in the *BNP Paribas/Fortis* case in December 2008 (Kroes 2010: 6; European Commission 2008d). The Commission also signalled that it was willing to consider a 'failing firm' defence, which induces special treatment in respect of the acquisition of firms likely to become insolvent where their assets might end up exiting the market (Reynolds et al. 2009–10: 1703–8). There was also some evidence according to Reynolds et al. (2009–10: 1711) that more mergers than usual were receiving a conditional clearance at the first (Phase I) preliminary stage of assessment.

A tough line continued to be taken on cartel policy (Reynolds et al. 2009–10: 1722); there was no tolerance of the crisis cartels that had been a feature of the 1970s crisis (Kroes 2010: 5). There was however increasing interest in the application of DG Competition's controversial fining policy with firms seeking to avoid the tough penalty of full fines, by making use of the immunity/leniency and settlement regimes introduced by the Commission prior to the crisis (Reynolds et al. 2009–10: 1724–30). In turn, the Commission was willing to use its flexibility in fining policy to respond to firms that requested a reduction in their fine (known as the financial constraints or bankruptcy discount). Although again only considered in exceptional circumstances, firms have even been permitted to pay in instalments where they can provide objective evidence of hardship (Reynolds et al. 2009–10: 1733–5).

In sum, the EU's competition regime has proven remarkably resilient. This resilience is surprising given the initial state aid onslaught, and the rather slow response of the Commission (DG Competition) in the early months of the crisis. Yet it is *because of* the Commission's state aid competence that the regime remained relevant. Its ability to respond effectively on this issue in late 2008 and early 2009 gave it a credibility, which had a knock-on effect in other areas of competition control. So when Commission officials claimed that 'The Commission is ... well placed to address the competition-related problems raised by the economic crisis in a comprehensive and effective way' (Tranholm-Schwarz et al. 2009: 3), they were able to substantiate their assertion. It was not only the state aid competence that mattered though, but also the relevant legal frameworks which managed to balance legal certainty and discretion and which had been strengthened by the reforms of the preceding years. This was further supported by the consistent and unflinching approach adopted by the Competition Commissioner, whose assertions of its relevance managed to sustain the credibility of the policy when it might otherwise have been undermined. Whether this policy resilience can also be identified in the external dimension of EU competition policy is a question addressed in the following section.

4. The External Dimension of EU Competition Policy

At much the same time as the Commission (DG Competition) was translating its modernisation agenda into a workable reform, that is, in the late 1990s and early 2000s, it was also seeking to promote an internationalisation agenda. It has various instruments at its disposal to do this. The most contentious of these instruments have involved the extraterritorial application of EU competition law. Extraterritoriality is the application of competition law to firms beyond the borders of the state or region's jurisdiction. It is contentious because extraterritoriality is generally perceived as an aggressive act. This is particularly the case where United States (US) firms are implicated in the Commission's decisions (even though the US antitrust authorities are experienced in the extraterritorial application of their own competition laws). States may even find ways of blocking their 'own' firms from complying with the laws of other regimes, for example by initiating blocking statutes prohibiting or limiting firms from assisting with investigations as a tit-for-tat response to, say, requests for information. This was what happened in 2012 when Russia issued a blocking statute in response to the Commission's investigation of Gazprom (Martiniszyn 2013). As the Commission's confidence and expertise has grown however, so too has its willingness to apply competition law extraterritoriality even in difficult cases. This is generally not a particularly positive instrument of external influence, even if it remains useful when dealing with individual cases.

At the broader policy level, the Commission has been keen to promote the negotiation and approval of bilateral agreements. These agreements have proliferated since the early 1990s and are discretionary in the sense that they constitute soft (international) law (Damro 2006a). The first and most important of these agreements was the EU–US bilateral competition agreement, first signed in 1991 which brought together the world's two 'antitrust superpowers' (Waller 1999: 165). The agreement has been revised since and other agreements, alongside looser memoranda of understanding, have been signed including a recent (2013) 'second generation' agreement with Switzerland.

Bilateral agreements have been successful in the simple sense that agreements have been reached, but also in that they have facilitated cooperation and provided the basis for greater understanding across competition regimes. Yet they have their limits. Competition cases that have an international dimension rarely involve only two regimes. The bilateralisation of global policy can therefore be a messy solution to the real world problems facing competition authorities dealing with tricky cases. Reflecting on the way multinational firms operate across borders (and so in light of 'globalisation'), the Commission sought in the late 1990s to go beyond the bilateral approach, to pursue a multilateralisation agenda for competition policy.

In the late 1990s the primary forum through which the Commission pursued its multilateral agenda was the World Trade Organisation (WTO) (Maher 2002). The WTO was a relative newcomer to the competition policy field as it was only in the mid-1990s that competition was included as one of its 'new issues'. This was in spite of the fact that one of the original ambitions of the forerunner of the WTO, the General Agreement on Tariffs and Trade (GATT) in the 1940s, was to deal with global-level competition issues. In 1996, at the Ministerial Conference in Singapore, the decision was taken to set up two working groups to examine how trade and competition interact, and in the Doha Ministerial Declaration in 2001 it was agreed to include competition as part of the Doha Development Agenda, focusing on such issues as hard-core cartels, voluntary cooperation, and capacity building (the reinforcement of competition institutions, especially in transition economies) as well as looking at core principles.

If the option of the WTO as the EU's forum of choice is not self-explanatory, neither is its commitment to a multilateral approach to competition enforcement. The rationale for such an approach is that it is a response to 'globalisation forces' (Dabbah 2003: 287). This meant that antitrust became a complement to trade policy, thereby explaining the relevance of the WTO as the international competition actor of choice (Dabbah 2003: 288). Damro (2006b: 880) has a view on why the Commission chose to focus on the WTO as opposed to other international organisations. He argues that regulators generally select venues which provide dispute prevention over and above dispute resolution. More specifically, the push to cooperate with the WTO came more from DG Trade than it did from DG Competition. Likewise Tarullo (2000: 479) argues that the choice of venue matters in terms of policy outcomes and that where a code was promoted by the WTO, market access would end up taking precedence over competition.

The WTO was reacting to the EU's agenda in taking these steps. However, while the Commission argued for a WTO competition code, the US firmly opposed the idea, preferring a looser form of cooperation across national competition authorities (Tarullo 2000: 478). One commentator has argued that the reason for this was that a code of this kind was alien to the US's common law tradition (Waller 1999). The US position may also be explained by the regulatory rivalry that persists across the two regimes in what Fox has called 'the race to be the model of the world' (Fox 1999). From 2001 the interest in developing a multilateral agreement waned, as it became less likely that any agreement could be struck. By 2003, the Cancun Ministerial Meeting of the WTO had expressed a desire to drop competition from the Doha agenda. This was confirmed in the 'WTO 2004 package', in which the WTO General Council decided that competition policy 'will not form part of the Work Programme set out in the Declaration – and so no work towards negotiations will take place within the WTO Doha Round' (WTO 2013). Since then the working groups have been inactive.

This does not mean that there was a collapse in international activity on the competition front. But since the mid-2000s and the onset of the Euro-crisis the strategy adopted by the EU has been much more in line with US preferences. Thus, the priority beyond extraterritoriality continues to centre on the negotiation of bilateral agreements. The Commission has continued to follow 'diverse strategies of external governance' (Aydin 2012: 78) however. In 2001 a new forum at the global level was established, in the form of the International Competition Network (ICN) (Hollman and Kovacic 2011; Yoshizawa 2011). The ICN is an informal network of competition regulators who meet to agree guidelines and principles, and to recommend common practices. Maher (2002) places particular emphasis on this kind of network of experts or epistemic community in this policy area (Van Waarden and Drahos 2002; Wilks 2005; Lehmkuhl 2008: 112–13), in wielding soft power and using persuasion to good effect – possibly even resulting ultimately in formal agreements. DG Competition views the ICN in a similar way, as ' … a new form of governance based on converging views leading to common standards as opposed to binding rules and sanctions'. The forum has the support and active involvement of the US authorities, as well as more than one hundred participants from both the developed and the developing world.

Since the mid-2000s and the onset of the financial and economic crisis, references to the Commission's earlier policy of multilateralisation have disappeared from the Commission's official documentation and from speeches made by Commissioners. International organisations, including the OECD and the United Nations Conference on Trade and Development (UNCTAD), continue to provide a forum for discussion, but there is no expectation that they will do more than this. There is no mention made of any potential role for the WTO. This shift in approach pre-dates the onset of the crisis, however, and can be interpreted in two ways: first, as evidence that the US was able to veto the Commission's preferred approach to the global governance of competition; and second, as the victory of DG Competition's preferred approach within the Commission (see Damro 2006b). However, it also needs to be understood in the context of the more general difficulties associated with international trade negotiations since the early 2000s.

The dropping of the multilateral agenda (with the exception of involvement in the ICN) has meant that there has been a certain consistency in the EU's approach to the internationalisation of competition policy. The focus has been on resolving internal matters. As we have seen, since the crisis began DG Competition has been able to assert itself effectively within the European Commission. Although competition policy is close to matters of economic governance, it is also somewhat detached from the travails of the Eurozone. In demonstrating both the consistency and flexibility of the policy, and in asserting its value as a solution to the crisis, Competition Commissioners have been able to save competition policy from the discrediting effect that seems to have impacted other EU (economic) policy domains. This has been helped by the fact that EU competition policy is distinctive in having a state aid control competence which made it more relevant than it would otherwise have been at the start of the crisis.

Informal modes of decision-making, the use of soft law and the network governance approach are rarely associated with effective supranational policy-making, and they are rarely understood as a way in which the Commission might become more powerful. Yet the adoption of these instruments and the use of these channels of influence by DG Competition, both in its dealings with national regimes and at the international level, have allowed it to continue to influence global competition policy, even in spite of the crisis. The capacity to make use of such opportunities derives from the DG's credibility, which is itself a product of its resilience. That said, it certainly helps that its approach is similar to that of the US in its preference for bilateral agreements and the spread of what it considers to be good practice through the ICN. This should not necessarily be taken as an indicator of the Americanisation of the policy, but it does point to the importance of transatlantic (US–EU) convergence as a prerequisite for the gradual building of a global competition culture (or multilateral convergence). It also suggests that improved transatlantic relations, and the growing similarity between the US and the EU approach to competition enforcement helps rather than hinders DG Competition, as it seeks to maintain its position, whether inside the Commission, with firms and governments across Europe, or indeed internationally.

5. Conclusion

This chapter began by asking whether the Euro-crisis has impinged on the international dimension of the EU's competition policy. It finds no evidence that it has. In the period since the crisis it has been business as usual for the EU's approach to global competition governance. The credibility of EU competition policy remains intact within the Union, demonstrating the quite impressive resilience of the policy, and though the EU failed to influence the international agenda on competition policy, this failure pre-dated the onset of the crisis and so cannot be attributed to it. This finding of 'no effect' might be considered surprising and even counter-intuitive as we might have expected to find that the EU policy externally faced particular difficulties because of the impact of the Eurozone on EU policies, particularly those linked to the economic sphere. Even if the scope for generalisation might be limited because of the unique characteristics of EU competition policy, this might tell us that EU policies have at least the potential to disassociate themselves from crisis, to operate somewhat autonomously and be judged on their own merits.

Chapter 3

The Transformation of EU Governance, the Open Method of Coordination and the Economic Crisis

Susana Borrás and Claudio M. Radaelli[1]

1. Introduction

Celebrated by some as a 'new' mode of governance (Sabel and Zeitlin 2008) and experimentalist architecture (Sabel and Zeitlin 2010), and denigrated by others as a 'red herring' (Idema and Keleman 2006), the Open Method of Coordination (OMC) connects with major themes in EU politics and public policy, namely the Europe 2020 strategy for economic growth and competitiveness, the transformation of the Eurozone, and the emergence of a new decision-making framework within the scope of the Treaty on the Functioning of the European Union (TFEU). In this chapter we set out to rescue the OMC from this polarised debate and situate the usages of this mode of governance within the debate on the future of the Eurozone. Our main research question is to establish the role of the OMC in the current responses to the Eurozone crisis. To answer this question, we need first of all to explore the conditions that determine the performance of the OMC. We elaborate on our analysis of the literature (in Section 2) by arguing in Section 3 that three dimensions are key: the externalities generated by EU-level collaboration, the level of uncertainty regarding the content of the public action, and the degree of asymmetric distribution of costs and benefits.

We then discuss the implications of the changes under way in the governance regimes of the Eurozone. This leads us to tackle two additional research questions. One is about the interaction of the OMC with harder instruments. The other is about the consequences of the asymmetries, especially in terms of divergence among member states, for the performance of the OMC. There is consensus for 'more' coordination in the embattled architecture of the Eurozone. And there is

1   We wish to acknowledge the formidable input provided by the GR:EEN workshop on *The Transformations of EU Governance*, Brussels, 18–19 April 2013. Frank Schimmelfennig kindly provided detailed feedback on our workshop paper. The usual disclaimer applies. Radaelli thanks the European Research Council, Advanced Section Grant on Analysis of Learning in Regulatory Governance (http://centres.exeter.ac.uk/ceg/research/ALREG/), for financial support.

little doubt that the political response is towards tighter surveillance and more coordination based on harder policy regimes. This applies to the roles of both the Council and the Commission in monetary crisis management, economic coordination, and structural reforms.

We will argue, however, that the re-definition of national budgetary discipline and macroeconomic surveillance calls the meaning of coordination into question: is coordination a way to promote learning, exploration or surveillance? We will show that the OMC can be used in all three dimensions of coordination. At the moment, however, the preference for surveillance casts the interaction between the OMC and the harder instruments of the Eurozone governance regime in the category of surveillance, rather than learning or exploration (see Section 4). The implication is that policy makers should adopt OMC-like approaches to converge on well-defined solutions rather than spawning a process of discovery of solutions at the domestic level. The presence of large asymmetries has somewhat divided the Eurozone members into those who design the policy solutions and those who have to implement it. To converge, the weakest Eurozone members have to follow a paradigm that is often dubbed one of 'austerity' – even if this is not the ideological monolith that the press presents to its readers.

The problem is that to bend the OMC towards surveillance can work only if the strong players of the Eurozone can define the solution in advance. If, instead, structural reforms require learning and exploration at the domestic level, it is a mistake to reduce the variety of OMC to a single dimension of usage, that is, surveillance. We also point to the risk of pushing for convergence towards pre-established solutions under conditions of uncertainty. There is no in-built mechanism to learn lessons and adjust (or even change) the so-called paradigm of austerity on the basis of exploration and learning, if these other two mechanisms are silenced. Under conditions of uncertainty, this creates the risk that the centre of the system can find out about mistakes only when the whole house is on fire. This leads us to conclude in Section 5 that uncertainty refers not only to the uncertainty of the socio-economic context as such, but to the views of decision makers on this socio-economic context and the extent to which they share the same core policy beliefs or not.

2. Literature Review

The history of the creation and development of the OMC begins in the early 1990s with a rapidly changing political and economic context. Firstly, national policy coordination became the central focus of attention in the Economic and Monetary Union (EMU), as enshrined in the Maastricht Treaty. A relatively strict form of economic policy coordination mechanism tackled the prevalent view that a monetary union is impossible among the highly heterogeneous European economies. Most of the efforts in the early 1990s aimed at setting up such a coordination mechanism through the Broad Economic Policy Guidelines (BEPG).

Secondly, in the aftermath of the successful single market project, the Delors Commission started considering the next steps for the socio-economic strategy of the Union. The 'economies of scale' and 'more competition' logic of the single market project 1985–92 was complemented by a vision grounded in environmental sustainability, the information society, and job creation. The key word became 'competitiveness', a term focusing on a wide set of framework conditions shaping the institutional context for economic activity. Admittedly, the 1993 White Paper on competitiveness did not have significant political impact at the time it was published, nor did it have any specific focus on policy instruments or modes of governance. Nevertheless, it struck a chord in many of the academic discussions addressing the 'knowledge based economy' and 'green economy', which were drawn into the centre of political discussions in the late 1990s.

Thirdly, the crisis surrounding the Maastricht Treaty ratification put massive pressure on EU elites to bring the Union closer to citizens. Employment, economic growth and environmental protection became three fundamental dimensions of that political effort, which appeared at the highest political level, later enshrined in the Amsterdam Treaty. This formed the backdrop against which a series of pragmatic voluntary coordination 'processes' were created at the Essen (1994), Luxemburg (1997), Cardiff (1998), Cologne (1999), Lisbon (2000) and Gothenburg (2001) Council meetings. Parallel processes for coordinating national environmental, employment and economic policies were developed in these various 'processes' and rapidly integrated into each other.

Yet the most decisive moment in the creation of voluntary coordination as an EU governance method was the launch of the 'Lisbon Strategy' in March 2000 and its subsequent procedural reform in 2005. The Lisbon Council of 2000 introduced the official definition of the OMC – clarifying its general terms – and the institutionalisation of the annual 'Spring Councils' dedicated to EU policy priorities. The Treaty on the Functioning of the European Union has introduced an interesting novelty. In the catalogue determining the competences of the Union and of Member States (Article 2 TFEU), the Open Method is implicitly referred to as a way of coordinating member states' policies in the areas of economic policy, employment and social policy (Article 4 TFEU). Hence, Article 5 is the closest that the OMC gets in terms of being enshrined in the Treaty, albeit in a rather generic way. This is the end point of the otherwise intense academic debates about constitutionalising the OMC that took place during the Convention and in the negotiations leading to the failed Constitutional Treaty. The Open Method of Coordination is also implicitly mentioned in economic governance (Article 121 TFEU for broad economic policy coordination, Article 126 on budgetary discipline and stability and growth pact and Article 136 for Eurozone budgetary discipline), employment policy (Article 148), social policy (Article 156) and research policy (Article 181). Beyond the specific Lisbon Treaty legal enshrinement, several EU policies have developed OMC-like activities.

The intergovernmental Treaty on Stability, Coordination and Governance signed in 2012 by 25 of the 27 member states, builds upon and facilitates the implementation of Articles 121, 126 and 136, and hence revisits the OMC potential in the macroeconomic policy area. This new treaty, together with the revised Stability and Growth Pact (SGP) of November 2012, has strengthened fiscal discipline via stronger commitment on balanced budgets, and clarifications on types of public debt, as well as via tougher monitoring and sanction mechanisms (that is, excessive deficit procedure). As we observed in the introduction, the conventional wisdom is that asymmetries across the Eurozone have grown because the coordination mechanisms were poor in terms of monitoring, surveillance and sanctions. Hence, we witness a re-consideration of the OMC amidst a broader push for harder forms of governance.

In the meantime, in the specialised literature the question of OMC effectiveness has continued to divide. One set of 'pessimists', like Lodge, argues that the OMC is deficient as a control system. It is not based on clear standards, on accurate information, and on willingness of actors to change their behaviour (Lodge 2007: 348). Idema and Kelemen (2006) make similar findings regarding the OMC's inherent 'failure by design'. The conditions for effectiveness are however different from Lodge's. For these two authors, effectiveness depends on the ability of the Commission to detect transgressions by member states; the Commission's discretion in reacting to member states' transgressions so that the threat of shaming is credible; and the Commission's authority not being discredited by member states (Idema and Kelemen 2006). Since the OMC does not fulfil any of these three criteria, this 'new' mode of governance is defective by design. Another set of 'pessimist' scholars is more focused on the issue of the poor effects of the OMC in terms of change. In her study of the impact of the OMC social inclusion in the reforms and changes of social policy in France and Germany, Sandra Kröger finds no effect (Kröger 2009a).

In spite of this, there is evidence of at least some degree of effects in terms of the transnational diffusion of information and mutual learning. This is particularly evident in studies that summarise the literature on various OMC processes (Kröger 2009a, 2009b; Radaelli 2008; Hartlapp 2009). Radaelli (2008) distinguishes between (a) learning at the top or EU-level learning; (b) compliance among member states with EU-level instructions or learning from the top; and (c) social learning or learning at the EU level as a result of innovations produced in the member states and at the local-regional level – the latter being the kind of reflexivity evoked by the theorists of deliberative-experimentalist governance. By reviewing a large number of empirical studies, Radaelli finds some evidence of learning at the top – limited, but not trivial evidence of cognitive convergence driven by the top – concerning economic policy paradigms and the constitutional boundary-drawing we mentioned earlier, and almost no evidence of learning from below, or 'bottom-up' learning. The OMC seems to support the development of new intra-governmental routines and subnational governance structures, but that differences across countries in terms of learning and change depend largely on the previous degree of ideational and institutional misfit with the principles put forward by the OMC (Lopez-Santana 2009).

Another useful approach to these questions is to focus on policy instruments. Hartlapp (2009) looks at instruments such as guidelines, benchmarking, peer review, reporting, and indicators. The focus on these five instruments is useful in understanding the different contributions to three types of learning, that is (a) learning from one's experience; (b) learning from the experience of the others, and (c) learning with others in deliberative problem-solving settings, a concept reminiscent of reflexive social learning and Radaelli's 'learning from the bottom'. Hartlapp's evidence shows that the instruments are designed and used in ways that often tilt interaction towards negotiation and bargaining. This attitude, she concludes, is incompatible with learning, since learning arises out of processes of communication, trust, and open argumentation in a problem-solving setting. However, the instruments of the OMC do contribute to learning processes, albeit in different ways: learning from experience is facilitated by guidelines and indicators; learning from others is found in benchmarking and peer review; learning with others appears in the national reform programmes (reporting) but not in the other four instruments.

The role of learning and other mechanisms should not be appraised in relation to a single notion of the OMC or one single set of specific OMC instruments. Naturally, since the OMC operates in different policy domains, learning mechanisms vary depending on the specific nature of the policy area at stake. Perhaps the widest set of evidence regarding effects on national learning and information diffusion is found in a collective work about the influence of the OMC in national employment policies (Heidenreich and Zeitlin 2009). The empirical findings point yet again towards diversity in terms of learning effects and in terms of procedural aspects at the national level. Most interesting in those findings, is that learning processes have been related to EU membership conditionality, as in the Baltic countries (Jacobsson and West 2009), and to the degree of political and economic dependence on the EU of countries like Spain and Poland (Mailand 2009).

This leads us to two dimensions: variation across countries and across time. Cross-country variation is mainly explained by the degree of fit or misfit between the pre-existing national institutional frameworks on the one hand, and the specific OMC goals on the other. This Europeanization hypothesis expects the OMC to have the highest impact in cases when there is a high degree of institutional misfit, as this would generate strongest pressure for national policy change. We have already mentioned in the introduction the asymmetries between different Eurozone members and how this has generated more pressure, even to the point of dictating the policy agenda, on countries with high institutional misfit.

The effects of misfit and pressure have been recognised by the literature well before the crisis of the Eurozone. Extant literature provides evidence of differential pressure and different capacity to produce structural reform in the field of employment policies (Mosher and Trubek 2003; Graziano 2009; Heidenreich and Bischoff 2008), social policy (European Commission 2010h), health policy (Hervey 2008), and research and technology policy (Borrás et al. 2009). Yet, even if institutional national variables are important, they might not be all determinant, as cross-national variation and uneven impact also seem to be explained by actor-based variables (Graziano 2009): the higher the degree of national political consensus on the content of policies, the lower the impact of the OMC (Mailand 2008). National political controversies about the content of these policies opens up opportunities for some domestic policy actors/entrepreneurs to use specific notions as leverage in pursuit of particular reform agendas.

Variation across time is another fundamental dimension in explaining uneven impact. Focusing on the 'politics' side, Büchs argues that the diversified national effectiveness of the OMC, to induce policy and institutional reform, depends largely on a two-level game performed by national governments (Büchs 2008). In this two-level game, national governments' strategies explain temporary differences in the pace, content and direction of policy reform. Recent empirical findings seem to confirm in part these cross-temporary variations of impact within countries. Gwiazda shows that changes in the pro-European/Euro-sceptic ideology of the political parties in power in Italy (Prodi government and Berlusconi government) and in Poland (Tusk government and PiS-LPR-SO government) were determinant in explaining these two countries' stop-and-go nature of labour market policies' reforms towards 'flexicurity' (Gwiazda 2011).

All this evidence acts as a warning that to impose pre-established solutions from the centre of political gravity of the Eurozone needs support from core governmental actors. One can indeed interpret the change of government in Italy from Berlusconi to Monti in late 2011 as an additional implication of the linkage between government strategies at home and policy vision at the centre of the Eurozone: when there are discrepancies between strategies and vision, the pressure moves from the policy arena to the politics arena, generating momentum for a change in government.

Finally, socio-legal studies have shed light on the implications of the OMC for the transformation of EU law. Because of its 'para-law' or 'extra-law' nature (Senden 2005), the OMC is not soft law: (a) it has an intergovernmental approach rather than the supranational approach of soft law; (b) it is monitored at the highest political level (Spring Council), rather than administratively as soft law; (c) it has an iterative process rather than the ad hoc procedures of the legal interpretation focus of soft law; and (d) it aims to link systematically different policy areas, rather than the traditional single-policy focus of soft law (Borrás and Jacobsson 2004). Yet, as the legal literature has advanced on these discussions, the focus is turning away from the debates about the legal or non-legal nature of the OMC or about the risk that the OMC erodes the basis of the 'rule of law'. Instead, the attention among legal scholars seems to be turning to studying the extent to which (and how) the OMC affects EU law and the overall form of the EU's legal integration (Trubek and Trubek 2005), mainly by examining the evidence of the actual interactions between the two.

3. Breaking Down the Monolith

As previously mentioned, there is no OMC monolith, an important point to consider when addressing our three research questions (see Section 1) about the role of this mode of governance in the Eurozone and EU crisis, the connection with harder instruments of coordination, and the implications of asymmetries and divergence across Europe. The OMC has changed across time, countries and policy areas. For example, important OMC-related mechanisms like 'naming and shaming' were introduced in an earlier phase, to be dismissed later because of national resistance (Borrás 2009), and to be reconsidered in some specific policy areas, mostly macroeconomic policy coordination. There is indeed a high level of instability, largely the result of a lack of clarity, regarding the meta-goals or overall purposes, as well as turbulent conditions in EU politics. The notion of 'coordination' has been operationally translated in many different ways. Hence, the different OMC designs have objectives ranging from mutual learning and the exploitation of already known solutions, to the exploration of new solutions not known in advance, or ranging from the concrete convergence of policy outputs, to the convergence around normative standards.

All this invites an investigation of scope conditions for different usages of the OMC, rather than strong black and white statements – about whether it is red herring or a fundamental transformation of governance. Indeed, practically all recent studies acknowledge the diversity of OMC processes across policy domains. The same reasoning about variation applies to the instrumentation of the OMC: guidelines, peer review, benchmarking, reporting-monitoring, and indicators (Hartlapp 2009; de Ruiter 2008). These instruments, we argue, should be calibrated depending on the usages. To illustrate, indicators and peer review have some purposes and features if the OMC is used to steer member states towards convergence, and other purposes and features if the main usage is exploratory or learning-oriented.

Let us then turn to our theoretical categories. Rational-choice theory provides some useful conjectures. Adrienne Héritier (2004) has examined two dimensions of the 'modes of governance', that is, political capacity and policy effectiveness. The former relates to high consensus and an acceptable timeframe to agree on solutions; the latter is the problem-solving capacity of modes. Working from the assumption that the characteristics of problems and social interactions determine political capacity and policy effectiveness, she argues that the new modes of governance are suitable for some types of problems, but not for others.

More concretely, she submits that the new modes of governance (here including OMC) are less suitable for policies related to redistribution and 'prisoner's dilemma' problems. In those types of policies, new modes of governance can only be effective if they are buttressed by the Community Method (or hierarchical forms of governance). For problems related to distributive and network-goods types of situations, the new modes of governance seem to be more suitable. We elaborate on this by observing that these situations have to do with the nature of social interaction and in particular the (a)symmetric distribution of the costs and benefits of the policy across different actors. We can think of asymmetry as revealed by the split between policy-makers and policy-takers across the Eurozone member states. Yet, as a general point, the concept of asymmetry also covers actors in the same country, for example, consumers or producers, elected policy makers versus independent regulators, or different regional actors within a jurisdiction. This brings us to a model with three variables:

1. *(A)symmetric costs and benefits for actors:* like Héritier, we focus on the type of social interactions moving from the most asymmetric to the most symmetric costs and benefits: re-distributive social interaction (where there is a clear zero-sum game between winners and losers); prisoner's dilemma (an incomplete zero-sum game as there might be situations of more symmetric effect); distributive interaction (with a partly symmetric distribution of costs and benefits across actors); and last but not least, network-goods interactions (a quasi-public good with highly symmetric costs–benefits).

2. The level of *externalities, or the overall gains from EU-level cooperation:* this is the main rationale for engaging in EU-level governance. The Commission has been blamed for trying to achieve integration by stealth (Majone 2005), that is, seeking EU-level coordination for political reasons, even in cases when there is no objective rationale for coordination. We can label this variable policy *externality*, since externalities are the major source of EU-level gains from cooperation – although, certainly, not the only source. We measure externalities as high, medium and low. Externalities are difficult to judge since there may be some externalities, but cooperation has its own costs and these costs in terms of suppressing diversity can be higher than the benefit of governing externalities.

3. The level of *uncertainty:* it is useful to be explicit about what we mean by 'uncertainty': it means that no-one has a pre-defined solution, that the system's reactions to policy cannot be predicted in sign and magnitude, and that there may be more than one solution that works, given certain conditions (equifinality). This is a fundamental variable in the OMC. The logic of experimentalism, discovery and open-ended learning is contingent on the assumption that the 'solution' to policy problems is not known. It has to be discovered via network-like activities at different levels of governance. By contrast, if uncertainty is low, the problem is relatively tractable and the 'solution' is somewhat known. In this circumstance, it makes sense to talk about convergence towards the 'solution'. The OMC can therefore be used in different ways depending on the level of uncertainty.

We can now enter the different usages of the OMC. They are placed on the following scale:

No usage: the OMC is not a panacea, of course. It follows that we should identify the circumstances under which it cannot deliver, drawing on the concept of policy externality as the main rationale for EU coordinated action.

Exploration: here the OMC spawns deliberation over possible courses of action – new possibilities and unknown solutions. It can generate reflexivity among member states during the adaptive process. This is essentially a usage oriented towards 'process-based exploration' in a situation where there is no pre-defined socially certified actor – the equivalent of the 'teacher' in the class (see Dunlop and Radaelli (2013) for these metaphors) – nor do we find pre-defined solutions, as uncertainty is high (March 1991; Freeman 2006).

Learning: this occurs when there are some good practices known to be able to solve difficult problems, and to generate mutual advancement of solutions by the intensive consideration of each others' practices and approaches, often in recursive iterations (Radaelli 2008; Dunlop and Radaelli 2013).

Convergence: The OMC can be used to promote convergence of national policies towards a specific set of EU solutions when there is relatively low uncertainty about what needs to be done, and how, and when there are medium-level of externalities. This mode implies that there is a socially certified actor that not only 'teaches' (to carry on with our metaphor), but it also is socially authorised to exercise surveillance.

By combining our variables on the levels of uncertainty and of externalities we come to Table 3.1, which portrays different types of usages. Our first variable, the (a)symmetry of costs and benefits, will be introduced later on, when examining the additional conditions for OMC usages, that is, when the creation of specific incentives or sanctions is needed to achieve the expected outcomes of the OMC.

When looking at the 'low externalities' column, there is no strong case for EU action. Externalities are a fundamental rationale for EU-level coordination – arguably not the only rationale, but certainly less controversial. If there are no externalities at EU level, member states can solve problems of coordination without operating via the classic Community Method or the OMC. One could go so far as to argue that activating EU coordination under these conditions is equivalent to integration by stealth (Majone 2005). If there is a possible usage of the OMC here, it is to assist in a process of scaling back from EU competence to re-nationalisation of policies (ancillary usage, as mentioned earlier). It has long been shown that the EU fisheries regime does not solve any externality problem – if anything, it aggravates the problem. Facilitated coordination may represent a way out of a binding EU legal system.

Looking at the first cell in Table 3.1, when externalities are high and uncertainty is also high, the OMC performs as a governance device for learning. The OMC can assist national policy makers in learning from different types of public action. It is worth noting that the use of OMC for learning is not written in stone for some specific policy areas. If EU-level solutions become available, not contested, and stable over time, EU competences could be recognised and formally enshrined, and the Community Method unfolded for that particular policy area. Thinking of the symmetry among actors, if there are asymmetric costs and benefits among actors, the OMC needs to be boosted by incentives. This is because, if there are some actors with more resources and capabilities than others, they may not engage in coordination for learning purposes, unless properly incentivised. Parts of health policy and pensions provide prima facie cases.

Turning to the second cell, here the OMC is an exploration device, with a moderate level of externalities and a high level of uncertainty. Here the solutions to policy problems are still not known, and the overall gains of EU-level policy action not entirely clear. Hence, the OMC can be used as a way to explore options of national-level policy action. Incentives for the OMC are needed if the resources of actors and their costs and benefits are asymmetric. Research and development policy, and social inclusion are our prima facie examples.

In contrast to this, when externalities are high and uncertainty low (the third cell), we are most likely to already find EU-level policy competences. The best way to proceed is via the classic Community Method if there are strongly asymmetric configurations of costs and benefits (re-distributive or prisoner's dilemma). If major disagreement about competence and subsidiary hinders the Community Method, the OMC can pave the way for legislation that may emerge in the future, building on the results of open coordination. Examples of this are employment and immigration policies.

Last, but not least, the fourth cell illustrates that if gains from EU-level action are neither particularly high nor particularly low, but the solution is well known *ex ante*, the main rationale for the OMC lies in convergence. In situations where there is a relative symmetry of costs and benefits across actors this might happen relatively un-problematically. However, in situations of strong zero-sum games (such as prisoner's dilemma configurations) the OMC would need to generate specific forms of sanctions (shadow of hierarchy), in order to avoid defection. A most remarkable example of this is the Stability and Growth Pact for fiscal coordination in the EU, reinforced as a result of the crisis.

Table 3.1   Scope conditions for OMC usages

		Externalities		
		High	Medium	Low
Uncertainty	High	1. OMC to learn (with incentives)	2. OMC to explore (with incentives)	No EU action
	Low	3. Community Method (with sanctions)	4. OMC to converge (with sanctions)	No EU action

Having looked at the different scope conditions for OMC usages, the next question is: What are the implications of this way or reasoning for the choice of concrete policy instruments that support these usages? In the extant literature, the instruments of the OMC (such as benchmarking, guidelines, reporting, and peer review) have been assessed as a whole. Instead, instruments are contingent on our scope conditions. Consequently, we consider next whether the OMC is used for learning, exploration or convergence.

If the OMC has to work (to learn or to explore) when the solution is not known *ex ante* (high uncertainty), we are under the conditions described by the theorists of experimentalist governance such as Sabel and Zeitlin (2010). We argue, however, that theirs is not a general prescription for the instruments of the OMC. We have to consider externalities and besides, asymmetries matter. If there is low symmetry, instruments will have to be supported by incentives to engage in learning or exploration. What are the more specific implications for instruments when using the OMC for learning and for exploring? Consider learning first. In this case guidelines should not be too prescriptive and concrete. A certain level of abstraction is actually an asset in these conditions. Final outcomes and targets are not essential in the learning-oriented usage, indeed they can be counterproductive. Benchmarking should be cooperative rather than competitive (see Radaelli (2003a) on this difference). It should be 'intelligent' (Lundvall and Tomlinson 2002). Peer review should have the function of discovering lessons and examine the conditions for extrapolation of innovations from one country to another.

Consider exploration now (cell 2 in Table 3.1). Let us keep in mind that here the OMC is used in conditions of high uncertainty and of medium-to-low level of externalities. This means that the instruments have to take into account that the overall gains of EU-level cooperation might not be that high. Seen from this perspective it is then obvious that the instruments shall be the 'softest' of all possible instruments.

Reporting and indicators should play a special role. A common set of indicators is important to give meaning and a sense of purpose to learning and exploration. As a general proposition, learning and exploring are essentially disruptive of regularity, and hence, cannot be subject to 'monitorability' (Sabel 1994). There are ways in which we can ease the trade-off between learning, exploration and monitorability. However, the more we move towards exploration, the less we should interpret monitorability as surveillance. To anticipate some of our considerations in the next section, this explains why some arguments about stricter monitoring and surveillance in the debate on the Eurozone crisis are misplaced if they refer to situations with high-to-medium externalities and high uncertainty.

Put differently, in using the OMC for learning and exploring, policy instruments such as indicators and reporting are eminently a device to clarify and perhaps re-interpret member states' own preferences. The selection of common baseline indicators is a formidable opportunity for learning. To achieve that, however, one has to dispose of targets and design a process in which the actors have incentives to learn and explore by re-elaborating their preferences and re-defining

their priorities as their joint experience 'outpaces their initial understanding' (Sabel 1994: 155–6). In this experimental approach to indicators and reporting, each year the discussion should not be about league tables and who is leading on reform programmes; rather, each Member State should focus on the 'story' behind the variations of the indicators. Thus the framework of facilitated coordination would assist in developing a common understanding. This comes close to a policy conversation, or 'the process by which parties come to re-interpret themselves and their relation to each other by elaborating a common understanding of the world' (Sabel 1994: 138).

The case of OMC for convergence pushes us towards the pole of monitoring as surveillance. The implications for the design of instruments and their utilisation vary accordingly. Indicators and reporting should be used to measure compliance with EU goals. Targets could play a role, although we have to acknowledge the limitations of causally relating a policy reform to a final economic outcome. Benchmarking should trigger competition among policy models as well as the spread of innovations. Guidelines should make clear what the 'solution' is, given that this usage operates under conditions of low uncertainty.

In the three cases – learning, exploring and convergence – the OMC should improve on the mechanisms to introduce innovations that foster national reforms. The reality is that political systems are sticky and idiosyncratic, which means that introducing innovations either by drawing lessons from the experience of others (learning), by taking part in a collective search for solutions (exploration), or by seeking to adapt to a specific set of EU solutions (convergence) is always a delicate process. The challenge for cross-national innovation is one of intelligent adaptation and a collective search for common solutions, not just a mere imitation or replication. This is important not only in situations of using the OMC for learning and for exploration, but also in situations of using the OMC for convergence, where national institutional frameworks are intrinsically different from each other.

4. Governance and the Economic Crisis

Since 2007, the financial and economic crisis has hit the EU very hard, exposing externalities and the high level of asymmetries across the European economies and their governments. This has tested in new and difficult ways the overall design of economic governance, which refers not only to macroeconomic policies but also to welfare state and competitiveness-related socio-economic reforms. The crisis has unleashed a political response in both areas, and this response has been double. On the one hand the political responses have strengthened the incentives and sanctioning mechanisms in existing usages of EU governance – be it Community Method, OMC or new forms of inter-governmentalism. In short, the modes of governance have been bent towards stronger surveillance, monitoring and sanctions. On the other hand, they have also created meta-coordination governance architectures like the new 'European semester' (which meta-coordinates all macroeconomic coordination), and the revised 'Europe 2020' (which meta-coordinates welfare state and competitiveness-related socio-economic policies).

There are two main consequences of the directions taken by governance during the economic crisis. First, the crisis has hardened the problems arising out of divergence, especially in the Eurozone, exposing the distributional consequences of policy choice, most visibly across countries. In terms of our framework, this implies a shift towards constellations of problems and actors characterised by asymmetric conditions. It is objectively more difficult to coordinate EU solutions to learn, to explore and to converge when this brings about a net transfer of resources to another country.

Whether this argument (that is, the net transfer claim) is true or not, given the high degree of inter-dependence of the banking sector and the real economies, is of course a moot point. Commentators have pointed to all sorts of transfers between French/German banks, citizens and public budgets and Greek actors – the matter is not one of simple transfer from the French or German citizens to the Greek citizens. However, what matters in these cases is the discursive construction of policy problems by domestic political elites – which may or may not be in line with the objective economic realities of interdependent economies in the Eurozone. The divergence and asymmetries we consider in this chapter may well be discursively constructed – they have material effects nevertheless! Discursive claims that current solutions generate net transfers of monetary resources across nations have the effect of increasing the role of externalities in our governance framework. Looking at our table, this implies a shift towards the cells with high externalities and a greater role of incentives and sanctions to comply.

Second, these shifts have gone hand in hand with an attempt to change the hierarchy of actors in the overall design of governance. Within the Eurozone, actors like the European Central Bank (ECB), the Eurogroup and the International Monetary Fund (IMF) have asserted their role in the design of economic and social policies to address the crisis. Consequently, coordination within the Eurozone involves new actors' constellations, like the so-called Troika. The coordination problems within the Troika are different from the classic problems of EU-level coordination – and the latter have gone away, of course, so they have to be factored in anyway. Looking at domestic political elites, it has been argued that they have engaged in deliberative inter-governmentalism (Puetter 2012), a mode of governance based around a new centre of political gravity consisting of the Eurogroup and the European Council – away from the Community Method (cell 3 in our table).

But what about the other dimension of our table, uncertainty? Most efforts during the economic crisis have been towards the re-design of sanctions and stricter monitoring. It is a kind of surveillance paradigm that works well if the 'solution' is known by the actors at the top of the hierarchy – be they the Eurozone ministers, the EU Council or the Troika. Within deliberative inter-governmentalism, the goal of convergence has gained prominence, whilst learning and exploration have been seen as either riskier propositions or secondary goals. We argue, however, that this is not the most appropriate way to design policy given the conditions of uncertainty during crisis.

Let us explore uncertainty, then. This operates at different levels. To begin with, systemic uncertainty has been high since 2007 and is bound to remain high given the responses to EU policies provided so far by financial markets and the real economies of the Eurozone. Instead of taking unambiguous decisions (a sort of federal big bang) about the kind of relationship between EU economic government and monetary union, the EU leaders have tinkered at the edges to fix existing instruments, like the Stability and Growth Pact, or exploring new solutions, like the banking union, incrementally. The austerity paradigm may not be contested within the Troika, and yet it is increasingly attacked by MPs, citizens and political parties.

These considerations lead us to the claim that hardening governance and moving towards surveillance and sanctions in order to impose a certain economic 'cure' like austerity has its own risks. Convergence towards economic outcomes requires convergence in deep-core policy beliefs about the roles of the market and the state. This is very difficult to develop when the crisis hits asymmetrically. To achieve that level of convergence in deep-core policy beliefs, 'exploration' and 'learning' might be more powerful than 'surveillance' from the centre, cemented by strong sanctions. Persuasion and re-orientation of core domestic policy beliefs are fundamental – otherwise there will always be a way to comply with the letter and not the spirit of the Eurozone policy solutions, and perhaps also ways to get around the letter too!

Exploration and learning are more robust in relation to risk. The problem is that in times of crisis there might be little time to react. Let us assume for a moment that the 'solution' for convergence (that is, the so-called austerity paradigm) is not the right one. If the EU operates in a regime of learning and exploration there might be ways to find out early that the solution is not workable and re-direct policies somewhere else (that is, the Icelandic solution to their meltdown in 2008 could have constituted a 'lesson' for the Cyprus crisis in 2013). By contrast, if deliberative inter-governmentalism insists on discipline and convergence on a very specific set of goals only, and with the solution devised solely at the centre, the way to find out about mistakes is when the house is on fire. This leads us to think that uncertainty refers not only to the uncertainty of the socio-economic context as such, but to the views of decision makers on this socio-economic context and the extent to which they share the same core policy beliefs or not.

5. Conclusions

Three research questions have motivated our chapter: the relevance of the OMC in the responses to the crisis; the connection between this mode of governance and other, harder modes; and the implications of divergence and political-economic asymmetries. The OMC remains relevant in the responses to the crisis – also in light of its acknowledgement in the Treaty on the Functioning of the European Union, its potential for the European semester, and the ambitious Europe 2020 agenda for structural reform. However, its usage is bound to be bent towards convergence, thus neglecting the potential for exploration and learning.

To understand this, we have to consider the second and third research questions. Empirically we observe that in the context of the crisis the Open Method of Coordination has been a way to assist a process of increasing surveillance and solutions 'pushed-down' from the Eurozone's policy makers to the member states that are the policy-takers. Yet our normative answer, that is, what ought to be done to increase the relevance of the OMC in response to the crisis, leans towards exploration and learning, for the reasons presented above, in Section 4. No matter what the level of pressure may be, it will never work as well as persuasion and genuine re-direction of core domestic policy beliefs. The literature has explained that pressure, misfits and incentives to adapt are not mechanical forces. The preferences of governments and ultimately of citizens determine compliance with the spirit and the letter of the 'solution'. Endogenous capacity to act and innovate at the domestic level is even more important when the 'solution' needs to be responsive and applied in a context of uncertainty, or is not known in advance and can only be found by experimenting locally. These conclusions are strengthened if we add the losses caused to legitimacy by pushing down solutions rather than persuading via exploration and learning.

Policy makers have operated following an austerity paradigm in a context in which financial, banking and sovereign debt crisis have recursively emerged since the beginning of the crisis in 2007. The notion of an economic centre and an economic periphery in the European Union has never been clearer, even when part of that 'centre' has been under severe financial and economic strains too. This has exposed, as never before, the intrinsic asymmetries, not only of the European economies as such, but also the asymmetries of the views of European citizens and elites on these matters.

As Maria João Rodrigues points out: so far, the instruments developed to address the Eurozone crisis have had an intergovernmental character rather than a 'federal' or more supranational character, 'a paradigm of mutual insurance has been preferred to a more federal or Community paradigm' (Rodrigues 2014: this volume). New and ad hoc mechanisms for rescuing member states and banking systems on the brink of bankruptcy have followed intergovernmental designs and have been accompanied by hard conditionality. This has run parallel with the more structural changes in some key governance architectures in the EU, like the new European semester linking and aligning of different macroeconomic and socio-economic coordination policy processes, and structural changes in existing methods like harder sanctioning procedures. In that sense, the crisis might have brought to the fore the growing role of open coordination and its cross-national way of addressing problems in the interdependent European economy. In so doing, the nature of the Open Method of Coordination has been changing rapidly too. For this reason, the previously polarised debates in favour of or against the Open

Method of Coordination seem to be largely out of scope when considering the institutional effects of the crisis.

One question that remains unanswered though is whether the past few years' hardening modes of governance during the financial and economic crisis (with more sanctioning and closer monitoring) will prevail once these troubled waters of the crisis have calmed, or whether it will remain an inescapable feature of European integration in the decades to come. Normatively, the key issue for the next few years is whether surveillance may generate legitimacy and support for the EU and its policies, and detect risks that if not addressed may bring it to European dis-integration rather than deeper integration – no matter whether federal, supranational or intergovernmental.

PART II
The Transformation of European Economic Governance

Chapter 4

Beyond Intergovernmentalism: The Puzzle of European Economic Governance

Sergio Fabbrini

1. Introduction

The European Union (EU) is a union of states and citizens structured around both inter-states (or intergovernmental) and supra-states (or supranational) institutional relations. Unions of states and citizens are federalised or federalising polities coming out of the aggregation of previously independent territorial units (as is the case with the United States or Switzerland), whereas the other established federalised or federalising polities are the outcome of a process of disaggregation of a previously unitary state (as is the case in Europe, of Germany, Austria, Belgium or Spain, and outside Europe, of Canada and Australia).[1] It is inevitable that the former polities have tried to guarantee the constituting units as much power as possible, in terms both of the policy's competence and institutional representation. This has been particularly true for the EU, which aggregates historically powerful nation states with rooted cultural and linguistic identities and sophisticated representative and administrative structures. Indeed, the Council of Ministers (now only Council) has been the fundamental institution driving the process of integration since the very beginning, thus strengthened in a later stage by the informal institutional development of the European Council (the institution constituted by the governmental leaders of the member states of the Union). Nevertheless, the existence of supranational institutions – such as the Commission, the European Court of Justice (ECJ) and at a later stage the European Parliament (EP) – has balanced the intergovernmental logic with a European/supranational perspective.

With the 1992 Maastricht Treaty the intergovernmentalist and supranationalist logics, however, were separately institutionalised. While they interacted within the single framework before 1992, in the period that followed the EU allocated different policies to different institutional frameworks. The single market policies have become more and more managed through the decision-making interaction of supranational and intergovernmental institutions (together forming the *supranational* EU), while new policies, such as (*inter alia*) financial and economic

---

1   I consider here the countries belonging to the Organisation for Economic Co-operation and Development (OECD).

policies have come to be controlled exclusively by the intergovernmental institutions (constituting the *intergovernmental* EU). This institutional differentiation was the expression of two alternative views of the Union, one (the former) interpreting it as a supranational federation in the making and the other (the latter) interpreting it as an international organisation (Schimmelfennig 2004) with the features of a confederation of nation states, although pursuing political aims. The 2009 Lisbon Treaty has abolished the distinction between formal pillars, but it has confirmed the substance of the Maastricht Treaty's compromise. Single market policies continue to be managed through a supranational decision-making regime, while 'most of the important substantive areas of modern governance remain firmly in the hands of national governments' (Moravcsik 2007: 34). In the former case, integration is based on law, in the latter case on coordination of member states' governments.

The Euro-crisis has represented an occasion for assessing the crisis management capability of the intergovernmental EU. The test has been unsatisfactory. The intergovernmental EU has not been able to guarantee an effective decision-making process, nor legitimacy to the latter's outcome. Indeed, the basis of the intergovernmental institutional framework, constituted by a centralised monetary policy (in the Frankfurt-based European Central Bank or ECB) and decentralised financial, fiscal and budgetary policies (in the member states), has been challenged by the Euro-crisis. Under the financial threat of the Euro's collapse, the heads of state and government of the EU member states eventually ended up in dramatically redefining the intergovernmental system of economic governance in Europe (and the Eurozone in particular). New radical legislative measures were approved (from the 2010 European Semester to the 2011 Six-packs and 2012 Two-packs) within the institutional frame of the Lisbon Treaty and new intergovernmental decisions (the 2010 European Financial Stability Facility or EFSF and the European Financial Stability Mechanism or EFSM[2]) and new intergovernmental treaties (the 2011 Treaty on European Stability Mechanism or ESM[3] and the 2012 Fiscal Compact

---

2   At the ECOFIN Council of 9–10 May 2010 was adopted a regulation to create the European Financial Stability Mechanism (or EFSM), as a new EU instrument of law and then, based on Article 122(2) Treaty on the Functioning of the European Union (TFEU). On the margin of that meeting, 'the members of the Council from the 17 euro area countries "switched hats" and transformed themselves into representatives of their states at an intergovernmental conference; in that capacity, they adopted a decision by which they committed themselves to establish the European Financial Stability Facility (or EFSF) outside the EU legal framework' (De Witte 2012: 2). The EFSF consisted of an executive agreement (not a new formal treaty), a form of private company established under Luxembourg law, authorised to negotiate with its (17) shareholders and serving the purpose of giving financial support to countries facing a severe sovereign debt crisis. Both EFSM and EFSF 'have been used simultaneously and cumulatively with respect to Ireland and Portugal' (De Witte 2012: 4) and Greece. The EFSM has been superseded by the ESM.

3   The Treaty on the European Stability Mechanism (ESM) was signed by all the EU member states on 25 March 2011 on the basis of a European Council decision, taken on 16 December 2010, to amend TFEU Article 136 for authorising the Eurozone member

Treaty[4]) were set up outside of the Lisbon Treaty. The new measures and treaties attempted to ameliorate market pressures on the weaker and indebted member states of the Eurozone, but they didn't work as expected. They were considered ineffective by the financial markets and illegitimate by the affected citizens (as shown by the strikes and riots in the capitals of the indebted EU member states). The Euro-crisis has called into question the intergovernmental EU and, through it, the EU as such.

The chapter is organised as follows: first, Section 2 describes the institutional structure of the intergovernmental EU, thus detecting its performance in the Euro-crisis. Section 3 then analyses the reasons and the implications of the complex and unusual measures introduced in the period 2010–2013 by the intergovernmental EU. Last, Section 4 discusses the strategies for going beyond intergovernmentalism in setting up an effective and legitimate system of economic governance.

2. The Intergovernmental EU in the Context of the Lisbon Treaty

The Treaty of Lisbon came into force on 1 December 2009 (Foster 2010).[5] Although the Treaty of Lisbon scrapped any constitutional symbolism, it has defined (in terms of roles and functions) the EU's institutional structure (as constitutions do). For a large majority of policies where integration proceeds through formal acts (*integration through law*), the Lisbon Treaty formalised an institutional structure organised around two distinct legislative chambers and two distinct executive institutions. Celebrating the co-decision procedure as 'the ordinary legislative procedure' (TFEU, Article 289), the Treaty has institutionalised a two-chamber

---

states to establish a specific stability mechanism for their currency. It is an international organisation located in Luxembourg, which provides financial assistance to members of the Eurozone in financial difficulty. After several revisions, the ESM was finally established on 27 September 2012 and functions as a permanent firewall for the Eurozone with a maximum lending capacity of €500 billion. It replaces the two previous temporary EU funding programmes: the EFSF and the EFSM. All new bailout applications and deals for any Eurozone member state with a financial stability issue will in principle be covered by the ESM, while the EFSF and EFSM continue to handle the transfer and monitoring of the previously approved bailout loans for Ireland, Portugal and Greece. It was finally established on 27 September 2012 and became operative by January 2013, replacing the EFSM.

4   The term 'Fiscal Compact Treaty' is generally used for the sake of simplicity. Indeed, its title is 'Treaty on Stability, Coordination and Governance in the Economic and Monetary Union', of which the fiscal compact is only one component. Signed by all the heads of state and government (except the Czech Republic and the United Kingdom) in the meeting of the European Council of 2 March 2012, it entered into force on 1 January 2013.

5   The Lisbon Treaty is constituted of the amendments to two consolidated treaties, the Treaty on the European Union (TUE) of 1992 and the Treaty on the European Community, renamed as TFUE, of 1957, plus the Declaration concerning the Charter of Fundamental Rights considered *de facto* as a third treaty.

legislative branch, consisting of a lower chamber representing the European electorate (the EP) and an upper chamber representing the governments of the member states (the Council). At the same time, by recognising the European Council (which consists of the heads of state or government of the EU member states, chaired by a president elected 'by a qualified majority' of them 'for a term of two and half years, renewable once', TEU Article 15(5), and which has become for the first time a formal institution of the EU) as the body responsible for setting the general political guidelines and priorities of the EU, the Treaty has finally transformed it into a political executive of the Union, in charge of defining the strategies of the Union, while confirming the Commission in its role of technical executive of the latter. The Lisbon Treaty has therefore built a four-sided institutional framework for governing the EU policies on the single market, operating under the supervisory role of ECJ together with member states' constitutional courts. This is the *supranational* EU, whose process of institutionalisation started with the 1957 Rome Treaty and was largely influenced by the so-called *community method* (Dehousse 2011: 4).

However, integration through law does not represent the only logic celebrated by the Lisbon Treaty. With the extension of the integration process to policy realms traditionally considered sensitive to the national sovereignty of the member states, such as Common Foreign and Security Policies (CFSP) and the Economic and Monetary Union (EMU),[6] the EU has looked to organise the decision-making process by new modes of governance, based on open methods of coordination, benchmarking, mainstreaming, peer review and, more generally, *intergovernmental coordination* (Héritier and Rhodes 2010; Caporaso and Wittenbrinck 2006; Idema and Keleman 2006). Indeed, integration in this context is based on as *voluntary coordination* between member states' governments, with a minor if not insignificant role played by the supranational institutions.[7]

The Lisbon Treaty's intergovernmental decision-making regime is based on a different institutional structure than the supranational one (Allerkamp 2009) in that the main decision-making body is represented by the European Council, which sets the overall direction of policy with the Council, transforming those policy's directions in policy decisions. The Commission is assigned a limited

---

6　The EMU is constituted only by those member states whose currency is the Euro.

7　Indeed, it was the 1992 Maastricht Treaty that institutionalised a *compromise* between those asserting the need to promote integration in policy areas historically at the centre of national sovereignty, such as monetary and economic policy or foreign and security policy, and those unwilling to downsize the powers of national governments in those policy's realms. The compromise also consisted on one hand, in integrating those policies at the Union level and on the other, in interpreting this integration as *voluntary coordination* between member states' governments, with a minor if not insignificant role played by the supranational institutions. Indeed, to distinguish between different models of integration, the Maastricht Treaty set up three distinct institutional pillars or decision-making regimes.

role in the elaboration and decision-making of those policies, although its role is magnified regarding the latter's implementation. Because integration proceeds through voluntary coordination, the intergovernmental EU has no significant place for the EP and the ECJ. Rather, an important role, in all three phases (elaboration, decision-making and implementation) of the policy's process, is played by key national policy-makers, with the support of the Council Secretariat which coordinates not only the Council's activities but also those of the European Council. What we have here is a simplified decision-making regime, based mainly on the European Council and the Council, within which national governments play an exclusive role.

Regarding EMU, the intergovernmental logic is indisputable (Heipertz and Verdun 2010). Although monetary policy was centralised in the ECB, economic and financial policies were left in the hands of national governments. TFEU, article 119, states that 'the adoption of an economic policy ... is based on the close coordination of Member States' economic policies', with the Commission allowed to play a technical, but not a political role, in monitoring the economic performance of member states. Consider the crucial excessive deficit procedures of the Eurozone member states (annexed as Protocol number 12 to the Lisbon Treaty, called the Stability and Growth Pact (SGP), as regulated by TFEU, Article 126): here the Council (in its configuration of economic and financial ministers, generally called ECOFIN Council) monopolises the policy's decision, although the latter is generally based on reports or recommendations of the Commission. According to the special legislative procedure, the Council, acting either unanimously or as a qualified majority, depending on the issue concerned, can adopt legislation based on a proposal by the Commission after consulting the EP. However, while being required to consult the EP on some legislative proposals concerning economic and financial policy, the Council is not bound by the latter's position. The ECOFIN Council is supported in its activities by an Economic and Financial Committee, whose task (TFEU, Article 134) is to supervise the economic and financial situations of the member states. EMU functions according to a decision-making pattern that Puetter (2012) has defined as 'deliberative intergovernmentalism'.

In fact, although it is recognised (TUE, Articles 126(6) and 126(7)) that the Commission may initiate a procedure against a member state running an excessive budget deficit, the Commission's recommendation has however the status of a proposal, because only the ECOFIN Council can take the appropriate measures (that may go from requests of information addressed to the member state that fails to comply with the fines imposed on it). It is thus up to the ECOFIN Council to decide whether or not to proceed along the lines of the Commission's proposal (as it did not do in 2003, when the Commission proposed opening an infringement procedure against France and Germany, who were not respecting the parameters of the SGP). This is even truer for Eurozone member states, whose main deliberations take place either in the Euro Summit or in the Euro-group (consisting respectively of the heads of state and government and the ministers of economics and finance of the EU member states adopting the common currency, as regulated by Protocol

n. 14 annexed to the Lisbon Treaty), with the technical support of the Commission. The Euro-group has the status of an 'informal institution', embodying a specific approach to policy-making defined as 'informal governance' (Puetter 2006). Protocol n. 14 doesn't even mention the EP, at least in terms of the institution that should be informed about the decisions made.

Overall, this section has shown that the Lisbon Treaty has formalised two different decision-making regimes or constitutional frameworks. The supranational one that deals with the policies of the single market and intergovernmentalist one that deals with the policies of financial stability (*inter alia*). The Euro-zone crisis has thus been a test for the intergovernmental EU. The following section will focus on the crisis and the intergovernmental response to it.

3. The Euro-crisis and the Intergovernmental Answer

When the crisis started to hit Greece, there was in place a decision-making regime for structuring the institutional and policy's answer to financial turmoil. As established by the intergovernmental Lisbon Treaty, the European Council and the ECOFIN Council immediately took centre-stage of the policy-making process, while the Commission was marginalised and the EP was left dormant. Continuous meetings of the European Council and ECOFIN Council were organised between 2010 and 2013, although none of them was able to stop or contain the crisis. Decisions of great magnitude were taken during those meetings. Some of them, such as the six-pack and the two-pack, were taken through the supranational constitution, given they consisted of regulations and directives approved predominantly through the co-decision or ordinary procedure. However, with the deepening of the Euro-crisis, the EU has shifted decisively in an intergovernmental direction (Fabbrini 2013).

A multiplicity of treaties was set up, as the EFSF thus substituted by the ESM for crisis management and the Fiscal Compact for crisis prevention. Nevertheless, these treaties were not sufficient to appease the financial markets that indeed began demanding higher interest rates for buying public bonds from peripheral Eurozone member states. Market pressures became so powerful that many of these countries with high ratios of public debt to Gross Domestic Product (GDP) had to register the collapse of their incumbent governments. Even the most audacious decisions arrived too late to answer for the market's pressures and they were perceived as illegitimate by the affected interests. Indeed, it is generally agreed that the reduction of the spread between the Italian, Portuguese and Spanish public bonds and German bonds, finally achieved in the course of 2012, has to be considered as the outcome of the firm position of the ECB 'to do whatever it takes to save the Euro',[8] rather than of the decisions taken by the intergovernmental

---

8   As the president of the ECB, Mario Draghi, said at an investment conference held in London on 25 July 2012.

institutions. The latter have created not only a very convoluted system of control of national financial, fiscal and budgetary policies, but have also introduced an extremely intrusive set of rules unevenly constraining Eurozone member states (as would be unacceptable in any federal system). This outcome cannot be explained by the magnitude of the financial crisis: indeed, neither the United States nor other countries, severely hit by the latter, have witnessed a similar institutional and policy transformation. Such institutional intricacy has to be considered the logical outcome of a decision-making regime that is based primarily on national governments' coordination. Coordination has been shown to be insufficient for solving basic dilemmas of collective action.

Consider the effectiveness aspect of the intergovernmental decision-making regime. A decision-making regime based on the voluntary coordination of member states' governments is based on a unanimity's logic. When unanimous consent is required for taking a decision, then it seems inevitable that the decision-making process will get stuck in interminable negotiations (if not in the veto of an actor aimed to prevent an undesired decision). This might explain why, although the financial crisis was initially circumscribed only to Greece, it gradually began expanding to other Eurozone member states because of the decision-making stalemate produced by divergent strategies for dealing with it. That stalemate was the expression of divergences motivated by the different domestic electoral interests of the various incumbent governments. One has only to think that, for neutralising the British veto on fiscal coordination, it was necessary to move outside of the Lisbon Treaty, setting up a new treaty (the Fiscal Compact Treaty).

At the same time, an intergovernmental decision-making regime cannot guarantee the proper application of a decision taken on a voluntary basis. The enforcement dilemma emerged dramatically with regard to the approval of the new treaties (the ESM and the Fiscal Compact) by their contracting member states. One has only to consider that, in order to avoid jeopardising the entire project by the possible rejection of one or another intergovernmental treaty by a few of their contracting member states, the Fiscal Compact Treaty (Title VI, article 14.2) had to state that it 'shall enter to force on 1 January 2013, provided that twelve contracting parties whose currency is the Euro have deposited their instrument of ratification'. Twelve, not all the then seventeen member states of the Eurozone. It is the first time (in the European integration experience) that unanimity has been eliminated as a barrier for activating an intergovernmental treaty (that would require, by its own logic, the unanimous consent of all the contracting parties). Anticipating plausible rejection of the Fiscal Compact Treaty, the ESM Treaty had to state (Point 5) that 'the granting of financial assistance … will be conditional, as of 1 March 2013, on the ratification of Fiscal Compact Treaty by the ESM Member concerned'. This threat was efficacious in cooling down the euro-sceptical mood of Irish voters (in the referendum on the Fiscal Compact held on 31 May 2012) or the anti-European mood of Greek voters. However, in moving in this direction, the intergovernmental logic had to contradict itself.

Also, an intergovernmental decision-making regime cannot guarantee the respect of the decisions or rules it generates, if that compliance no longer fits the interests of one or other of the voluntary contracting parties. This dilemma emerged dramatically in the case of the disrespect of the rules of the SGP. It became apparent in 2009 that Greece had cheated the other member states' governments (manipulating its statistical data regarding public deficit and debt) to remain in the Eurozone. However, the same dilemma had emerged in 2003, when France and Germany were saved from sanctions by a decision of the ECOFIN (and in contrast to a Commission's recommendation) notwithstanding their disrespect for the SGP's parameters.

In sum, since the beginning of the crisis, the intergovernmental decision-making regime, originally justified by the need to guarantee the political discretionary power of national governments, has ended up by introducing *automatic* legal measures of intervention in member states' economic governance systems that dramatically curtails their *political* discretion. Those automatic legal measures, imposed by the Commission, have resulted extremely intrusive of the domestic policy-making of indebted member states (but not of course of the creditor member states). The Fiscal Compact Treaty tries to deal with the non-compliance possibility, providing for a binding intervention of the ECJ upon those contracting parties that do not respect the agreed rules. This also applies when the Commission issues a report on a contracting party failing to comply with the rules established by the Treaty. In the latter case, if the Commission, after having given the contracting party concerned the opportunity to submit its observations, still confirms the non-compliance by the contracting party in question, the matter will be brought to the ECJ. Article 17 of the Fiscal Compact Treaty has come to stress that, in order to neutralise a recommendation of the Commission to intervene against a member state breaching a deficit criteria, 'a qualified majority of the member states (should be) opposed to the decision proposed or recommended'. Thus, for preventing non-compliant behaviour by a contracting party, the discretion of the ECOFIN Council has been severely restrained, if compared with the rules concerning the SGP institutionalised in the intergovernmental side of the Lisbon Treaty.

Moreover, the intergovernmental institutions (the European Council and the Council) had to recognise the need to rely on third actors (the ECJ or the Commission or the ECB) to keep the contracting parties aligned with the agreed aims of the Treaty, with the implication that a new organisation (set up by the Fiscal Compact Treaty or ESM Treaty) claims to use an institution (such as the ECJ, the Commission or the ECB) of another organisation (the EU of the Lisbon Treaty) to bind its own contracting parties. Certainly, the intervention of the ECJ is justified by TFEU, Article 273, which states: 'the Court of Justice shall have jurisdiction in any dispute between member states which relates to the subject matter of the Treaties if the dispute is submitted to it under a special agreement between the parties'. Nevertheless, the ECJ, the Commission and the ECB are institutions operating within a legal structure that is also defined by the UK and the Czech Republic, who did not agree upon the Fiscal Compact Treaty that utilises them.

Consider now the legitimacy side of the decisions taken by the intergovernmental EU. Throughout the Euro-crisis, the decisions reached by national executives in the European Council or the ECOFIN Council were never discussed, let alone approved, by the EP, the institution representing the European citizens. The lack of legitimacy of those decisions became evident as the crisis deepened and the citizens of the indebted member states had to pay high costs for making the necessary structural adjustment of their country possible. Not only did they have to abide by decisions imposed by impersonal financial markets, but above all by decisions which were imposed by the Council and the European Council where the national executives of the larger member states (they never voted) played a predominant role. In fact, as the financial crisis deepened in the period 2009–2011, the bi-lateral leadership of Germany and France came to be transformed into a compelling *directoire* of EU financial policy. It was common to read in the press of a 'Merkozy' government within the European Council. This *directoire* has thus become only German after 2012. The intergovernmental EU has not only set up a highly centralised crisis prevention regime, but it has come to operate under the control of the larger and creditor member states, not the supranational institutions, with the implication that intergovernmental centralisation has been uneven: some member states have retained their political discretion whereas others have not.

In sum, the intergovernmental EU has not satisfied the needs of an effective and legitimate decision-making process. In the throes of the Euro-crisis, it has ended up by creating, paradoxically, an extremely centralised system that overrides national prerogatives, based on the policy's domination by one group of member states over other member states, unable to control the threats coming from the financial markets, but also devoid of the necessary legitimacy necessary to be accepted by the citizens of the indebted member states.

4. Beyond Intergovernmentalism: The Puzzle of Economic Governance

The Euro-crisis has dramatically challenged the coexistence of the supranational and intergovernmental unions formalised in the Lisbon Treaty. Moreover, the crisis has deepened the divide between the Eurozone and the non-Eurozone member states. It has not only halted the expectation of a gradual convergence of the intergovernmental union into a supranational one, but it has also shaken the idea of the unitary and ever expanding EU. How do we deal with these institutional strains?

Three strategies can be considered. The first strategy consists in rationalising the *status quo*, preserving the dual constitutional nature of the Lisbon Treaty, albeit fine-tuned on the basis of the measures introduced to manage the Euro-crisis and to prevent similar outcomes in the future. This strategy is made explicit by Article 16 of the Fiscal Compact Treaty assessing that 'within five years at most following the entry into force of this Treaty ... the necessary steps shall be taken ... with the aim of incorporating the substance of this Treaty into the legal framework of the

European Union'. This article was imposed on the national governments by the EP (Krellinger 2012). Once achieving the main objective (that of making the signatory states introduce – as the majority of them already did, through constitutional or equivalent means – the golden rule of balanced budgets), the Fiscal Compact should become part of the Lisbon Treaty, assuming the characteristics of an enhanced cooperation agreement, not unlike that obtained with the Schengen Agreement originally signed in 1985 by five (out of nine) member states, thus incorporated into EU law through the 1997 Amsterdam Treaty. In this case, the integration process will continue to be regulated by a single legal framework, with functional internal differentiations concerning specific policies. Financial policy will continue to be controlled by the ECOFIN Council and the European Council, with the Commission playing mainly an implementing role and the EP constrained to play a secondary legislative role. This strategy has the merit of keeping the EU together, but it also has the demerit of leaving unaltered the intrusive and yet ineffective intergovernmental features of the economic governance system, which emerged from the Euro-crisis. Moreover, it leaves unresolved the question of legitimacy, because national governments have not been elected for dealing with European problems, but with domestic ones. The recourse to the enhanced cooperation clause cannot help if the development of a set of systemic (economic, fiscal, budgetary) policies regarding a monetary union of 17 (18, starting in January 2014) member states is at stake. Enhanced cooperation can work regarding a specific and peripheral policy, but it seems ill-fitting for organising a set of different policies that are central to the integration process (as those constituting the Economic and Monetary Union). An intergovernmental Fiscal Compact, combined with the other measures approved, would end in strengthening the Lisbon Treaty's intergovernmental constitution. This strategy would move the centre of gravity of the EU to the intergovernmental side, consequently constraining the same functioning of the supranational side. One might argue (Crum 2012) that this transformation would envisage the institutionalisation of an *executive federalism* model. In any case, the intergovernmental EU that emerged during the Euro-crisis has gone far beyond a 'confederal constitutional settlement' (Moravcsik 2007), assuming that there ever was one.

Two alternative strategies have been (or might be) considered for promoting a more effective and legitimate system of economic governance in the EU. Both presuppose the existence of an independent budget of the Union, based no longer on the direct contribution of member states but on Union taxes derived from the activities made possible by the existence of the Union (as argued persuasively by Maduro 2012). A limited (no more than 5 per cent of the total GDP of the Union) but independent *fiscal capacity* of the Union would allow the Brussels institutions to pursue anti-cyclical policies compatible with the pro-cyclical ones of balanced budget at the member states level. This distinction of roles should be strengthened by the constitutional recognition of the no bail-out clause, on the basis of which member states 'are free to fail' but the Union 'is also free' to help member states in financial difficulty through autonomous strategic programmes.

At the same time, the ESM might be transformed into a European monetary fund (Pisani-Ferry 2013), governed in a federal manner as the ECB (with no country allowed to have a veto power). In addition, the ECB should become a lender of last resort, as it has been already *de facto*.

However, as the Four Presidents Report 'Towards a Genuine Economic and Monetary Union' of 5 December 2012 stressed, 'the creation of a new fiscal capacity for the EMU should also lead to adequate arrangements ensuring its full democratic legitimacy'. Here the two strategies diverge. According to what may be called the *parliamentary federation*' strategy, democratic legitimacy can be guaranteed only by the fiduciary relationship between the EP and the Commission. Under a recommendation adopted by the European Commission on 12 March 2013, 'political parties should nominate a candidate for European Commission President in the next European elections (2014)'. In its Resolution of 22 November 2012 on the elections to the EP in 2014, 'the EP urges the European political parties to nominate candidates for President of the Commission ... expecting those candidates to play a leading role in the parliamentary electoral campaign'. The transfer of the centre of gravity of the EU not only in the supranational side but above all in the relationship between the EP and the Commission implies a downsizing of the role of the European Council, to become again one of the specialised formations of the legislative Council, while executive power should be exclusively allocated to the Commission, whose formation should mainly derive from the results of the elections for the EP. In this strategy, the economic governance of the EU is based on the Commission, with the latter's president and the commissioner for financial affairs playing a governmental role, because it is legitimated by the outcome of the elections for the EP. Although very popular among European political elites, this strategy does not consider the powerful constraints within which a union of asymmetrical states has to operate. Any centralisation of power, in the EP or otherwise, has the effect of strengthening the power of larger member states to the detriment of smaller member states. Both strategies of *executive federalism* and *parliamentary federalism* are uncongenial with the asymmetrical nature of the EU.

A third strategy might thus be considered for granting legitimacy to the European system of economic governance (which I called *compound democracy*, Fabbrini 2010). This strategy aims to recompose the intergovernmental and supranational unions within a new constitutional project based on the institutional logic of *separation of powers*. This project has been finalised to prevent any decision-making centralisation, either in the EP-Commission or in the European Council-Council relations. This strategy consists in the formation of a strong executive system balanced by an equivalent strong legislative system. The institutionalisation of an original system of separation of powers at the Brussels level might take different forms. One form might be the following (Fabbrini 2012): it would be necessary to strengthen the role of the president of the European Council, extending his/her legitimation to national electors or parliaments, although maintaining the power of the European Council in selecting the candidates for the office and the collegial nature of the institution. That implies also the strengthening of the coordination between the presidents of the European Council and the Commission, and identifying a Treasury commissioner or high representative, nominated by the European Council with the consent of the legislature, with the tools for managing economic and financial policies. In this strategy, it is the office of the president of the European Council that should become the focus of the process of politicisation, shielding the Commission from it. The Commission has to preserve its civil service and technical nature, maintaining its special relation with the EP. The outcome would consist of a plural executive, yet politically centred around the president of the European Council. At the same time, it would be necessary to strengthen the congressional (that is, checking and balancing) role of the EP, recognising to it the power of legislative initiative. A separate political decision-making system can resort to political decisions, and not only on the automaticity of legal rules, yet can avoid the trap of centralisation. Political or policy decisions should emerge from the checks and balances between separate (legislative and executive) institutions sharing decision-making power.

5. Conclusion

The three reform strategies would have different implications for the constitutional bases of the EU. The first strategy requires minor constitutional changes, whereas the second and the third imply important constitutional changes – changes which might be recognised as having been already imposed by the Euro-crisis as the formation of new institutions for the Eurozone through the Fiscal Compact (Piris 2012). The Euro-crisis has not only brought the formation of new institutions but it has also deepened dramatically the distinction of interests and perspectives between the Eurozone and the non-Eurozone member states. Either the parliamentary or the compound union's perspective implies the recognition of the separation of interests between the Eurozone and the non-Eurozone member states (the UK in particular). At the same time, the latter member states cannot defend a *status quo* that has already been altered by the measures introduced and the treaties approved for managing the Euro-crisis and preventing a new one. The Eurozone has set up its own institutions (the Eurosummit of the heads of state and government and the Eurogroup of the finance ministers of the Eurozone member states) and is moving in creating a banking union under the supervision of the ECB. The Eurozone and the non-Eurozone areas need to have a reciprocal autonomy for dealing with the different financial challenges they are facing. A contrast between the two areas would worsen the conditions of both. It is thus necessary to find appropriate ways for differentiating the two areas, without breaking their connection in the single market. It remains an open question whether this differentiation might take place in the context of a revised Lisbon Treaty or through the definition of diverse institutional settings.

Chapter 5

Europe Waiting for Hamilton: Assumption of State Debts, the Federal Leap

Christian Stoffaës

1. The Hamiltonian Precedent

The Hamilton Plan

European political leaders, as well as European public opinion, are becoming aware that the accumulation of last chance summit meetings and of cosmetic measures are not sufficient to save the Euro. The precedent of the Hamilton Plan of 1790, which saved from bankruptcy the young American nation, can be a useful reference for the European debates. The Declaration of Independence of 1776 and the Constitution were limited to the mere definition of the rights of citizens and the balance of power in the newly independent nation. The founding acts left the bulk of sovereignty to each of the 13 colonies. As the salvation of the nation was at stake, the leaders of the Revolution were not concerned by the weight of public expenditure, thus the former British colonies had borrowed heavily to finance troops and arms purchases. When peace was established, the issue was how to pay back the debt.

The 'Articles of Confederation' of 1777 granted each of the former 13 colonies – now sovereign states – exclusive powers, delegating to Congress sole federal jurisdiction over war. This was a mere declaration of principles, not a state. Rapidly, the Articles were revealed to be dysfunctional: heavily indebted by military spending, states were struggling hard to repay their debts. The American nation was torn by conflicts of jurisdiction between states and commercial disputes, paralysed by the weight of reimbursements and heavily drawing on meagre tax resources. Ten years later, the Philadelphia Convention established the Constitution of the United States, which defines the rights of citizens and the balance of power within the Union. But it does not yet speak of public finances and federal power.

One more decade would pass before a Founding Father of America, Alexander Hamilton, New York delegate to the Constitutional Convention and first Treasury Secretary, proposed in his 'Report on the Public Credit' presented to Congress in 1790 to transfer the debts of states to federal power. The issue was to avoid bankruptcy, which might have been lethal to the young nation. At the time, pensions payable to veterans were valued at a quarter of their value. Public debt had risen to

$54 million, equivalent to one third of gross domestic product (GDP) at the time. The Union agreed to take over the debts at face value, for the purpose of issuing government bonds at the rate of 4 per cent. The federal debt was a perpetual debt: interest costs were financed by new resources, such as customs duties.

Birth of the American Federal State

The principal argument of the Hamilton Plan for the preservation of the public credit was to obviate the risk of defaults for the purpose of preserving the honour, public credit and future borrowing capacity of the young nation. In addition its aim was to consolidate the Union against the centrifugal forces and foreign intrigue, especially from the British and their local allies. The bearer of federal bonds, financial oligarchies and local landowners, Hamilton argued, would have a vested interest in supporting the central government against the temptations of secessionists. The establishment of a financial administration and federal tax would become a powerful integrative link.

The Founding Fathers were quite naturally divided on the proposed federal pooling of state's debts. Two major issues were at stake: surrender of local sovereignties to the federal power following decades of fighting to gain independence, and sharing of the debt burden. Opposite to the present-day situation in Europe, the South of the Union, rich from their colonial crops, was the creditor then, the North was the debtor. Those states which had already repaid their national debts, such as Virginia, were reluctant to share the debt of the impecunious, such as New York. Between Hamilton, who favoured a strong central government, and Jefferson, representing agrarian supporters of local sovereignties, a compromise was plotted, including the transfer of the federal capital from New York to Virginia (although not far away from the borderline…).

The true founding act of the Union, and the resounding success of the plan, was that Hamilton rooted legitimacy in the federal government, then a new idea in a republic deeply hostile towards the strong state, synonymous with oppression. America had taken a new direction: government credit restored the abundance of available funds, and there was general prosperity. For Hamilton, a permanent federal debt and a reasonable size was 'the powerful cement of our nation'. Hence, the Treasury Department grew in stature and staff to administer the public debt and to raise taxes. Then Congress created the Bank of the United States, which is the antecedent of the federal bank.

2. Comparative American-European Defaults

Causes of the European Quasi-Default

The American federal leap of 1790 was caused by unsustainable public debts, and by the quasi-default of the over-indebted states. Similarly, it is essential to understand the origin of the European debt, which led some member states to the verge of bankruptcy in 2010. The Euro-crisis has affected the countries of the Eurozone since the Wall Street crash of Lehman Brothers in September 2008. It started with a banking crisis in late 2008, followed by an economic downturn which lasted until mid-2009, which was subsequently transferred to budget deficits caused by recession and massive bailouts. In Europe this crisis – common to most developed countries, including the United States of America – was aggravated by the divergences which appeared between the economies and public finance of the countries and was exacerbated by the common currency – the Euro – which had lost its flexibility granted by the capacity to devalue the national currency.

The crisis made it difficult or impossible for a group of countries in the Eurozone to repay or re-finance their government debt without the assistance of third parties: Greece, the most symbolic example, was the first country to suffer, followed by Ireland, Portugal, Cyprus, and also, to a certain extent, large economies such as Italy and Spain. In 1992, the Maastricht Treaty created the common currency. The signatories pledged to limit their deficit spending to 3 per cent of GNP and debt to 60 per cent of GNP, a condition to becoming a member of the Eurozone. However, a growing number of EU member states failed to stay within the limits of the Maastricht criteria. Sovereign countries, such as Greece, managed to mask their deficit / debt levels through a combination of techniques, including inconsistent accounting and off-balance-sheet transactions.

In 2009 a number of rating agencies downgraded the governments in various European countries, thus stimulating the fear of sovereign debt crises among financial markets. Causes of the crisis varied by country. In several countries, private debts arising from a property bubble were transferred to sovereign debt as a consequence of banking bailouts. In Greece, high public sector wage and pension commitments and the inability to recover taxes were the major cause of government deficits. Without the common currency, the sanction of such public finance mismanagement would have been immediate, taking the form of devaluation of the national currency. However under the Euro, that adjustment had been made impossible. Sanctions took the form of raising interest rates of national treasury bonds on the financial markets.

Concerns among financial markets converged to ignite the Greek financial crisis of May 2010. The major Eurozone members, led by Germany with the support of France, decided, following a few dramatic summit meetings, to save Greece from bankruptcy. Eurozone members decided to commit themselves to rescuing the countries threatened by the attacks of financial markets on their sovereign debts, which took the form of the European Financial Stability Facility (EFSF) (transformed into the European Stability Mechanism (ESM)).Greece was the detonator of the Eurozone crisis. At a time when many thought the economic crisis was over in the wake of the economic recovery of the summer of 2009, the size of the deficit rose to 13 per cent of GNP. The treacherous handling of Greek public accounts suddenly revealed a huge gap, which shook financial markets.

The estimation is that the level of the budget gap, that is, the difference between the 'declared deficit' and the 'true deficit', was 2 per cent of GNP.

Greek debt slipped dramatically from 110 per cent of GDP in 2008 to 127 per cent in 2009, then 143 per cent in 2010, then 161 per cent in 2011. Interest rates of Greek bonds on financial markets grew dramatically to unsustainable levels, from 5 per cent to 40 per cent during a few weeks in 2010. To rescue the country on the verge of default, the 12 members of the Eurozone, behind Germany and France, agreed to act to save Greece from default and lent the country €110 billion, and imposed upon the banks the cancellation of €7 billion of private debts (called a 'haircut' in banking language) under conditions of fiscal rigour. A European Financial Stability Facility (EFSF) was set up in May 2010. Soon, it was the turn of Ireland and Portugal to risk default. In both countries bank speculations, especially on real estate, had created a huge bubble. A bailing out of the banks transferred their debts to the governments to save them from bankruptcy.

A European global rescue scheme seemed necessary, but debate raged on in Germany, the main creditor country. Many supporters were in favour of dropping Greece from the Eurozone and initiated procedures to declare the plan unconstitutional against the European commitments negotiated by the Chancellor. For the majority however, the impact of sovereign defaults and the uncertainties of what would follow would hurt the national economy more than the rescue plans. Gradually a national consensus took shape: Germany would agree to pay to save the Euro but only if the 'impecunious' member states, also nicknamed the 'ClubMed states', gave serious guarantees of fiscal discipline. In December 2011, during the negotiation of another bailout plan for Greece, Germany offered its partners the option of adopting a system of sanctions ensuring compliance with the criteria of deficit and debt ceilings in the Eurozone: this was the Treaty on Stability Coordination and Governance (TSCG), also denominated the 'fiscal compact'.

Aside from bailout programmes by governments, the European Central Bank (ECB) has also done its part by lowering interest rates and providing cheap loans of more than one trillion Euros to maintain liquidity among European banks. In September 2012, the ECB calmed financial markets by announcing free unlimited support for all Eurozone countries involved in a bailout programme from the EFSF/ESM. From rescue plans adopted in emergency situations the Eurozone agreed on a stable system duly negotiated and ratified to manage financial aid between member states in the Eurozone: the European Financial Stability Mechanism (EFSM), to be replaced by the ESM in 2013, a new institution of the European construction. It was finally accepted that the structure of the Eurozone as a monetary union (that is, one currency) without fiscal union (for example, different tax and public pension rules) had contributed to the crisis and harmed the ability of European leaders to respond.

Origin of the European Debt

The debt issue will dominate European agendas a long time in the future. For years to come, Europe will have to live with the Great Debt. As mentioned earlier, the origin of the American debt of 1790 was the repayment of war debt. Where does European debt come from? By what strange paradox did the monetarist revolution, sparked 30 years ago to curb inflation and to repay the debt incurred by the Keynesian welfare state, end in huge public debt? The mechanism is not yet fully understood.

After 2000, banking deregulation led to speculation without restraint: securitisation and derivatives had exploded, the repeal in 1999 of the Glass Steagall legislation separating deposit banks from investment banks irrigated financial markets with considerable amounts of liquidities to invest in securities of various kinds. The 'too big to fail' mechanism created a moral hazard phenomenon which led banks to speculate on financial markets, being sure they would be bailed out by governments in case of default. The resulting financial crisis crash of 2007 led to bank bailouts of massive proportions, resulting in transfer to governments of the burden of the debt accumulated by the private sector. Ireland and Iceland provide extreme examples of banking speculation while Spain is an example of real estate speculation. In response to the crisis the Bush administration introduced in October 2008 a comprehensive plan to support banks, the Troubled Assets Relief Programme (TARP), for an amount of about 5 per cent of GDP. Later on, the Obama administration implemented the Stimulus Plan in the form of a supplementary budget also exceptional in the amount of 5 per cent of GDP.

On top of the 2008 crisis the Euro also created a moral hazard for impecunious states within the Eurozone. Before, the sanction of mismanagement was immediate by means of devaluation. With the Euro, devaluation became impossible. Mismanagement of public finance was sanctioned only indirectly and after a delay, through the interest rates of government bonds sanctioned on financial markets. This is what happened to Greece, on a spectacular scale, then to Spain, Italy and Portugal. It is indicative that public debt has increased by about 30 per cent of GDP since the beginning of the crisis within the Organisation for Economic Development and Cooperation (OECD) countries. More specifically from 70 per cent of GDP in 1990, it rose to 76 per cent in 2005 and 96 per cent in late 2011. Budget deficits in Europe and the United States (US) are close to 100 per cent.

3. Revisiting the Debt Growth Dilemma

Is it reasonable to deepen recession and unemployment when austerity prevails? That great political controversy is at the heart of economics and has been there since the Great Depression and the Keynesian revolution. The United States and Europe offer a clear illustration of the controversy. In deep contrast with German rigorous orthodoxy, the US expansionary management has systematically favoured growth, full employment and Wall Street. The policy mix includes increased budget deficits, with the institutionally embedded reluctance of Congress to reduce spending and to increase taxes, and a monetary policy of quantitative easing by the federal bank. Japan provides a contrasting example for consideration. Since it follows an old growth model based on a fast growing undercompetitive industry, its economy has dragged along for 20 years in stagnation, aborted stimulus and recessions. In Europe the burden of debt accumulated by the state and the banks in the periods of speculative euphoria explains the deadlock. But it is impossible to compare what is not comparable. Can the German relative prosperity and stability throughout the crisis be explained by financial orthodoxy or the cultural characteristics of the Germans?

In economic debates, diagnoses and remedies are often rooted in economic history. However, history does not repeat itself exactly: one must take into account the uniqueness of each situation. In the debate for or against the budget agreement, historical references therefore carry substantial weight. In Europe, the debt that followed the Second World War resulted in hyperinflation, while that which followed the First World War resulted in deflation, the Depression and the rise of political extremism. In both cases the debt was eased through the spoliation of creditors which allowed the cancellation of part of the debt. These historical lessons are in sharp contrast with the arguments of the advocates of austerity, who top the pressure of financial markets. The present situation also puts this economic rationale in question. In 2013 the level of public debt in Europe reached more than 90 per cent of GDP (that is, up by half from the 60 per cent Maastricht limit before the financial crisis), which is the historical post-war level. At the same time a vicious circle of deficit reduction, weaker growth and lower tax revenues is developing. As the Keynesians would argue, restricting budgets in times of recession aggravates the disease instead of curing it. Without productive investment there is no future, especially at a time when the old industrial and technological pre-eminence of the continent is being challenged by emerging powers.

The main historical reference for the vicious circle of deflation was British austerity after the First World War. The United Kingdom came out of the conflict with a public debt equivalent to 140 per cent of gross domestic product. Determined to repay government debt and to bring the national currency to its pre-war level, conservative governments imposed extreme fiscal and monetary discipline. The result was a stagnant economy, high unemployment during the 1920s, and the increase of public debt to 170 per cent of GDP in 1930 and to 190 per cent in 1933. The concept of conservative economists was to pursue the restoration of public credit through re-establishing the gold parity of the pound sterling, a guarantee of the prosperity of the City and the power of the British Empire. On the other side, trade unions advocated full employment and refused austerity. The main political divide opposed the supporters of a strong currency and the supporters of full employment. The debate also raged among academics: the so-called 'classical' economists advocated a return to a balanced budget and the repayment of debt, while the disciples of Keynes advocated a budget deficit and the rise of public debt to stimulate growth. It is evident that the difficulties and debates of the interwar period created the foundation of the economic policy debate in its modern form as a part of our collective memories. Opened by the 'classical' economists and John Maynard Keynes, this controversy dominated the economic stage of the twentieth century and is still with us in Europe.

The other founding event of this cleaving took shape with the debate which dominated the US presidential election of 1932. Three years after the 'Black Thursday' crash of 24 October 1929, the US economy had failed in the Great Depression. Supported by the mainstream economists, Republicans advocated the return to equilibrium in order to restore confidence. President Hoover said in 1929 that 'prosperity [was] in the corner'. Instead, President Franklin D. Roosevelt, who won the 1932 elections, imposed punitive laws on Wall Street and launched social welfare programmes and major public works programmes. The federal budget increased from 20 per cent of GDP in 1933 to 40 per cent in 1936, after a series of deficit reductions from 3 to 5 per cent in annual fiscal years. The Second World War raised the public debt above 100 per cent of GDP (110 per cent in the US in 1949). The latter was to be reduced by inflation.

Comparison certainly is not the same as reason. However, there are striking analogies with our contemporary European economic debate. The obsession with the gold standard, the 'barbarous relic' denounced by Keynes, bears some similarities with the Euromania that dictates its law on fiscal and monetary fiscal policy. Worse than the gold standard is the fact that member states of the Eurozone are linked to the Euro by an international commitment and hence the decision to eventually abandon the gold standard is no longer a matter of pure sovereignty. The analogy with the Great Depression is also significant. Excessive speculation on the stock market in the optimism of the roaring twenties triggered the 1929 crash, as did the real estate euphoria with the 2008 crash.

4. Birth of a Federal Economic Policy

Designing a European Fiscal Union

The major steps of European construction have been performed often inadvertently. If the European public had been aware of what they had been committed to by their political leaders in terms of their economic sacrifice and surrender of sovereignty, they probably would have expressed their opposition. Let us remember that Europe was born from a minor initiative, a sectoral project born out of the coal and steel industries, which resulted in the common market and the single currency, and then, maybe in the future, on a federation. Similarly, Schengen is forcing a definition of the identity of Europe.

Similarly, the signing of the Treaty on Stability Coordination and Governance (TSCG) in March 2012 took place almost unnoticed, and for several reasons. The fiscal compact was enacted as an urgent response to the financial crisis of the

Eurozone, so it appeared not as a deliberate, conscious decision but as a natural, inescapable, automatic response to the constraints of the crisis of the Eurozone. First, to avoid cumbersome procedures for community review, it took the form of an intergovernmental treaty, negotiated following a rapid timetable under the pressure of the emergency financial markets alert. Then the qualification of 'historic' did not really seem to apply to a text that does not change the Maastricht criteria but establishes a mechanism for more effective sanctions for their breach.

However, history will record the TSCG as a milestone in European integration, because in reality it changes everything. The obligation to submit budgets for prior approval by the European partners creates an inexorable process of convergence of public spending and national taxation. Any future government will experience serious difficulties in abstracting the multilateral surveillance of its peers, let alone cheating, and there will be similar consequences regarding monetary policy. Unofficially, the treaty was also the condition set to open the floodgates to credit and prevent it from flowing into a bottomless pit. This is because, since its adoption, the European Central Bank (ECB), under its new president Mario Draghi, provides banks in the Eurozone with unlimited funding and declares itself willing to buy unlimited sovereign bonds on the secondary market, thereby releasing pressure from the markets.

Shaping the European Economic Government

The issue at stake is how to correct the malediction of European economic policy: a monetary union without a fiscal union. Historically, the concept of economic policy was defined as the submission of monetary policy to governments, and was the result of political debates of the interwar period between the two World Wars. This was the time when central bankers addressed severe warnings to impecunious governments. To overcome the obstacle, governments placed central banks under their supervision. They nationalised money creation to ensure the financing of budget deficits, public works and social transfers to assist the return to full employment. This was the result of the Keynesian revolution. The European economic policy that is taking shape within the Eurozone has exactly the opposite form as it entails the submission of the budget and fiscal policy to the Euro. The widespread application of the golden rule will profoundly change society. Economic government does not exist yet. But there is a European economic governance, whose institutions have taken on an increased importance all through the crisis.

With the Maastricht Treaty of 1992 Europe created a powerful institution in charge of the management of the European common currency. The European Central Bank rapidly took an important role, successfully implementing its mandate of guaranteeing stable money and low inflation. It is responsible for monetary policy and is governed by a president and a board of the heads of national central banks. The principal task of the ECB is to keep inflation under control. The ECB cannot receive instructions from national governments nor from other

European institutions, such as the Commission or the Parliament. Though there is no common representation, governance or fiscal policy for the currency union, some cooperation does take place through the Euro-group, which makes political decisions regarding the Eurozone and the Euro. The Euro-group is composed of the finance ministers of Eurozone states, however, in emergencies national leaders also form the Euro-group.

All along the financial crisis the ECB showed remarkable adaptability to the new, fast evolving situation despite the rigidity of its mandate, by practising 'quantitative easing' and buying sovereign debts not directly from governments – which is strictly forbidden – but on the secondary market. New European institutions have appeared as a consequence of the financial crisis: the EFSF (stability facility) and the ESM (stability mechanism). They have merged into the European Stability Mechanism which may become a major federal economic instrument in the future. The European Financial Stability Facility (EFSF) was created by the Eurozone member states following the decisions taken on 9 May 2010 within the framework of the ECOFIN Council. The EFSF's mandate is to safeguard financial stability in Europe by providing financial assistance to Eurozone member states within the framework of a macroeconomic adjustment programme.

To fulfil its mission, the EFSF issues bonds or other debt instruments on the capital markets. The proceeds of these issues are then lent to countries under a mutually agreed programme. The EFSF may also intervene in the primary and secondary bond markets, acting on the basis of a precautionary programme and financing recapitalisations of financial institutions through loans to governments. The EFSF was created as a temporary rescue mechanism; October 2012 saw the creation of a permanent rescue mechanism. The European Stability Mechanism (ESM) entered into force on 8 October 2012, as an international organisation located in Luxembourg which was established as a 'permanent firewall' to provide instant access to financial assistance under urgency situations in financial difficulty, with a lending capacity of €500 billion, replacing the earlier temporary programmes.

Also the economic governance of the Eurozone has taken the form of the stable presidency of the Euro-group. As the French President said: 'This economic government will debate the main political and economic decisions to be taken by the member states, harmonize tax policy, start the convergence of social policies from the top and launch a battle against tax fraud.' The TSCG already imposes a ceiling on budget deficits and public debt reduction. Germany had imposed these rules on its partners in 2012 in exchange for its agreement to the establishment of the EFSF in 2011, which was followed by the ESM, and was designed to organise and distribute the load in supporting indigent southern states, primarily Greece. At the same time however the Eurozone government casts little shade on national governments or other Community actors.

A paradoxical lesson has emerged from the past three years of the crisis: the Euro has been voted on by the European public. The markets have found that they had underestimated the commitment to the Euro, and the European nations have realised that there was a price to pay to keep it alive. No politician and no member state can take the risk of breaking this carefully constructed edifice, knowing that they would gain an unenviable record in the history books. In other words, the Eurozone was the first step: the inevitable consequences of the Euro are under way. The next step is how to deal with the European debt.

5. Designing a Hamilton Plan for Europe

Not only are sovereign debts not reduced, they are increasing. Worse, divergences are growing steadily. And an anti-Euro sentiment is developing in some nations and political parties.

Unsustainability of European Debt

Indeed, the public debts accumulated during the past decade in Europe are irredeemable, since reducing them from 100 per cent to 60 per cent of GDP requires not only balanced budgets, but budgets with a proposed lifespan of more than a decade, as well as the reduction of pensions and public sector salaries by about 20 per cent, and austerity and deflation for more than 10 years. If we also take into account what contortions are needed to reduce the deficit to 3 per cent, as well as the inevitable rise of the interest rates, we come to the conclusion that the servicing of public debts will be totally unbearable, thus reinforcing the vicious circle of austerity. Table 5.1 depicts the champions of public debt in Europe in 2012.

Table 5.1   Champions of public debt in Europe (per cent of GNP)

Country	Deterioration
Portugal	123
Ireland	127
Spain	86
Greece	157
Italy	127
EU average	90.6

The deterioration of public debt is still more worrying. From 2010 to 2012, the average deterioration of European public debt is 5.4 per cent of GNP. Not only is public debt not reduced, it is still increasing, and sharply. The highest levels of deterioration occur roughly in the same group of member states, with a few differences, mainly explained by the enormous bank rescue schemes in Spain and Ireland real estate lending (see Table 5.2).

Table 5.2   Deterioration of public debt (per cent of GNP)

Country	Deterioration
Portugal	29.6
Ireland	25.5
Spain	22.7
Greece	8.6
Italy	7.7
Average	5.4

Nevertheless, the question of how to deal with European debt cannot be asked openly in all its brutality without simultaneously offering a solution, otherwise it destroys public trust, and destabilises financial markets. This is because large over-indebtedness invariably ends up with the spoliation of creditors: 'When I owe you $100 billion that's my problem, when I owe you one trillion, it's yours', as the cynics say. The spoliation of creditors causes a loss of public confidence and deep frustrations: there is either the hard approach, such as the refusal to honour commitments (Argentina, Russian loans), or the soft approach (European post-war hyperinflation) – both are options with heavy consequences. Faced by the possibility of anarchic, chaotic and confrontational theft, the preference should be for an organised and negotiated plundering, through a scheme of restructuring public debt. This is the historical issue that the European reconstruction is facing. Various debates are taking place between Europeanists and separatists, federalists and sovereignists, between those who want to stick to the Euro and those who argue for leaving it; there are even disputes between states and citizens, and chaos on the constitutional balance of powers. Meanwhile, the weight of accumulated debt stifles the South, exacerbates divisions, possibly prepares splits, develops populism and political extremism.

Devising Inter-European Compromises

Horresco referens: the restructuring of debt robs creditors, whether it be rescheduling or, worst case, writing-off. This is why the financial community does not like to talk about it. Talks announce future decisions – even low-level talks. It thus belongs to politics and to the productive forces of the real economy to bring the idea to the table. Huge indebtedness often ends the plundering of creditors under two schemes, both with heavy effects: the 'hard' option is to refuse to honour the commitments (for example Argentina and the Russian loans); the soft option is to allow hyperinflation to grow (for example, Europe after the First World War). Already private creditors have been forced to accept a 'haircut' of $100 billion in exchange for the bailout of Greece by governments and the IMF. The rescue plan for Greece has already resulted in the write-off of a significant part of the sovereign debt and the haircut of reckless bankers. The rescue plan for Cyprus, an indirect consequence of the abandonment of Greek debt by the haircut tax of depositors, has had a small but heavy impact on citizens' trust, perhaps foreshadowing the return of banking panics of the past.

A parallel between the Hamiltonian situation of 1790 with our great Euro debate is tempting but one has to be mindful of the fact that the federal debt to be borne by the US was a fledgling war debt, as was most of the public debt of those times, doomed to dissipate after the end of hostilities. In contrast, contemporary European debt is a debt of peacetime, and as such it remains to be disciplined. When we talk about Eurobonds we must know what we are talking about. Eurobonds can be designed to cover future expenditures or to amortise past indebtedness. The Hamilton Plan is a pooling of depreciation and rescheduling of past war debts. Where we are not, strictly speaking, talking of Eurobonds, some fear that a huge 'moral hazard' is generated by the impecunious nations whereas they are not (yet) convinced that they have completed the cure for their addiction to debt without risk.

The German analysis of the Eurozone crisis is that the essence of the debt crisis lies in a spirit of complacency. Therefore the very existence of the Euro created a moral hazard of gigantic proportions by suppressing the sanction of devaluation, the usual punishment of impecunious governments. Over the period of a decade, the Euro had freed national economic managements of the assent to devaluation, and therefore the governments and demagogic political forces have forgotten the most basic rules of prudence, whether in social spending, hiring public officials, managing the release valves of credit, real estate speculation, etc. Therefore according to the moralistic German approach, the Eurobonds would only prolong the spirit of complacency that led us to the present situation. These concerns must be addressed. How do we prevent the return of speculative excess and spending? How do we ensure a conversion to moral discipline?

What institutional form might a Hamilton Plan for Europe take? Already, some German economists have proposed pooling government national sovereign debts exceeding the Maastricht state limit of 60 per cent in a mutual fund. Reducing the total debt of the Eurozone from the existing level (90 per cent of GDP) to the targeted level (60 per cent) would require funding of €4000 billion. Amortised over a period of 25 years, debt service costs would be approximately 200 billion per year at 2 per cent of GDP. Certainly such a rescheduling/restructuring would mean a spoliation of creditors, but a reasonable and defensible one.

The ESM could fulfil this role by being transformed into a European Debt Agency. A major step to undertake would of course be to create a dedicated resource for the service of the European debt. The sinking fund, the European Debt Agency (EDA) would be financed by the European Debt Amortisation Tax. To start with, funding of the EDA debt service (capital amortisation plus interest) would be provided by transfers from national budgets. But it might be transformed into a federal tax, which of course would be a major leap towards federalism. As Hamilton put it: 'a common debt of reasonable proportion is the cement of our nation'.

6. Timing of the European New Deal

There is not much time left to act. Not only have sovereign debts not been reduced: they are increasing, despite (or possibly because of) the fiscal measures imposed as the conditions for rescue. Worse, North and South are diverging more and more, not converging, and that deterioration is worrying. It will make the problem more difficult to solve in the future. After years of austerity providing disappointing results, the popular consensus in support of the Euro may shrink. An increasing number of populist leaders and political parties, on the left and the right, are advocating a return to national currencies and declaring competitive devaluations, both in creditor member states, whose populations are tired of paying for European solidarity, and in debtor nations, who are tired of austerity, unemployment and impoverishment.

Since the 2008 financial crash and the ensuing economic crisis, European governments have managed an efficient international cooperation to save the Euro. The member states which were on the verge of defaults have been rescued from bankruptcy by European solidarity. The Euro has been saved from disintegration. The peoples of Europe, whatever the vicissitudes, voted overwhelmingly to save the Euro, as well as the Greeks, Spaniards and the Irish, at whatever cost. Important political leaders who were considered obstacles have been dismissed (ask Berlusconi and Papandreou, or the Irish, Spanish and Portuguese heads of governments). It thus appears that the crisis has strengthened popular support for the Euro and it will generate the 'federal leap' as expected. At least, so far…

Management of the Euro-crisis has been led by the major member states, mainly Germany, inspired and supported by France, undertaking countless summit meetings. European established political institutions – the Commission, the Parliament – did not play a major role. The ECB played its part following German and French positions, without receiving formal instructions, as prohibited by the Treaty. The European Monetary Union has achieved the maximum that was allowed without more political integration. A major step was accomplished when it was realised that the crisis was not simply illiquidity but insolvability, starting with Greece in 2010, then continuing with Ireland, Portugal, the EFSF, the fiscal compact, the ESM. A similar step has to be accomplished globally with European sovereign debt. The ECB's policy of quantitative easing and money injection is not sufficient. European debt needs a deep restructuring.

The time has therefore come for a European New Deal, building on the recent European achievements, meaning more integration of a federal nature – the fiscal Union. The intergovernmental instruments which were designed during the crisis might be transformed into federal instruments: the Financial Stability Mechanism, successor of the European Financial Stability Facility (EFSF), and endowed with a funding of €500 billion (3 per cent of the European GNP); the Fiscal Compact, submitting national budgets to peer review and multilateral monitoring under coordination by the Commission; and the Council of Ministers of the Eurozone led by a stable, permanent Chairman.

The missing link in transforming the existing governance scheme might be the proposed European Debt Agency, possibly with the restoration of a European Debt Amortisation Tax dedicated to this service, thus creating a new instrument of European integration with a highly symbolic value, meaning 'never again'. The European New Deal will require compromise; compensation; interstate golden rules; constitutionalised and powerfully controlled national budgets; loss of sovereignty; and fiscal, budgetary and social coordination and harmonisation. The US compromise between the indebted states and solvent states, between Hamilton and Jefferson, was the highly symbolic transfer of the federal capital from North to South, from New York to Washington. Nobody remembers the terms of the Hamilton Plan: everyone knows that the US capital lies in Washington, DC, not in New York City.

The issue at stake will of course provoke a number of political debates and electoral programmes, transnational convergences and divergences, political parties, trade unions and social actors taking positions on a number of puzzling questions related to the European New Deal. For example, what compensation should be granted for Germany to be persuaded to accept the pooling and the restructuring / rescheduling of the European sovereign debt? A rigorous government of the Eurozone, certainly. Enhanced independence rules for the ECB that should be remembered in the right way after the recent monetary excesses? A transfer to Frankfurt of the Federal Capital of the Eurozone? Possibly a stronger president of the Eurozone, elected directly by EU citizens, a truly historical first Euro-election, as was proposed by some political parties. Could Angela Merkel – already proclaimed by the European public as the saviour of the Euro, and triumphantly re-elected after two four-year mandates as the Chancellor of Germany – be the front-runner candidate, benefiting from wide transpartisan-transnational support, thus finally sign the rehabilitation of Germany, ironically a cursed power in the twentieth century, and a model for the economy and democracy of the twenty-first?

Chapter 6

Political Lessons from the Economics of the Euro-crisis

Stefan Collignon

There is something impressive about the Euro: after nearly five years of pounding and hammering, it still exists. Compare this to the previous European Monetary System, which collapsed within three weeks after being attacked by speculators in the financial markets. This institutional stability stands in sharp contrast to the social and political turmoil it has brought about in many member states. Thus, one should not condemn the Euro too quickly, even if it is in crisis. Is the source of Europe's economic suffering due to its currency or is it a consequence of mistaken policies? Blaming high unemployment, slow growth, fiscal austerity and high taxes on the Euro is understandable, given that Europeans are told that *only* austerity and deep structural reforms cutting into the welfare system can save the common currency (Schäuble 2011). There comes a point when, despite the greatest love for European unification, people will no longer put up with daily hardships as their sacrifice for a distant goal. But what if the problems were not due to the institutional arrangement of common money, but to mistaken policies? In that case, we should conclude that the Euro-crisis is political, not economic.[1]

That the half-built house of monetary union without political union may not be sustainable has been understood from the beginning. During the Maastricht negotiations, the German Chancellor, Helmut Kohl, sought to complement monetary by political integration, but the project was intellectually not yet as advanced as monetary union (Featherstone and Dyson 1999). Nevertheless, most protagonists of European Monetary Union (EMU) have always thought that a single currency will ultimately force member states to move to a political union (Collignon and Schwarzer 2003). If this has not happened (yet), it is not the fault of the Euro, but of European politics. In this chapter, I will suggest that the real crisis of monetary union results from the fact that the European economy's deep tissue integration has no counterpart at the political level.

For economic liberals the lack of political integration may not appear as a disadvantage, because they resent interference with the 'invisible hand' of the market. They believe that the creation of the European single market is all it takes to maximise welfare. But if private transactions generate externalities and national policies affect citizens in other member states, a more 'visible hand' in the form of

---

1   See also Bergsten and Kirkegaard 2012, who come to a similar conclusion.

rules, regulations and discretionary government action is needed. For nationalists, only the nation state has the legitimacy to impose rules and policies on citizens and they simply ignore the external effects of domestic policies on neighbours – and even indirectly on their own citizens. For nationalists on the left, preserving the welfare state in times of economic crisis is incompatible with more European integration. They are therefore willing to accept the disintegration of the Euro and ultimately the European Union. That, of course, would undermine the very foundations on which European welfare is built. None of these solutions will ultimately help European citizens to lead a better life.

The fact is, that European integration, and especially the Euro, has generated many economic interdependencies and externalities – some positive, some negative. Unfortunately, these externalities, many of which are related to European public goods such as macroeconomic stability, cannot be managed in a coherent and efficient manner without a political union that defines common welfare and gives sense and direction to economic policies in the Eurozone.[2] I will argue that the problems revealed by the Euro are primarily based on the disjunction between an integrated economy and a splintered polity and show why the Euro is a source of potential strength, which cannot unfold properly, because the political institutions for governing the Eurozone are inadequate for the conduct of welfare improvements.

1. The Amazing Robustness of the Eurosystem

It was part of the pre-Maastricht discourse to think of the EMU as a fixed exchange rate system, where member states have permanently pegged their exchange rates to each other.[3] It follows that one could exit the Euro and re-peg the exchange rate *in extremis*. Yet, this description of monetary union is not correct. There are no national currencies in the Eurozone. The Euro has replaced all previously existing currencies. The Eurozone functions exactly like any other currency area, where credit contracts can be enforced and extinguished by paying the legally defined and generally accepted currency. On 1 January 1999, the earlier monetary laws were abrogated and the Euro became legal tender (TEU, Article 3.4) in the participating member states. The European Central Bank (ECB) was set up as the directive organ and head office for the conduct of monetary policy. The existing National Central Banks (NCB) were merged with the ECB to form the Eurosystem. The abrogation of national monetary laws has, therefore, lifted the distinction of monetary jurisdictions and turned the Eurozone into an 'economic country'.

The difference between a fixed exchange rate system and a currency union is important, and it hinges on the difference between domestic and foreign money.

---

2   For a discussion of European public goods and their efficient administration, see Collignon 2002b; 2011.

3   See Delors Report 1989.

Domestic money is the liability of the central bank. It is created when central banks grant credit to commercial banks. Broad money includes the liabilities of commercial banks, which hold deposits on behalf of their clients in the 'real' economy. Thus, whether narrow or broad, money is always the liability of the banking system. Payments are made by transferring these liabilities between economic actors. Currency, that is, coins or the pieces of paper we carry in our pockets, are nothing else than a certified document of such liabilities, which banks can draw against their reserves at the central bank and then put into circulation with their clients.

By contrast, foreign money is the liability of a foreign central bank. It cannot be 'created' by domestic banks. In order to make a foreign payment, one has to earn foreign currency or get a loan from a non-resident. When a European firm sells products or European securities in the United States of America (USA), it will be paid dollars, which are foreign assets for the exporter, but domestic liabilities (money) for the American banking system. If the European exporter decides to exchange her foreign currency against Euros, she must find a partner who is willing to swap his domestic asset (Euros) against her foreign asset (dollars). Usually banks do this exchange. For example, a bank can buy the exporter's dollars and sell them to the European Central Bank. The foreign currency will then end up as an asset (foreign exchange reserves) in the balance sheet of the ECB. Hence, the difference between domestic and foreign currency is clear: *domestic money is a liability, and foreign money is an asset in the balance sheet of banks.*

The different sources of domestic and foreign money have far-reaching consequences: a currency area can run out of foreign currency but not of domestic money. If economic agents wish to exchange more domestic currency against *foreign* currency than the central bank can cover with its reserves, the price for domestic money will depreciate until the excess demand for foreign currency is eliminated. By contrast, if a bank needs more *domestic* liquidity because its clients have transferred their money balances to another bank or into neighbouring regions, it can borrow from other banks *or from the central bank.* Since Bagehot (1873), it has been universally understood that central bank lending to solvent banks must be without limit in the very short run, but can be controlled over the medium and long run by setting interest rates in pursuit of price stability. The open discount window ensures that the central bank is the lender of last resort to the banking system[4] and thereby preserves the stability of the financial system. This makes the Eurozone so robust. Despite the mitigating role of the IMF, there is no equivalent lender of last resort for foreign currencies at the international level.

---

4   See Santos and Peristiani, 2011. The ECB's role as a lender of last resort to banks is beyond dispute; there is less agreement, however, whether it should also be a lender of last resort to governments. This has been the contention between the ECB and the Bundesbank with respect to the *Outright Monetary Transactions* (OMT) programme of buying government bonds under certain conditions.

As a consequence of the difference between domestic and foreign currencies, the adjustment mechanism does not function in a currency area as it does in international economics. If a country runs current account deficits, they must be financed by capital inflows from abroad. If these inflows suddenly stop, as occurred during the Asian crisis in 1997, deep currency depreciations will follow, usually coupled with steep recessions and reductions of financial wealth. Within a currency area, a region that imports more than it exports will experience an outflow of money, but it is not dependent on capital inflows, because local banks can borrow from the central bank. This is why currency areas are sustainable, even if regional deficits persist for a long time. If a currency area did not work in this way, no nation state would ever have survived. Italy's north and south would have separated, the United Kingdom would have split into England and Scotland, and Bavaria and Catalonia would have introduced their own currencies.

In the Eurozone, southern member states ran large current account deficits, which were largely financed by banks borrowing savings from local residents or neighbouring countries or new funds from the ECB. Against the background of the Global Financial Crisis, the Euro-crisis started as a public debt crisis in Greece. As banks and lenders started to doubt the solvability of debtors, they stopped providing credit. Soon the crisis turned into a private debt and banking crisis in Ireland, Spain and Portugal. Risk-averse households and non-financial corporations started to save massively and hold their savings in liquid form or they accelerated repaying outstanding liabilities. Thus, the credit boom was followed by a credit crunch. As aggregate spending shrank, economies fell into recession. Although the ECB cut interest rates, the lower cost of credit did not compensate lenders' risk-averseness and investment fell.[5] The resulting crisis was deep in terms of output and employment losses, but financial wealth in the Eurozone, and relative prices and costs between different member states remained stable, at least initially.[6] This stability was achieved by the Eurosystem lending to crisis economies and recycling the excess liquidity from the north. These payment flows are reflected in the so-called TARGET2 balances, which record claims and liabilities among national

---

5   The argument can be formalised as follows. Let us assume that the required return on investment r is the cost of borrowing i plus the risk premium ρ. The return is the operating surplus, i.e. the share of income going to capital. Income is a function of capital. We then have in equilibrium $r I = (i + \rho)I = mkI$ where m is the profit margin and k the productivity of capital and I investment. This can be expressed as $\rho = mk - I$.

It is immediately clear that an increase in risk ρ would require a lowering of interest rates or an increase in profit margins and/or capital productivity. If interest rates are at their lower zero bound, monetary policy is powerless. If there are limits to how much wages can be lowered to increase profit margins, capital productivity has to be increased. But if capital productivity follows the law of diminishing returns, the implication is reducing the capital stock, which means negative investment.

6   In Greece and Cyprus, financial wealth was destroyed by haircuts for government debt, but this loss was significantly less than the depreciation of all domestic assets in the Asian case.

central banks in the Euro system. Far from being a threat, these monetary transfers between central banks are precisely what ensure the sustainability of the system.[7]

One may argue that flexible exchange rates could make the adjustment in the crisis easier. In the context of an integrated economy, such as Europe, that is no longer true. Currency depreciations are changing relative prices between domestic and foreign economies and small independent countries may be able to free-ride on undervalued real exchange rates without major side-effects for global trade. But for big economies this is not the case. Flexible exchange rates, which are largely driven by asset markets, will generate competitive distortions and disturbing uncertainties in goods and capital markets. The purpose of European monetary union was to eliminate such barriers to trade and investment. This has worked. Large European corporations have restructured their supply side to reap the full benefits of comparative advantages. They have outsourced and delocalised parts of their supply chain to regions with lower cost and more adequate skill profiles and this has allowed them to resist or minimise the loss of world market share in view of the dynamic performance of emerging economies. The consequence has been a fragmentation of national production, but also a deepening of European integration and also the growth in the internationalisation of the European economy (Esposito and Guerrieri 2013). Germany has been the leader in this process, but the logic applies to all member states. However, this process would not have been possible without a single currency.

In fact, while economic theories suggest that changing the *level* of exchange rates may be a useful tool for adjusting relative prices, they often ignore the detrimental effects of exchange rate *volatility*. Volatility increases uncertainty for future returns on capital; the longer the time horizon, the larger the uncertainty. This has two consequences. On the one hand, there is value in waiting until the situation becomes clearer, so that holding back investment will lower growth and employment. On the other hand, given the uncertainty of future returns, investors will ask for a risk premium in order to be compensated for the possibility of not being able to realise the expected rate of return. But at these higher *required* rates, there will be less profitable investment opportunities available. So, once again, investment, growth and employment will be reduced.

In order to counter these negative effects of exchange rate volatility, governments are often pegging their currencies to one of their main trade partners. This reduces uncertainty at the micro level, and generates currency blocs at the macro level.[8] However, currency blocs do not last forever because the net benefits are unfairly distributed between the centre and the periphery. The key currency benefits from stability with neighbouring trade partners, but its exchange rate becomes more volatile with respect to other global currencies. Peripheral currencies must tolerate these movements passively, but when the volatility between key currencies becomes

---

7   The discussion about TARGET2 balances was launched by Sinn and Wollmershaeuser 2011. For a critique see Collignon 2012.

8   For a formal model describing the emergence and demise of currency blocs, see Collignon 2002a.

too large, the blocs break up. Furthermore, the country with the key currency in the bloc usually sets the interest rate in accordance with its own stability requirements, while the peripheral countries need to keep their interest rates higher in order to prevent sudden outflows of capital. As a consequence, peripheral economies suffer from a structural comparative disadvantage due to the high cost of capital, which cannot be compensated by occasional currency adjustments.[9]

This monetary instability is a permanent threat to the sustainability of the single market. Economists like Tommaso Padoa-Schioppa (1987) have therefore concluded soon after the European Single Act had set up the internal market that the free flow of goods and capital and the need for stable exchange rates were incompatible with autonomous monetary policies. Creating the Euro was the answer to this problem. Eliminating exchange rate uncertainty has boosted trade (Rose 1999). Nitsch and Pisu (2008) found that the *propensity* by firms to export into the Eurozone and the *number of products* that exporters ship to EMU member countries increased after the introduction of the Euro. These effects are stronger for small and less productive firms. In other words, they have supported not only Germany, but also the peripheral economies where the share of small enterprises is large. Hence, there is empirical evidence that the creation of the Euro has achieved precisely what it was meant to achieve: improved competitiveness, more trade, and higher welfare. So if the Eurozone is in crisis, what has gone wrong?

2. Explaining the Euro-crisis

Several models dominate the analysis of the Euro-crisis: At first, it was believed to be a *public debt crisis*. However, financial markets also quickly worried about private debt which was accumulated during the previous boom. The Euro-crisis became a banking crisis. When it appeared that many banks had become vulnerable because they had lent excessively to member states with large *current account* deficits, the analytic focus shifted to macroeconomic imbalance, since the new policy consensus sought to balance current accounts of member states. While this meant reducing expenditure in the midst of a crisis, international economics also taught that macroeconomic adjustment may require a change in real exchange rates and this raised the issue of *competitiveness* cost and labour market developments. Each of these approaches contains parts of truth, but partial policy responses have

---

9   The German Chancellor, Angela Merkel, has regretted that the Euro keeps interest rates in Germany lower than what would be required by the German economy (http://www.faz.net/aktuell/wirtschaft/europas-schuldenkrise/vor-ezb-zinsentscheid-merkel-fuer-deutschland-muessten-zinsen-hoeher-sein-12161702.html). This view involves a double mistake. On the one hand it ignores that in a currency area excess liquidity is recycled through the central bank. On the other hand, it ignores the detrimental effects of not having the Euro: German interest rates would go up, the German currency would appreciate and monetary stability in the single market would collapse. This could hardly be in the German interest.

not been able to pull the Euro out of the crisis. For this reason, we will have to place these explanations in the context of the *financial and banking crisis*.

Fiscal Policy and Debt

The Greek debt crisis was triggered when the newly elected Prime Minister Papandreou revealed that previous Greek governments had knowingly and secretly violated the rules of the Stability and Growth Pact (SGP). Trust in the institutions of Europe's fiscal policy vanished, markets were in turmoil and policy makers sought to tighten fiscal policy and balance public deficits. The idea that fiscal profligacy has led governments to accumulate unsustainable mountains of debt is particularly popular in Germany. But in this crude form it is too simplistic. Figure 6.1 shows that prior to the Global Financial Crisis, public debt-to-GDP ratios were falling in most Eurozone states, with the exception of Germany, France and Portugal. Yet, Germany is unscathed by the crisis, France has struggled and Portugal collapsed. Ireland and Spain were well within the limits of public debt set by the SGP before the crisis and nevertheless they got into deep trouble. The fact is that in all countries inside and outside the Euro, including the USA, debt ratios did shoot up after the Lehman bankruptcy in 2008. Thus, it is not so much excessive borrowing by irresponsible governments, but rather the economic impact of the Global Financial Crisis on output and tax revenue that has pushed up the debt burden.

Even if there was no fiscal profligacy, one may argue that public debt did not fall enough, especially in highly indebted countries like Greece and Italy, and that consequently highly indebted countries did not have the necessary margins to stimulate the economy when they were hit by the crisis. Comparing Italy and Belgium highlights this: Belgium started monetary union in 1999 with a debt-GDP ratio of 130 per cent, Italy with 120 per cent. By 2007, the Belgian debt level was down to 88, the Italian to 106. Thus, Belgium consolidated 42 percentage points during the happy boom years, Italy only 14 points. During this time, Italy had consistently higher positive output gaps (1.7 per cent of GDP on average) than Belgium (0.9), and that exerted higher inflationary pressures on the Italian economy and has hampered competitiveness. The cyclically adjusted deficit, which according to Europe's fiscal rules should have been in balance, was on average –0.75 per cent in Belgium, but –3.84 per cent in Italy. After 2008, Belgium could therefore increase its cyclically adjusted deficit to –0.8 percentage points of Gross Domestic Product (GDP) on average, but in order to prevent the risk premium from rising to unsustainable levels Italy had to cut its deficit back by 1.6 percentage points to –2.2 per cent. Thus, fiscal prudence before 2008 allowed Belgium to better absorb the crisis shock: after 2008 the average output gap, that is, the difference between actual and potential output was –0.8 per cent in Belgium, but –2.2 per cent in Italy.[10] Hence, by avoiding fiscal consolidation during the boom

---

10   These figures are based on the Commission's AMECO database and take averages for the period 1999–2007 and 2008–2014.

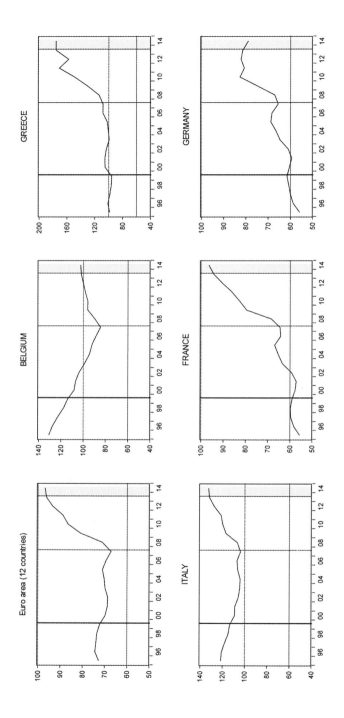

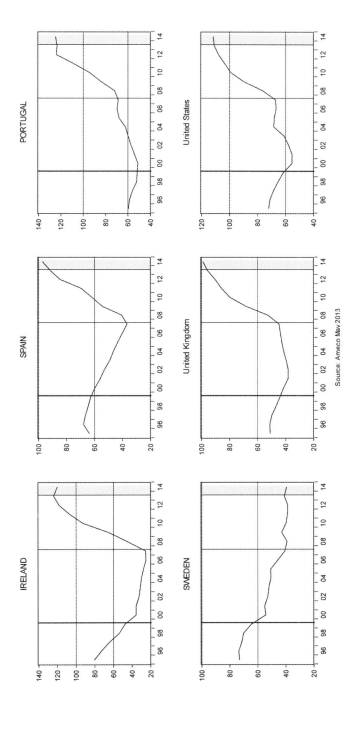

Figure 6.1   Debt-to-GDP ratios
Source: AMECO, May 2013.

years, Italy had no margins for fiscal stimulus in the crisis. Playing by Europe's rules before the crisis would have made it easier to avoid austerity after the crisis.

From this point of view, the tightening of fiscal rules in accordance with the new Fiscal Compact (Treaty on Stability, Coordination and Governance in the Economic and Monetary Union) may appear as a step in the right direction. Member states are committing themselves to introduce the stringent rules of the SGP into their own constitutional framework. The treaty defines a budget as not being excessive if the general budget deficit is less than –3.0 per cent of the GDP, and the cyclically adjusted deficit is less than –1.0 per cent of GDP, provided the debt-to-GDP ratio is significantly below 60 per cent; otherwise the cyclically adjusted deficit shall be below –0.5 per cent of GDP. The treaty also defines the rate at which debt levels above the limit of 60 per cent of GDP shall decrease.[11] These rules constrain the margins of national fiscal policy and could thereby reduce negative externalities for the Eurozone.

The problem with this arrangement is its rigidity. While the rules are reasonable during the boom, they may not give enough breathing space in a severe crisis. For example, Belgium would have had to consolidate its cyclically adjusted deficit even more during the boom years, but it could not have run an average structural deficit of –2.9 per cent to stimulate the economy after 2008. This rigidity will cause pro-cyclical consolidation and increase the amplitudes of output gaps, which will translate into high levels of structural unemployment. This is precisely what happened in 2010, when European governments responded to the Greek crisis by an early exit from the stimulating fiscal policies adopted in 2009. The result was a double dip recession with ever worse social consequences. European fiscal policies were the opposite of what the Obama administration did in the United States when it responded flexibly and efficiently to the economic situation. Thus, the political lesson European authorities have drawn from the European debt crisis was the imposition of austerity and tighter fiscal rules, while the proper way out of the crisis would have required discretionary measures as in the USA.

A better reform of Europe's fiscal rules would have been a policy framework that allows stabilising the economy by responding with anti-cyclical measures to large booms and busts. Fiscal rules should be conditioned on output gaps. When output gaps are positive, budgets should be in surplus and debt should be repaid. When output gaps are negative, fiscal consolidation should not be imposed and some leeway for discretionary stimulus should exist. It is easy to understand why the reform of fiscal policy rules has gone wrong. The Eurozone has no institution with the power to make discretionary decisions. For that a genuine 'economic government' would be required. Because they are afraid to lose power, the 17 dwarfs of European governments are tying down the Gulliver of the European economy until it can no longer move. Unemployment is the price to be paid for this mistake.

---

11   See http://en.wikipedia.org/wiki/European_Fiscal_Compact.

After Greece, the crisis spread. Ireland became the paradigmatic case for private debt problems, which spilled over into the banking system after the property bubble had burst. When interest rates had come down in the early years of EMU, credit was cheap and banks were lending generously, especially to the real estate sector. House prices in many southern countries had risen, and this had broadened the scope for collateral lending. Following the Lehman shock, the credit boom collapsed, collateral became insufficient and banks' balance sheets came under severe pressure. In Ireland, Spain, Greece, Portugal, Belgium, the Netherlands, Germany and later also in Cyprus, governments had to bail out banks in order to avoid a systemic meltdown of the banking system which would have had severe spillover effects for the rest of the Eurozone. When the national funds needed for the stabilisation of the system exceeded national capacities, a European bail-out fund – first the temporary European Financial Stabilisation Facility (EFSF) and later the more permanent European Stabilisation Mechanism (ESM) – had to step in. This established a close nexus of public and private debt crises, which now had external effects on member states in the north, because taxpayers in the non-crisis countries had to bail out debtors in the south. Severe political tensions developed, for suddenly Europe was no longer played as a benign positive sum game, but driven by nasty distributional conflicts. In nation states such conflicts get solved by the democratic process, but in Europe policy makers sought new methods to deal with this issue by setting up a *Troika* that imposed austerity without a democratic mandate and by creating the new *Macroeconomic Imbalance Procedure*.

Macroeconomic Imbalances

Analysts were quick to recognise that member states with private debt problems had also run large current account deficits during the boom. As any economic textbook teaches, current account deficits increase the external debt of a country. If these countries had run large current account deficits, they must also have accumulated foreign debt, and the solution to high debt was to rebalance current accounts between member states in the Eurozone. Through the so-called six-pack legislation, the European Commission set up a new procedure to avoid macroeconomic imbalances. However, the prominent focus of the procedure on current account balances within the Eurozone was another policy mistake, for it has reinforced austerity unnecessarily.

Current account balances are identical with the sum of public sector savings and the private sector savings–investment balance. From national income accounts we can formulate this identity like this:

$$CA = (T - G) + (S - I)$$

where a current account surplus (CA) is determined by the government's budget balance between tax revenue (T) and spending (G) and by the difference between private savings (S) and investment (I). It is clear that if the current account deficit is to be reduced, the public sector must cut the deficit and the private sector must increase savings or reduce investment. Hence, policies focusing on reducing current account deficits in the Eurozone will reinforce austerity and restrain economic growth. But this is a mistake, for exiting the crisis requires higher growth and increased investment, especially when concerns about debt sustainability prevent expansive fiscal policies.

The policy error of aiming at balanced current accounts between member states of the currency union originates in the mistaken belief that regions in the same currency area are economically to be treated as if they were foreign countries. We have seen above that this is wrong, because the economic distinction is the currency. The current account balance matters between different currency areas, because it indicates the growth of foreign debt in foreign currency. To service this debt, an economy must earn foreign currency. Therefore it is at some point necessary to generate positive current account balances. In fact, the simple rule of foreign debt sustainability says that the discounted value of all future expected current account positions should be equal to the amount of outstanding debt. However, as we have seen above, within the same currency area the story is different. Current account deficits between member states of the currency area are not building up foreign debt, because local governments or companies borrow domestic currency, which is supplied by the central bank and not by trade surpluses. Of course, credit must be paid back. But because the funds to do so are denominated in Euros, it does not matter whether the debtor's income is earned by net exports or by the expansion of sales in the non-tradable sector. Therefore, the need to balance current accounts has disappeared; instead, there is the need to generate cash flow sufficient to service the debt.

There is another argument why balancing current accounts between member states is a fallacy. For such a balance implies that local borrowing by the corporate and public sector is financed by local savings, so that member states become financially autonomous. But this is contrary to the idea and principles of a fully integrated market. In a single market, savings should be allocated where they yield the highest return. There is no reason why, say, investors in Ireland should only borrow savings from Irish households. In fact, Irish growth would be severely constrained by such a limitation. The proper functioning of a currency union would imply that capital moves into regions with above average returns to capital and as a consequence current accounts may deteriorate. But in this case, it is the region's comparative advantage which creates the deficit and not a lack of competitiveness.

The basic lesson from our analysis of how a monetary union works is that, rather than balancing current accounts, macroeconomic policies in the Eurozone must focus on balanced growth. The necessary and sufficient condition to ensure debt sustainability in a currency area is that local debtors' cash flow exceeds or at least equals debt service obligations. On the macro level this implies either that output grows at the same rate as interest rates in firms' liabilities, or that profit margins increase if output growth slows down. Because profit margins are the difference between prices and unit labour costs, the issue of wage bargaining and competitiveness has rightly entered policy debate.

Unit Labour Costs and Competitiveness

Competitiveness has had its role in the Euro-crisis. If regional costs and prices diverge significantly, investment will leave uncompetitive regions and local growth will slow down. The question is then how the cost adjustment is to be achieved. Europe's prevailing policy consensus has used austerity as the main adjustment tool and the European Commission (2012b) has rejoiced that it is working. Others have argued that the social costs are too high, and they have called for 'an orderly exit from the Euro' (Flassbeck and Lapavitsas 2013). This would be the end of monetary union.

The exit argument hinges essentially on the assumption that wage and price dynamics in the Eurozone have generated huge competitiveness gaps. Usually, unit labour cost indices are shown as evidence. These indices have their base year in 2000 and then trace the evolution of nominal wage compensation relative to productivity in different member states. Figure 6.2 is an example. It shows that in most southern member states unit labour costs have increased faster than the ECB-inflation target (thick straight line), while in the north (Germany and Austria), wage restraint has prevented unit labour costs from rising. Hence, labour cost gaps have emerged. For example between 1999 and 2007, unit labour cost increases in Greece have exceeded German developments by 27 per cent and in Italy by 22 per cent. Some conservative economists have suggested wage cuts of similar proportions to restore competitiveness (Sinn 2013). On the left, the reasoning is similar, although the policy solution of wage cuts is rejected in favour of dismantling the Euro (Flassbeck and Lapavitsas 2013).

However, the argument is flawed. First of all, we observe that in Slovenia and Slovakia the competitiveness gap would have been even higher than for Greece, but so far these countries have not been pulled into the Euro-crisis. On the other hand, the Netherlands, which have a huge trade surplus with the Eurozone, also seem to have accumulated competitive disadvantages. Secondly, adjustment is already taking place in many crisis countries. For example, unit labour costs in Greece are close to German levels and in Ireland they are comparable with Austria. But this does not seem to have stopped the crisis in these member states. Thirdly and most importantly, there is no good reason to assume that the year 2000 represents an equilibrium position so that the diverging indices show unsustainable divergences in labour cost. A country may have accelerated wage inflation because its unit labour cost level was well below average or because capital productivity has gone up. Cost indices like Figure 6.2 are not suitable to assess *levels* of competitiveness. We therefore need to find an equilibrium benchmark against which cost developments can be judged.

De Grauwe (2011) has tried to solve the base year problem by taking a long historic average as base, but this is just another *ad hoc* index without theoretical foundation. There is, however, a simple solution: in an efficient market economy, returns of capital are supposed to converge in equilibrium. Taking the Eurozone as the benchmark, we can calculate the national level of unit labour costs, which would

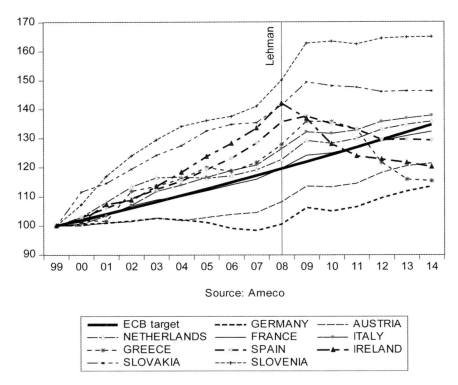

Source: Ameco

▬▬▬ ECB target	---- GERMANY	----- AUSTRIA
---- NETHERLANDS	—— FRANCE	----- ITALY
--*-- GREECE	—-- SPAIN	—▲-- IRELAND
—•-- SLOVAKIA	---+-- SLOVENIA	

Figure 6.2   Unit labour cost indices

generate the return to the national capital stock equal to the Eurozone's average. By calculating the ratio of actual unit labour costs relative to the equilibrium level, we obtain an index that correctly reflects the excess of a member state's unit labour costs above or below equilibrium.[12] It has the advantage not only of being grounded in sound economic principles, but also of taking into account the difference between labour costs and prices, that is, profit margins and the impact of capital productivity. Figure 6.3 shows the index for some Euro members. As expected, we find that in most southern member states, competitiveness has deteriorated before the crisis, but only in Spain and France did this lead to overvaluations, while Germany and the Netherlands have moved from over- to undervaluations.

Table 6.1 shows that, with the possible exception of Greece, labour cost overvaluations are relatively moderate in the Eurozone. They are far from the drama painted by the index in Figure 6.2. Italy, for example, has lost competitiveness since the Euro started, but in 2013 its labour cost levels are close

---

12   An index value of 1 indicates that the national ULC level generates the same return as the Euro average. For a detailed description, see Collignon 2012 and Collignon and Esposito 2013.

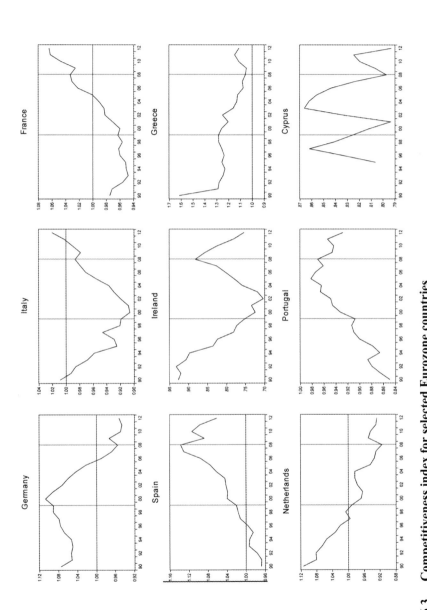

Figure 6.3 **Competitiveness index for selected Eurozone countries**
Source: AMECO and own calculations.

to the equilibrium position, at which the Italian capital stock generates the same return as Eurozone average. Slovakia, which has a huge 'competitiveness gap' according to Figure 6.2, is actually deeply undervalued. The Netherlands, on the other hand, seemed overvalued in Figure 6.2, but in reality the country has improved its competitiveness. Austria is still overvalued, even if it has improved its situation, and the same was true for Greece before 2007, although at higher levels. Surely, these proportions of overvaluation do not warrant an exit from the Eurozone and in some crisis countries unit labour costs are actually undervalued.

Table 6.1   Over- and undervaluation of unit labour costs

	1999	*Change*	2007	*Change*	2011
Slovakia	−33.0	*−8.5*	−41.5	*0.2*	−41.2
Luxembourg	−32.9	*−6.3*	−39.3	*3.8*	−35.5
Malta	−28.6	*1.1*	−27.4	*−1.0*	−28.5
Estonia	−19.6	*−2.9*	−22.5	*0.1*	−22.4
Ireland	−24.8	*7.4*	−17.4	*−4.4*	−21.8
Cyprus	−17.4	*−0.2*	−17.6	*0.1*	−17.5
Finland	−13.3	*−2.5*	−15.7	*3.2*	−12.5
Netherlands	−0.8	*−6.1*	−7.0	*0.0*	−7.0
Germany	9.1	*−12.3*	−3.2	*−2.2*	−5.4
Slovenia	−12.3	*−0.4*	−12.8	*7.6*	−5.2
Portugal	−9.2	*5.3*	−3.9	*−0.7*	−4.6
Belgium	0.4	*−4.2*	−3.9	*−0.2*	−4.1
Eurozone	*0.0*	*0.0*	*0.0*	*0.0*	*0.0*
Italy	−8.1	*6.0*	−2.1	*2.4*	0.3
Austria	12.7	*−6.5*	6.2	*−1.9*	4.3
France	−3.7	*6.8*	3.1	*3.2*	6.3
Spain	2.1	*11.0*	13.1	*−3.4*	9.7
Greece	28.5	*−20.3*	8.2	*6.6*	14.8

Source: AMECO and own calculations

The debate on unit labour costs has nevertheless some merit. For it highlights that incoherent wage policies can cause competitive disadvantages which would slow down regional growth and, as we have seen, this can turn into a systemic risk in a monetary union. No doubt, with sufficient labour and capital mobility, the market's 'invisible hand' would eliminate such distortions. There is, in fact, evidence that labour mobility has increased since the crisis (Bräuninger 2011; European Central Bank 2012a). But losing skilled workers is hardly a welfare enhancing tool for the periphery. In the long run, nominal wage flexibility may therefore be preferable to migration as an adjustment instrument and in this context it is worth reflecting on the methods and systems of wage bargaining. One reason why unit labour costs in the south may have increased faster than in the north, is the fact that in the south, the protected public sector takes leadership in wage bargaining, while in the north, especially in Germany, wage bargaining is led by industrial sectors, which are exposed to international competition (Visser 2013). If the other sectors follow the leader, unit labour costs in the different regions diverge.

A second reason for labour cost divergence is the suspension of the Phillips curve, according to which wage increases slow down when unemployment is high and increase when it is low. There is evidence that in the first decade of the Euro, this relationship did not work in the south (Collignon 2013a; CER 2013). One explanation is that following the convergence in interest rates, the European credit boom has generated 'irrational exuberance', not only for investors, but also for wage bargainers. Since the crisis, however, the Phillips curve has returned. High unemployment is lowering wage claims again. Nevertheless, a better explicit coordination of wage bargaining in the Eurozone could render the wage adjustment less costly in terms of employment and would therefore contribute to more balanced growth. Hence, as a first step, a reform of the European wage bargaining system should establish the principle that the tradable sector, which is exposed to international competition, shall be the leader for wage bargaining in all member states. Additional steps could be undertaken by establishing closer concertation and coordination between trade unions in the Eurozone.

Financial Crisis and Banks

All the theories we have discussed so far are based on non-financial explanations of the Euro-crisis. However, not taking proper account of monetary and financial developments can lead to policy errors. Money integrates the economy, but it also creates conflicts. Because money acts as the general budget constraint on the market system, it often requires making hard choices. Money is also an engine of growth, for money is credit and without growth interest claims cannot be paid (Riese 2004; Collignon 2013b). Banks, which create money as the intermediaries between savers, investors and central banks, therefore play a central role in the adjustment process of the Euro-crisis. If banks no longer lend, or if firms no longer wish to borrow, a recession is inevitable.

There are two reasons why growth in peripheral regions of a currency union may underperform. Both are related to uncertainty. The standard argument is that banks may not lend to regional firms because they fear their bankruptcy; similarly, firms may not expect to make sufficient profit to be able to reimburse their loans. Essentially this is an argument of insufficient profitability and cash flow *in a given risk environment*. As was pointed out above,[13] increasing profit margins is not necessarily the answer to this problem when economic and political uncertainties generated high risk premia. Neither cutting labour costs, nor lowering interest

---

13   See footnote 5.

rates by the central bank will then pull the local economy out of its local slump or even depression.

There is also a second explanation for reduced borrowing and investment even if the cash flow of firms is high. Koo (2002) has called such a situation a *balance sheet recession*, which often follows a financial crash. A financial crisis usually originates in a shock to the prices of specific asset classes, such as real estate. If these assets are financed by nominally fixed liabilities, the net worth of the asset owner will deteriorate. This generates pressure to deleverage the balance sheet, that is, to reduce liabilities. The higher the leverage, the more vulnerable is a firm to shocks. To reduce their risk exposure, firms will use their cash flow to pay back debt rather than borrow and invest in new assets. If uncertainty is high, increasing profits and cash flows will simply accelerate the deleveraging process. Yet, without borrowing, there will be no investment, growth will collapse and insolvency risks will increase further. With the growing probability of corporate and bank defaults, uncertainty and risk premia increase again. Money will start flowing from risky regions into safe havens, which means the liquidity crisis in the periphery accelerates. Thus, the interaction between the financial and the real economy will set off a negative feedback mechanism, which cannot be stopped until some form of borrowing resumes.

How can one break this vicious cycle? Budget policies could have stimulating effects, but only if the public debt is considered safe and unlikely to default. In most of the European crisis countries this is not a viable option. Policies must, therefore, concentrate on creating an environment that reduces risks and lowers liquidity preference for households, corporations and banks. The ECB has already done the maximum to accommodate liquidity preference in the Euro economy: it has cut interest rates repeatedly; it has implemented unconventional monetary policies by giving banks access to cheap and large amounts of liquidity for long periods; it has set up the OMT for the stabilisation of the sovereign bond market. However, it is unfortunate that the ECB had to step in to stabilise the market for government debt, while this should have been the task of governments. The proper way to stabilise the bond market for European sovereign debt would be the issue of Eurobonds. But national governments are by definition not in a position to assume responsibility for the Eurozone as a whole, because they represent partial interests. Responsibility for the Eurozone can only be exerted by a European institution.

The ECB's actions have dealt with liquidity requirements, but they cannot fix the risks of insolvencies. In the real economy, insolvency risks will only come down when growth returns, so that firms and households are assured of the income necessary to service their liabilities. In order to restore the growth dynamic, the banking sector is a key variable. One of the dominant features of the crisis has been the disappearance of trust between banks. The interbank money market dried out early on and banks borrowed or deposited excess liquidity at the ECB. While this preserves the integrity of the banking system in the short run, overcoming the credit crunch requires restoring trust and creditworthiness in the European banking sector. This is dependent on recapitalising weak banks, closer and tighter banking supervision and the creation of a banking union. Many European banks need to be recapitalised. The question is how this should be done. Shareholders may prefer deleveraging rather than see their equity diluted, but that drags out the credit crunch. A better approach would be to nationalise and/or Europeanise banks, for example by using funds from the ESM. But this is resisted by many governments because they do not wish to pay for a collective benefit. The same collective action problem has emerged with respect to banking supervision. After years of haggling, the European Council has finally decided to transfer responsibility for supervising large banks to the ECB, but many questions of practical implementation of the banking union remain. The persistent uncertainty dampens the propensity to invest in peripheral economies. Hence, it is the politics of the European Union that drives the crisis, not economics. To find ways out of the crisis, the governance of the Eurozone has to be changed in profound ways.

3. An Economic Government for the Eurozone?

The economic governance of the Eurozone is handicapped by the inconsistency between centralised monetary policy and most other economic policies (especially fiscal policy) which have remained under the decentralised control of national governments. The Delors Report, which set up the blueprint to European Economic and Monetary Union in 1989, had already discussed the need for 'a coherent set of economic policies at the community and national levels' (Delors Report 1989: paragraph 25). With respect to fiscal policy, it noticed that:

> it would seem necessary to develop both binding rules and procedures for budgetary policy, involving respectively:
> • Effective upper limits on budget deficits of individual member countries ... ;
> • The definition of the overall stance of fiscal policy over the medium term, including the size and financing of the aggregate budgetary balance, comprising both national and the Community positions. (Delors Report 1989: paragraph 33).

While the first part of this quote has become the core of the SGP, the Maastricht Treaty did not transfer powers to the European Commission and entitle it to define or implement the aggregate policies described in the second part. As a consequence, Europe has been powerless in fighting the crisis.

It is not difficult to see what has been the obstacle to a more efficient policy framework, which could have accelerated the way out of the crisis: intergovernmental policy making has prevented the pursuit of optimal policies because the partial interests of member states dominate the common interest. Collective action problems have caused cooperation failure. Even when agreement for common action was reached, the way to get there was noisy and uncertain and the result resembled a *Nash equilibrium*, where each actor optimises his own payoff given what others do.[14] However, as is well known, *Nash equilibria* are not necessarily *Pareto optimal*, which means that at least some partners could be made better off by a different set of policies.

The typical example is the setting up of a bailout fund. When uncertainty hit financial markets and investors started to massively sell sovereign debt of the crisis states, a bailout fund could have stabilised financial markets. Early intervention would have calmed markets and stopped the crisis at minimum cost, but Europe's messy intergovernmentalism has prevented such benign solutions. The insistence of the German government on the so-called no-bail-out clause in the Treaty (TFEU paragraph 125) seemed, at first, to make it impossible to set up such a fund. However, when the danger of a systemic meltdown became imminent, German authorities gave in and the temporary EFSF was created. When this needed to be put on sounder institutional foundations, Germany again haggled to keep potential liabilities for taxpayers to a minimum. This clearly served the German government, but not the Euro, nor European citizens in Germany and elsewhere. In a similar fashion, the rapid completion of the banking union with a single supervisor, a unified resolution mechanism and credible deposit insurance has been delayed again and again. The uncertainty created by these repeated game transactions has been extremely costly (Collignon et al. 2013). These costs are not only unavoidable in an intergovernmental framework, but in a monetary union they are also likely to exceed the benefits of monetary union in the short run. From a narrow point of view it may then seem justifiable to exit the Euro, but in a long-run perspective, this would destroy the economic foundations of European wealth and welfare. Hence, the primary policy objective should be to set up a system which minimises uncertainty. This would require transforming the European Commission into a proper, democratically elected government.

It is important to understand why the traditional governance of intergovernmental voluntary cooperation no longer works in European monetary union. We have said earlier that the process of European integration has generated many interdependencies and externalities, which have become particularly prominent in the Euro-crisis. We now have to look at the nature of these externalities more closely. Externalities are related to the nature of goods people consume. The economic literature distinguishes between private goods, pure public goods, club goods, and common resource goods (Collignon 2011). Because private goods are defined by exclusive property rights, they can be efficiently provided by the invisible hand of the decentralised market mechanism. By contrast, pure public

---

14   As Bergsten and Kirkegaard (2012) have pointed out: 'The euro-area crisis ... is a political crisis. Therefore, the most appropriate theoretical framework for analysing it is game theoretical concepts describing strategic bargaining among multiple actors, as found in Schelling (1966), or broader considerations of strategic actions as described in Liddell-Hart (1967) – not macroeconomic theories like optimal currency area theory (Mundell 1961), the debt sustainability theorem (Chalk and Hemming 2000), or other equilibrium-seeking modelling exercises aiming to restore full employment as soon as possible'.

goods are characterised by free access and unlimited benefit. For club goods, access can be restricted, but benefits are unlimited for club members. Common resource goods are freely accessible, but limited in supply and benefit. It is well known that public goods are not efficiently provided by markets, because with free access individuals could free-ride on others who are willing to pay for them. But if every individual behaved this way, the public good would not be supplied at all. This is why political economists since David Hume have emphasised the need to set up a government to ensure that public goods are supplied. Democracy is the mechanism that makes sure that the supply of public goods coincides with the collective demand of the people concerned.

In principle, it is also possible to provide public goods by agreeing to cooperate, if compliance to the agreement can be guaranteed (Ostrom 1990). However, the incentive structure to cooperate voluntarily is very different in the case of club goods and common resource goods. In the first case, cooperation yields potential benefits for everyone who contributes to the supply of the public good. In other words, cooperation is a positive-sum game. Cooper and John (1988) call the incentives to cooperate *strategic complementarities*. By contrast, common resource goods are defined by *strategic substitutabilities*, which means the utility augmenting action of one actor will lower the benefits for another. This is a zero-sum game. In this case, voluntary cooperation will fail and a centralised allocation mechanism must provide the public good.

In its early stages, European integration was characterised by the creation of European club goods. The Commission, as a custodian of common interests, had the task of ensuring that the governments of the Member States cooperated with one another. Yet, with the creation of the Euro, the dynamics of European integration have changed. Money is the general budget constraint of an economy, which means the supply of money by the central bank is limited under the mandate to maintain price stability. Hence, all public goods which are subject to the monetary budget constraint are effectively following the logic of common resource goods and strategic substitutabilities. Public debt is a typical example: access to the capital market is open to all, but the loanable funds are limited by the availability of central bank liquidity. If aggregate credit demand exceeds available funds, interest rates will go up, which has negative consequences for borrowing anywhere in the monetary union. Hence, strong binding rules are necessary to prevent such negative externalities.

However, preventing negative externalities is one thing, generating positive ones is another thing. We have seen that in an economic crisis, discretionary policies may be needed to overcome the recession. Discretion is the opposite of rules. During the Euro-crisis, the Troika was established to introduce a small degree of discretionary control into the application of stabilisation policies in crisis countries. But only democratic governments can act with discretion on behalf of the citizens they represent. The Eurozone's governance, therefore, needs more than just a set of (binding) rules to ensure sustainable debt, balanced growth and low unemployment. It needs a government and European democracy.

The idea of an economic government was first proposed by the French Prime Minister Pierre Bérégovoy during the negotiations of the Maastricht Treaty (Featherstone and Dyson 1999; Verdun 2003). For a long time it was opposed by the German government, partly because it looked as if France wanted to be that government. The idea is no longer taboo, given that Chancellor Merkel has publicly declared 'The economic government is us' (that is, the European Council).[15] But an economic government for the Eurozone that consists of a council of member states and only implements *Nash equilibria* negotiated by autonomous nation states cannot be an efficient representative for the general will of European citizens. Without full democratic legitimacy by all citizens concerned, it is not possible to make fair and just choices in a zero-sum game. For that purpose, a government of the Eurozone must be democratically elected so that it can overrule the partial interests of partial constituencies in European nation states.

I have called the limited government for European public goods the European Republic (Collignon 2002b; 2011). The Euro-crisis has revealed that the old ways of governing Europe no longer work. The republican paradigm points in a new direction. It focuses on public goods, Europe's *res publica,* which affects and concerns all European citizens. This approach does not recommend the creation of a fully integrated federal state. It simply seeks an instrument for preserving and improving the welfare of Europeans. Whether Europe is capable of seizing the moment, I do not know. Emanuel Rahm, President Obama's first chief of staff in the White House, once made a candid point: 'Never waste a good crisis'. Europe's crisis is also an opportunity.

---

15   http://www.faz.net/artikel/S30638/die-ergebnisse-des-gipfels-status-quo-und-stossgebete-30486686.html.

Chapter **7**

EU Financial Market Regulation and Stakeholder Consultations

Rainer Eising, Daniel Rasch and Patrycja Rozbicka

1. Introduction

The regulation of the EU financial markets has come to the forefront of internal market policies in response to both the global financial crisis and the Euro-crisis. There is wide disagreement on whether the measures taken are merely 'gesture politics' (Buckley and Howarth 2010) or whether they introduce alternative regulatory paradigms (see Quaglia 2011: 678). Whatever the disagreement, the financial crisis has definitely brought financial regulation under public scrutiny (Woll 2012: 1). In this chapter we analyse the reform of EU financial governance by studying three cases of financial market regulation in the making: Alternative Investment Fund Managers (AIFM) (European Commission 2009c); Investor Compensation Scheme (ICS) (European Commission 2010a); and Deposit Guarantee Scheme (DGS) (European Commission 2010b).[1]

We endeavour to answer the following questions: Who or what put these legislative proposals on the political agenda of the European Union (EU)? What were the main issues that were debated during the policy debates? Why is it that the AIFM directive has been passed by EU policy-makers after a rather short span of time while the directives on DGS and Investor Compensation Scheme (ICS) have encountered greater difficulties in the legislative process? More generally, we want to shed light on the relevance of framing processes, public salience, political mobilisation, and issue characteristics in the making of EU financial market regulation. We study these factors using process tracing, population and media study, and framing analysis. We focus on EU level processes and the policy developments in four member states: Germany, the United Kingdom, Sweden, and the Netherlands. The comparative case study suggests that issue characteristics mattered more to the differential state of affairs on the three directive proposals than framing, salience or mobilisation.

---

1   They are part of a larger research project on interest representation in the EU (http://www.intereuro.eu). They are among the 20 directive proposals that received the greatest media coverage in a random sample of EU directives that were proposed between 2008 and 2010.

The chapter begins by establishing how the three directive proposals arrived on the EU policy agenda and what issues were debated on each proposal. Then we discuss whether public salience or the extent of political mobilisation mattered to the legislative state of affairs. Thereafter, we compare the frames that have been present at EU level and in the national arenas. We conclude by discussing the lessons derived from the case studies to examine the relation between frames and EU policy processes.

2. Regulation of the EU Financial Market: Alternative Investment Fund Managers, Investor Compensation Scheme, and Deposit Guarantee Schemes

The EU's regulatory regime of the financial market that had been put in place before the financial market crisis in 2007, was based on the Financial Services Action Plan (FSAP) that was proposed in 1999 and the *Lamfalussy* framework, which has altered the procedures for EU financial legislation and regulation since 2001. The FSAP detailed a number of measures for the integration of financial markets in the European Union that were largely implemented by 2005. The *Lamfalussy* framework consisted of a set of procedures and institutions designed to speed up the enactment of financial services legislation (initially only in the securities sector).[2] There is wide agreement that these measures aimed at strengthening financial market efficiency and integration rather than financial market supervision (Posner and Véron 2010) and led to a 'decentralized model of supervision' (Schammo 2012: 775).

When the financial crisis started in 2007 (Begg 2009), after initial firefighting, a first set of reforms changed the institutional framework of financial market supervision and regulation. An expert committee, the *Larosière* committee, was set up in 2008 to review EU financial market regulation (de Larosiére 2009). Based on its recommendations, the European Commission (EC) (2009) proposed to set up a new regime of supervisory and regulatory institutions. A European Systemic Risk Board (ESRB) would be put in charge of macro-prudential supervision, that is the monitoring and assessment of systemic risks in European financial markets complementing the firm-level micro-prudential supervision. The European System of Financial Supervisors (ESFS), which includes the European Banking

---

2 For this purpose, the *Committee of Wise Men* that was headed by Baron Alexandre Lamfalussy, the former President of the European Monetary Institute, proposed to introduce and co-ordinate institutions and procedures at four levels: Level 1 referred to the adoption of framework legislation in the securities sector by means of the codecision procedure. Level 2 related to the details of the implementation of these financial services laws through delegated legislation. Level 3 was about the greater cooperation among national supervisors of the securities sector in EU level committees to ensure the consistency of the implementation of level 1 and level 2 legislation. Finally, level 4 was about a better enforcement of financial services legislation in the securities sector.

Authority (EBA), the European Insurance and Occupational Pensions Authority (EIOPA), and the European Securities Authority (ESA), would be put in charge of micro-prudential supervision. In essence, the ESFS has transformed the previous *Lamfalussy* level three-committees into bodies with greater supervisory, rule-setting and coordinating powers while day-to-day supervision remains in the hands of member state authorities. An important argument against greater centralisation of regulatory capacities at EU level during the debate on these reforms was that the costs of regulatory failures would not be borne by the EU institutions but by national taxpayers (Schammo 2012: 780). ESRB and ESFS were adopted in late 2010 (Regulation No. 1095/2010).

The three directive proposals that we study here are part of the effort to strengthen financial market stability following the global financial crisis. They extend EU regulation to the hedge fund and private equity sectors and revise existing EU directives on investor protection and deposit guarantee schemes (see below). The EU institutions discussed these regulatory areas well before the financial market crisis of 2007, but then did not plan to take significant actions. An expert group set up by the EC on finding ways to improve the efficiency of the EU investment fund markets advised against the regulation of hedge funds in 2006 (Alternative Investment Expert Group 2006). Similarly, after a review of the 1994 Directive on DSG, the EC decided in 2005 that no changes were necessary at the time. It is fair to say that only the global financial crisis prompted greater action by the EU authorities in these areas to prevent further market failures and to increase the stability of the entire financial system.

The Alternative Investment Fund Managers (AIFM) directive proposal aimed at harmonising the requirements for entities engaged in the management and administration of alternative investment funds (for example private equity, hedge funds or real estate funds), but excluded entities covered by the EU directive on Undertakings for Collective Investment in Transferable Securities (UCITS) (European Commission 2008e). They included hedge funds, but also private equity funds. The AIFM directive was proposed in June 2009 and passed by the EU's legislative one year later. The other two directives were proposed in 2010 and are still in the legislative debate. The EC tabled both proposals together as a 'package to boost consumer protection and confidence in financial markets' in July 2010 (European Commission 2010c; European Commission 2010d: 1). The proposal for a DGS directive was introduced to revise earlier legislation on this subject. It is meant to protect savers and to prevent bank runs in case of a bank's bankruptcy as well as to harmonise more than 40 national deposit protection schemes that exist in the EU. The proposal for the ICS directive aimed at revising the existing ICS directive (97/EC/9 from 1997) and harmonising the 39 existing investor compensation schemes in the EU member states. Its focus is to compensate retail investors (small investors) in those circumstances where investment firms are not able to return money or financial instruments as a result of a significant fund failure. Both proposals were blocked in the legislative process after the European Parliament's (EP) first readings in 2011. So far, the EU Council and the EP only reached an informal agreement on the DGS proposal in December 2013. In the following section we analyse why these topics reached the EU policy agenda and what policy issues were debated.

Directive on Alternative Investment Fund Managers

Several observers find it puzzling that the AIFM sector has become the subject of EU regulation. There were no significant international regulatory requirements for the hedge fund sector that the EU had to adopt, and the sector has not been identified as a root cause of the financial crisis. Moreover, while there was no EU regulation of the sector in place, it was already subject to national regulation in several member states. However, in the international arena, consensus gradually emerged that hedge funds might impact significantly on financial markets and therefore be brought under official oversight (Ferran 2011: 389). The *Larosiére* committee that reviewed the EU financial regulation system found it guilty of important transmission effects 'through massive selling of shares and short-selling transactions' (de Larosiére 2009: paragraph 86). The committee came close to recommending United Kingdom (UK) style national regulation as best practice (de Larosiére 2009: paragraphs 86–7). In addition, it recommended establishing an oversight institution that would gather relevant information from the industry and evaluate it.

   Given the lack of international requirements and clear-cut causal effects of the sector on the financial crisis, what brought AIFM-regulation onto the political agenda of the EU? Most authors point to a mix of domestic economic structures, regulatory approaches, and issue characteristics, even though there is disagreement on the relative importance of these factors. First, hedge funds would seem to be important financial players in the corporate governance structures of Liberal Market Economies (LME) while they might disentangle the close relations between banks and enterprises or across enterprises that supposedly prevail in Coordinated Market Economies (CME)[3] (see Hall and Soskice 2001; Vitols 2001). LMEs like the United States (US) or the UK where more than 80 per cent of the European hedge fund industry is located would generally support the industry's position in favour of no, light, or self-regulation, because they aim more at financial market innovation, emphasise competition in financial markets, and rely greatly on the industry's self-regulation (see Quaglia 2011: 669). In contrast, CMEs like Germany or the Netherlands or countries with 'state capitalism', even

---

   3   The varieties of capitalism approach posits that relationships among firms vary systematically across countries. In liberal market economies (LME), economic activities are mostly coordinated by hierarchies (firms) and competitive market arrangements, based on arm's length relationships 'in a context of competition or formal contracting'. In contrast,, coordinated market economies (CME) are characterised by non-market relations, entailing incomplete contracting, reliance on collaborative relationships to build up a firm's competencies, and information exchanges in networks (Hall and Soskice 2001: 8).

if transformed, like France (Schmidt 2002: 5), would suggest tighter control of the hedge fund sector and perhaps support established financial institutions in order to prevent major disruptions of the established finance-enterprises nexus. France and Germany, who aim at financial stability and consumer protection by means of rule-based regulation with a strong role for public actors, argued for a stricter regulation of the hedge fund industry well before the financial crisis.

Second, the importance of the hedge fund sector as a major symbol for global 'shadow banking' and the systemic risks it entails must be stressed. The French President Sarkozy and the German Chancellor Merkel were crucial in placing this issue on the EU's political agenda (Quaglia 2011: 670–71). Tighter control of hedge funds fit nicely with a 'pro-regulation rhetoric' of the French President to win public support for the upcoming elections (Woll 2012: 15). In all respects – the pursuit of domestic economic interests and established regulatory ideas, as well as the politics against a symbol of global financial capitalism – the financial crisis was a window of opportunity for the French and German governmental actors. They flagged the idea of stricter hedge fund regulation in both international fora like the G20 and in the EU. Given the Franco-German tandem's pressure and two critical reports in the EP on hedge funds and institutional investors (European Parliament 2008a, 2008b), the EC reversed its initially reluctant position to regulate the sector and put forward a Directive proposal.

The Spanish and the Swedish Presidencies of the EU Council brought several revisions to the directive proposal that allowed for a compromise between the member states. The compromise was mostly negotiated between France and Germany, which were critical of hedge funds and blamed them for the proliferation of the financial market meltdown on the one hand, and on the other, a coalition of countries led by the UK, which argued that stricter regulation would drive financial companies out of Europe (McDermott 2009). The compromise solution established minimum standards for all member states and subjected all alternative investment fund managers who manage funds above a minimum size to authorisation by their home member state supervisor and supervision according to commonly defined principles. This allowed both France and Germany to propose harsher requirements in their national regulations shortly before and after the directive publication (for example the German Investment Code introduced in July 2012).

It is contested whether the revisions to the Directive proposal significantly watered the original proposal down (Bucklay and Howarth 2011) or if the directive may be regarded as a sea change in the regulation of the hedge fund industry (Quaglia 2011). According to the EC, the two most controversial policy issues – the scope of the directive and the opening of the European market to funds from third countries after obtaining a European passport – have been settled very closely to its original proposal (Interview European Commission, 9 February 2012).

Directive on Deposit Guarantee Schemes

Although after reviewing the 1994 Directive on Deposit Guarantee Schemes in 2005 the EC arrived at the conclusion that no further actions were necessary, the financial crisis triggered a new review in 2008. In 2009 the EU Council and the EP passed Directive 2009/14/EC. This directive raised the previous coverage level from €20,000 to €50,000 and eventually to €100,000 from 2011 onwards. It reduced the allowed payout delay to a maximum of 35 working days and ended the co-insurance system, according to which savers would have to bear a 10 per cent loss of their deposit guarantees. The EC was requested to present a report on the effectiveness of these provisions and present, if necessary, proposals for amending the directive.

Why did this topic reach the EU's political agenda and why was it decided so quickly? This revision of the 1994 Directive was part of the immediate firefighting against the financial crisis and was meant to restore confidence in the banking sector. The bankruptcy of a number of banks during the financial crisis (for example, Icesave in Iceland, or Northern Rock in the UK) and the varied national responses to the question of how to secure the liquidity of national financial systems, put national deposit schemes into focus. The fact that banks' level of liquidity rushed down during the crisis raised concern that the established levels of deposit insurance schemes might not be sufficient and that savers needed additional reassurance. The member states were concerned about capital flights and had an interest in limiting state liabilities and a regulatory competition with regard to national guarantee schemes. When Ireland decided to guarantee savings deposits as well as a range of liabilities held by the country's six biggest banks (*European Voice* 2008a and 2008b), the UK felt pressurised to increase its minimum deposit guarantee from £35,000 to £50,000 and several other member states followed. Given these troubles, the member states quickly agreed on a directive that raised the level of guarantees for bank account savings of individuals significantly up to €100,000 and provided for a minimum harmonisation of the national schemes. The EC was asked to review the directive's provisions and develop proposals for further legal amendments by 2009, if necessary.

After public consultations, expert hearings, and recommendations by the *Larosière* committee for further harmonisation, the EC presented a recast proposal (European Commission 2010b), which aimed at a significantly greater harmonisation of the national deposit protection schemes. The EC argued that the minimum harmonisation provided for by earlier legislation was ineffective in protecting depositors' wealth and also inconsistent with the proper functioning of the internal market (European Commission 2010b: 3–4). In particular, the EC proposed to further shorten the payout period (the time frame to pay the creditors) to seven days and to amend the funding mechanisms of existing protection schemes. While the previous directives had not directly addressed the funding of DGS, the recast proposal suggested regulating the financing of these schemes in order to protect a larger percentage of the eligible deposits. The EC aimed at an *ex ante* fund size of 1.5 per cent of eligible deposits, amounting to approximately €150 billion and suggested a transition period of ten years to reach this level (Gerhardt and Lannoo 2011). Another 0.5 per cent could be extracted through *ex post* bank contributions. According to the EC, the proposal would increase the banks' contributions to DGS by four or five times and lower their profits by about 2.5 per cent in normal times (European Commission 2010b: 6).

This proposal met with substantial criticism from the member states. The German and the Swedish parliaments (October 2010) issued reasoned opinions under the subsidiarity control mechanism. In the UK, disagreement on the effects of the directive on the small banks caused a re-examination of the proposal by the UK Financial Services Authority and the initial rejection of parts of the proposal. The Dutch debate on deposit guarantee schemes started prior to the EC's proposal and was prompted by the collapse of Icesave, an online branch of the Icelandic bank, Landsbanki. Emphasis was on the guarantee schemes for non-Dutch banks operating in the country and the bail out of Icesave's customers in the Netherlands.

The most controversial issue of the proposal has been the level of deposits that are to be covered and the setting up of an *ex ante* fund. The political significance of the level of deposits became evident during the banking crisis in Cyprus when bank accounts up to €100,000 were exempted from contributing to the financial consolidation of the banks on grounds of the EU deposit guarantee scheme directive provisions that had just been passed. On the introduction of an *ex ante* fund, Belgium, Spain, Finland, Portugal, and Romania as well as the EP supported the EC's proposal that 1.5 per cent of *all* bank deposits of individuals and enterprises should be covered (Agence Europe 2011). Sweden claimed that even 1.5 per cent was insufficient. In contrast, France, Germany, and the UK all rejected this threshold as being far too high and established that a fund should cover only 0.5 per cent of bank deposits. In Germany, the proposal was debated as introducing a 'transfer union' through the back door by which German savers and banks would guarantee the safety of bank accounts in Southern Europe. Germany also insisted on the continuance of mutual deposit guarantee schemes, as they were already in place for German Savings Banks and Co-operative Banks, and of the voluntary deposit guarantee scheme as it was in place for German private banks in the BdB (Bundesverband deutscher Banken). Here, Savings Banks and Co-operative Banks, respectively, can loan money from each other to prevent a bank failure. Furthermore, German private banks have a voluntary deposit guarantee scheme for creditors that has a larger scope than the German statutory DGS. The mutual deposit guarantee schemes met the approval of the EP in its first reading, and the voluntary scheme met the criticism of the European Commission due to a lack of legal enforceability. In its first reading, the EP stuck to a fund size of 1.5 per cent but only for deposits up to €100,000, as these were guaranteed by the DGS directive that was in place. It lengthened the transition period for the build-up of the fund to 15 years rather than 10 years as had been proposed by the EC and set the payment period at 20 working days rather than 7 days. In 2012, the EC raised the symbolic significance of an agreement on the DGS directive by presenting this proposal as an elementary component of a European Banking Union, consisting of a single supervisory authority for banks, a single deposit guarantee scheme, and banking restructuring mechanisms. The Banking Union, in turn, was portrayed as a crucial condition for allowing direct payments to banks under the European Stability Mechanism (Agence Europe 2012). Hence, over time, the status of DGS moved from quick fixes to maintain investor confidence to becoming an elementary stabilisation mechanism. In the context of agreements on other aspects of the Banking Union such as the establishment of a Single Supervisory Mechanism and the Single Resolution Mechanism, the EU Council and the EP managed also to reach informal agreement on the revision of the DGS directive in December 2013 (EC 2013). The coverage level of €100,000 per depositor and bank remains unchanged. The target level for bank-paid *ex ante* funds has been set at 0.8 per cent of the covered deposits which is 0.7 percentage points below the Commission's proposal and 0.3 percentage points above the resenting member states' demand. The Commission can grant exemptions from that level which, however, cannot be lower than 0.5 per cent of covered deposits. The repayment deadline has been shortened to seven working days from 2024. Finally, the directive introduces a voluntary but not a mandatory mechanism of mutual borrowing between different national DGS.

Directive on Investor Compensation Schemes

Following the financial crisis, there have been increased calls for steps to be taken to restore investor confidence in the system and to revise the 1997 ICS directive (Directive 97/9/EC). Concerns were raised over the safety of investments, the funding of schemes and the delays in receiving compensation (European Commission 2010a). However, even though there is little evidence that investors demanded greater compensation due to the financial crisis, an amendment of the 1997 directive was generally felt necessary. A further rationale for the ICS proposal was the potential for competitive distortions arising from member states imposing their own compensation requirements on third country firms.

The proposal for the investor compensation scheme directive was presented as part of the EC's package to boost consumer protection and confidence in financial services. The proposal stipulated to compensate investors in case an investment firm that held and managed the money and the financial instruments of its clients should be unable to repay or return the invested money or the financial instrument due to fraud or other administrative errors in the investment firm. The proposal also covered investments in funds regulated by the UCITS and Markets in Financial Instruments (MiFI) directives (European Commission 2010a). According to the Commission, the protection of consumers required an increase of the existing coverage level and stronger common rules concerning the funding of the schemes at national level. Moreover, it suggested that investors with cross-border investments should enjoy the same level of protection in all member states. The main issues were how to fund the ICS and what investments were to be covered by the ICS

(Interview European Commission, 10 May 2012). A risk-based approach should be applied to fund the schemes, in that the calculation of contributions should be based on the potential compensation risk incurred by a firm. The Commission suggested *ex ante* funding. The member states should ensure that each investor compensation scheme establishes a target fund level of at least 0.5 per cent of the value of the money and financial instruments that were held, administered or managed by the investment firms or collective investments covered by the scheme. If the amount of compensation funds should prove to be insufficient for the claims, the funds should call additional money from the financial institutions or borrow it from other schemes. In that respect, the Commission proposed a compulsory lending level of 10 per cent among the member states' ICS. Additionally, the Commission discussed an upper limit to be imposed on the compensation coverage and proposed to compensate investments up to €20,000 which is significantly less than the €100,000 for bank deposits in the case of the DGS.

In response, both UK parliamentary chambers discussed issuing a subsidiarity complaint. The British parliamentarians argued that an investment compensation scheme might undertake inappropriate, careless or risky actions, because it was relying on the fail-safe mechanism of cross-border lending.[4] To avoid introducing moral hazards it would be better not to have recourse to other member states' schemes, but to have each member state ensure that the members of the national compensation schemes take full responsibility themselves. Similarly, Dutch and Swedish stakeholders rejected the proposed method of financing by a mutual loan system among national investor compensation schemes. In particular, the Dutch government was afraid of becoming the victim of invalid claims from other EU countries.

Furthermore, British, German, and Dutch governments claimed that national investor compensation provisions were already in place and that the proposed EU level regulation would neither improve the situation nor guarantee the future stability of the financial market. Swedish authorities appreciated the potential of the EC's proposal to improve the functioning of the single market for investment services, but they also argued that the relationship and proportion between the investor compensation scheme and the deposit guarantee scheme proposals had to be adjusted in a new document. In sum, all four governments rejected the ICS proposal.

The EP (April 2011) was also critical of the EC's proposal. It highlighted two issues: first, if the mutual loan system proposed by the Commission would not trigger moral hazards, and, second, if the level of the proposed *ex ante* target fund level of 0.5 per cent was adequate. The EP placed the first issue on its agenda due to the intervention of the UK Financial Services Authority that was supported by the UK MEPs. The proposed borrowing mechanism was recognised as a

---

4   Fail-safe mechanism specifies that a state or a creditor covers all the losses in the event of failure. All negative effects of a high risk investment for example would be assured by the state or another creditor.

useful tool. However, the EP underlined that member states should maintain the responsibility for having appropriate financing mechanisms in place and suggested that only 5 per cent of a scheme's funds should be available for a compulsory lending mechanism. On the second issue, the EP suggested that the *ex ante* funds should be put in place up to a target fund level of only 0.3 per cent in all member states, but within a period of five years instead of ten years. According to the EP, this formed a justifiable level of funding. Furthermore, the EP rejected broadening the scope of the directive to cover UCITS, arguing that the existing UCITS and MiFI Directives covered the topic sufficiently. The EP also favoured a full harmonisation of investor compensation at a level of €100,000 rather than the minimum standardisation at the level of €20,000 that had been proposed by the Commission.

The Commission opposed the amendments suggested by the EP (European Commission 2011a). Until 2013, the EP and the Council have not been able to find a compromise on the ICS proposal. The EP maintained its position on a maximum level of compensation (€100,000) and on excluding the UCITS unit holders from the ICS scope. The Council has not reached a common position. The member states disagree on the compensation level (ranging between €20,000 and €50,000), and the majority of them reject extending the scope of the Directive to UCITS unit holders.

In the next section, we discuss three potential causes of the different state of affairs in the three proposals: public salience, the extent of political mobilisation, and policy frames.

3. Media Coverage, Stakeholder Involvement, and Policy Framing in the Three Policy Debates

Media Coverage

How important was the public salience of the proposals for the outcomes? The coverage of the three proposals in the media may be considered as an indicator for the salience of the debates in the national arenas (Figure 7.1). The media analysis indicates that the public salience of the three proposals varies. The AIFM proposal attracted the greatest attention of all three proposals, while there is almost no coverage of the ICS proposal. However, it is important to bear in mind cross-country variations. The cross-national comparison indicates that the British press is responsible for the largest part of the AIFM coverage, while the Swedish, German, and Dutch newspapers pay fairly equal attention to the ICS and DGS proposals. Given the economic importance of the hedge fund industry in the UK, it is not surprising that it attracted the greatest media attention there.

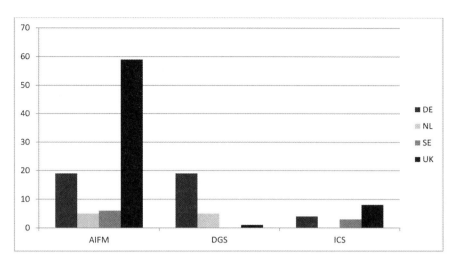

Figure 7.1   The number of articles on the AIFM, DGS, ICS proposals in national newspapers[5]

Stakeholders' Involvement

What role does the extent of political mobilisation play in the state of affairs? The EU has developed explicit consultation regimes to strengthen stakeholder involvement in the formulation of EU policies, and member states have also organised specific consultations. A total of 704 actors participated in these consultations or were mentioned in the media as actors involved in these proposals (excluding the EU institutional actors). The number of involved actors differs significantly across the three legislative proposals (Figure 7.2). Sixty-three per cent of the actors were visible in the consultations on the AIFM directive (449 actors), which attracted considerably more attention than the other two proposals, particularly so in the UK. The most visible categories of actors are interest groups, companies, governmental actors, and public agencies. The types of actors involved in the different proposals vary to some extent. Interest groups were the most active type of actor on DGS and ICS, while companies were the most active type on the AIFM directive.

In sum, the salience of the three proposals varies significantly across the four member states, and so does the involvement of national stakeholders. The policy proposal that received the greatest media and stakeholder attention, the AIFM directive, could be passed by the EU institutions in a rather short span of time,

---

5   The articles were retrieved from: *Süddeutsche Zeitung, Frankfurter Allgemeine Zeitung, Volkskrant, NRC Handelsblad, Dagens Nyheter, Svenska Dagbladet,* the *Guardian, Daily Telegraph.*

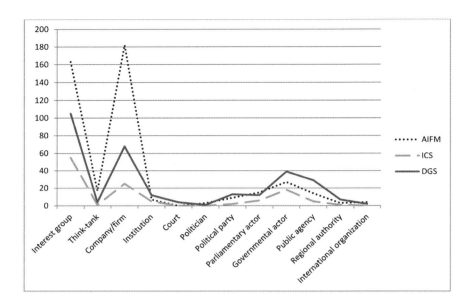

Figure 7.2   The types of actors involved in the formulation of the AIFM, DGS and ICS directives[6]

while the two proposals that were far less visible proved to be more controversial in the EU legislative process. The financial and re-distributive implications of the ICS and the DGS proposals seem to have stirred greater controversy among the member states than the regulatory aspects of the AIFM proposal.

Policy Framing

In this section we explore if the framing processes account for the different state of affairs in the three policy processes. For our purposes, we define a frame as an argument that emphasises a specific aspect of a policy proposal in a public policy debate (Entman 1993). Frame analysis highlights the ways in which political issues are presented (Price and Tewksbury 1997:184) and seeks to find out if these (re)presentations make a difference to policy outcomes. We identify frames by

---

    6 Details of the categories: Interest organisation (NGOs, umbrella organisations, unions, business associations), think-tank (research groups, expert groups, consultancies, law firms), company/firm (banks, enterprises, hedge funds), institution (hospital, university, charities), court, politician (prime ministers, presidents), political party, parliamentary actor (single parliamentarians, parliament committees, parliamentary chambers and working groups), governmental actor (individual ministries, governmental commissions, committees), public agency, regional authority, international organisation.

means of a content analysis of the arguments that different stakeholders employed in their position papers and public statements.[7]

What are the most important policy frames in these three legislative proposals? All three policy debates were rooted in an encompassing EU-level frame that presented the Commission's proposals as important means of achieving financial market stability and contributing to the security of the Single European Market. In conjunction with the financial market crisis, this frame brought the entire set of reforms of EU financial market regulation under way. The main frames in the four EU member states have been consistent with the EU level frames pointing to the homogeneity of the national and EU level policy debates. The political controversies concerning the three directive proposals were situated below the level of frames and focused on specific policy issues.

The Commission introduced the AIFM proposal as a directive that would shield consumers and institutional investors from high risks and contribute to the stability of the financial system. The national debates varied on this theme. In the UK, an additional frame focused on sustaining the global competitiveness of the UK and EU financial markets. The argument that the future directive ought to be fully compatible with the global approach to the regulation of fund managers aimed at preventing the introduction of European hedge fund regulation. After it had become clear that a European directive was under way, the British debate shifted to the tools that the directive would provide for supervisory authorities in order to shape the details of the directive. In all four countries the necessity of the directive was then agreed upon.

The national frames on the DGS proposal also resonated with the Commission's proposal. The Commission's main frame was to improve the protection of depositors, through reliable funding of the deposit guarantee schemes. Variations of this frame were present in all four member states. The most frequently used national frame in the DGS debate was focused on boosting consumers' confidence. The EU level debate on the ICS directive concentrated on strengthening the confidence of investors in the EU market through a better protection of their investments. The 'protection of consumers and investors' frame was used in all four countries.

4. Conclusions

In this chapter, we raised three questions. What brought the AIFM, DGS, and ICS directives on the agenda, what were the main issues during the policy debates,

---

7   We collected 746 documents on the three directive proposals (207 media articles and 539 position papers from different stakeholders). The majority of the statements were given in the consultation processes of the European Commission or the national authorities. For this article, we used a sample of 170, randomly selected, policy documents from the four countries and of the EU level actors.

and why was it easier for the AIFM directive to pass than for the others? First, the directive proposals are part of the EU's effort to respond with a unified voice to the global financial crisis and the crisis of the Eurozone. They were put in place as part of the second phase of the fire-fighting of the global financial market crisis. While the AIFM directive was put on the EU's legislative agenda by the French head of state, the German Chancellor, and by critical reports in the European Parliament, the European Commission took the initiative for the further harmonisation and regulation of the existing DGS and ICS schemes. Secondly, the main issues of the three proposals were: for the AIFM proposal, the scope and opening of the European market for third countries, in the DGS debate, the level of deposits that are to be covered and the setting up of an *ex ante* fund, and in case of the ICS discussion, the funding of the ICS and what investments were to be covered by the schemes. There is disagreement on whether these directive proposals are 'gesture politics' or whether they introduce a new regulatory paradigm. And yet, it is possible to categorise them as examples of reforms that are embedded in the master frame of stabilising financial markets by strengthening EU financial market supervision and regulation. The AIFM directive extended EU level regulation to the hedge fund sector in June 2011. The DGS recast proposal and the proposal on investor compensation schemes aim at a significantly greater harmonisation of the existing national schemes than their predecessors. National interests and positions play a more important role than in the first phase of fire-fighting.

Thirdly, why did the EU manage to pass the AIFM directive in a relatively short span of time but found it difficult to reach agreement on the DGS and ICS directive proposals? The master frame of financial market stabilisation and consumer protection guided all three policy debates. In conjunction with the international financial crisis and the Euro-crisis, it prompted and legitimised EU policy-makers to take action in the three areas that we analysed, but it cannot account for the fact that the AIFM directive was passed quickly while the other two proved to be highly controversial. Neither can the varying public salience of the three policy proposals in the four member states or the different degrees of political mobilisation on each directive proposal account for this difference. We witness the greatest media attention and the greatest political mobilisation in the UK, which was reluctant to agree to hedge fund regulation. However, the political salience of hedge fund regulation to the core executives in France, Germany, and the UK clearly mattered to the passing of the AIFM directive. Furthermore, our analysis suggests that issue-specific implications impacted greatly on the present state of affairs. Issue-specific national interests and positions played a more important role in the legislative debates on these proposals than in the first phase of fire-fighting. The potential financial and (re-)distributive implications of the DGS and the ICS proposals, involving the deep intrusion into long-established national protection schemes, the setting up of *ex ante* funds, and enabling cross-national monetary loans and transfers proved to be a greater obstacle than the extension of EU regulatory and supervisory powers to a hitherto little regulated financial sub-sector.

PART III
The Transformation of European Social Policy Governance

Chapter 8

EU Social Policy Content and Governance: A Complex Relationship with EU Economic Integration Over Time

Janine Goetschy

European Union (EU) governance issues have been a recurrent subject over the last 55 years in the field of EU studies. Much attention has in particular been devoted to questions of governance during the 2000s in the field of EU level social policy as a result of both the Lisbon Strategy and the various Open Methods of Coordination (OMCs). Since the 2008 crisis and the following set of EU economic reforms, of which Europe 2020 is a part, governance debates have remained central. They bear crucial implications for employment and social issues.

This contribution entails three parts. First, we shall recall the intrinsic governance features of European Social Policy and their developments over time (a policy area covering employment, social protection, industrial relation issues). Second, we shall devote some more detailed attention to the governance changes which the LS and the various OMCs have been inducing for European Social Policy. Finally, we shall reflect upon the role of European Social Policy in the crisis period and the characteristics of the governance debate since 2008.

1. EU Social Policy: Idiosyncrasies and Historical Developments

In order to reflect upon the governance dimension of EU social policy (that is, its rules, processes and their impacts on outcomes in terms of legitimacy and efficiency) and to disentangle its main features, as well as its evolution over time, several intellectual exercises can be carried out.

First, one can try to understand EU social policy and its developments *in their own logic*, on the basis of the wealth of European studies, concepts and theories. This requires capturing the specific EU polity features which have been shaping it progressively over the years and which have given it its distinctive traits, both content-wise and governance-wise. Among those structuring pillars, the following elements can thus be identified: the different phases in the building of EU economic integration (common market, internal market, monetary union, economic reforms following the 2008 crisis); the successive EU enlargements and the socio-economic level of the acceding countries; the treaties' content which define EU competences and institutional roles; the political will of the national, supranational, political and social players to actually seize potential powers from the treaties, and their individual organisational ability to do so; the stakeholders' 'institutional creativeness' in inventing novel procedural solutions outside the treaties in view of the urgency of the social problems to be solved; the impact of more general factors, such as economic globalisation, new economic policy paradigms, new information technologies, demographic change and sociological lifestyle changes.

Second, to capture the intrinsic features of EU social policy, one can also compare them with the features of other EU policy fields such as economic policies, and thus figure out how they compare. What makes them similar to other EU policies is the fact that they are inclined towards shared competences, to the subsidiarity principle, that they are subject to a twofold parliamentary and governmental legitimacy, that their *acquis communautaire* is cumulative geographically and temporally. But more interestingly, what makes them unique is the following: the stakeholders involved in the decision-making process are not only the classic EU institutional actors, but also the social partners; all together those actors carry a triple legitimacy (parliamentary, governmental and neo-corporatist). Besides, the various modes of governance which can be mobilised in EU social policy are more numerous than in any other policy field as they gather together the legislative method, the contractual method, OMC processes, policy cooperation, comitology, the ECJ mechanisms and the financial possibilities of the structural funds. As pinpointed by many authors, social policy has, more than some other domains, relied heavily on ECJ judgments (Leibfried 2005). Finally, the policy outcomes of Social Europe are directly related to social citizenship and employees at work, which constitute strategic electoral themes at national level.

Third, one can also wonder how EU social policy fares in comparison to national social protection and industrial relation systems. Here we can stress the following idiosyncrasies. Given its more recent existence (albeit 55 years) and its permanently evolving character due to enlargements to new countries and to treaty reforms, Social Europe is often described as being in permanent construction, unachieved and unstable, compared to national systems which are relatively more accomplished and more stable (though having gone through many reforms in the last 25 years depending on countries and policy issues). Social Europe policy content is further depicted as being more fragmented, piecemeal, lacking a comprehensive project, internally less coherent and less encompassing than national level social protection and industrial relation systems. However, the Lisbon Strategy and Europe 2020, by extending the social policy agenda and increasing its potential outcomes through soft regulatory devices (compared with the various OMCs on employment, social inclusion, pensions, health care, education/training), have tended to render Social Europe much less fragmented in its content.

In this chapter, we shall concentrate essentially on the study of Social Europe seen in its own logic. Looking at 55 years of Social Europe's development, we have in earlier works identified four phases (Goetschy 2009; Goetschy and Cochoy 2009). During a first period, a market ethos was at the core of Europe's first social provisions with the Rome Treaty (1957) and the Single Act (1986); social Europe was principally meant to deal with labour as a production factor and to facilitate the mobility of workers through social security devices and recognition of diplomas.

In a second period with the Maastricht Treaty (1992), a social ethos constituted part of a deliberate trade-off for legitimising rapid progress in economic integration with EMU; apart from a fairly important enlargement of EU social competences, the Maastricht social agreement introduced the contractual method to make it possible for EU social partners to negotiate EU collective agreements with legal strength; thus, it granted them the possibility to pre-empt the Commission right of initiative and also to have a say in national transposition procedures.

In a third period with the Amsterdam Treaty (1997), the Nice Treaty (2000) and the Lisbon Strategy (LS) (2000–2010), Social Europe was essentially meant 'to help the national level' in carrying through difficult social protection and labour market reforms; to do so, the Amsterdam Treaty inaugurated a new policy cooperation process for employment matters, which was to become the European Employment Strategy, a cooperation method taken up later by the LS for other social and economic subject matters.

A fourth period (still ongoing) started in 2008 where the EU was hit by the most severe financial, economic and social crisis of its history. This fourth period can be described as 'the Eurozone first, Social Europe after' with EU macro-economic and budgetary austerity imperatives implying national budgetary cuts and social protection and labour market reforms; new devices for member state improvements in competitiveness were also set up. Beside the vast array of EU level economic governance reforms among which was Europe 2020 (2010–2020), this period saw the coming into force of the Lisbon Treaty (2009).

This classification in four phases is essentially based on the changing political functions of Social Europe over time (market building function; legitimising EU economic integration function; enabling the national level function; constraining the national level function), with the idea that those political functions are not exclusive among each other, but that one function tends to be pre-dominant during a given period, or at least indicates a change of regime.

The two sections below (Sections 2 and 3) will draw particular attention to the transformations at stake in the realm of economic and social governance, during both the third and fourth phases.

Those four historical sequences reflect two elements: the constant spill-over effects between EU economic integration and EU social integration, as well as the overarching EU level asymmetry between economic and social integration, which treaty reforms and political actors have, with variable zeal, been attempting to reduce over time. This has led to a series of permanent tensions and ambiguities for Social Europe, which seems to have been increasing over recent years. Many authors have highlighted increasing tension between EU economic rights and EU social rights in the 2000s which were exaggerated with the Laval and Viking cases, and also lie in the objectives of the Lisbon Treaty (see Section 3). The role of Social Europe itself has been reckoned to be basically ambivalent – it was meant, on the one hand, to endorse a protection role for citizens and employees, especially vis-à-vis globalisation, and on the other hand, to be a tool for accelerating national labour markets and social system reforms under the pressure of markets and more so in moments of crisis. And the set of EU economic reforms (undertaken since 2008) with their social implications for national level budgets has also to be added to the list of highly ambivalent measures from a social point of view.

2. Major Governance Shifts for EU Social Policy in the 2000s with the Lisbon Strategy and its OMCs

In its White Paper on EU governance, the Commission has provided its own definition of governance, meaning the whole set of rules and processes that influence EU actor decision-making at various levels (European Commission 2001); it designated five principles of good governance, namely openness, effectiveness, coherence, accountability of rules and participation of stakeholders, which were supposed to complement two governance principles already in the EU treaties and the subsidiarity and proportionality principles (Wincott 2001). The Lisbon Treaty contains the term 'governance' in its Articles 15 and 21. Besides, in the academic realm, EU governance has of course been at the heart of an abundant literature in EU studies which was revitalised at the end of the 1990s (Sabel and Zeitlin 2011).

In the year 2000, an encompassing EU socio-economic project – the Lisbon Strategy – was introduced in the EU (Rodrigues 2009). The Lisbon Strategy (2000–2010) which led to a substantial enlargement of the EU employment and social agenda on matters of national priority, such as employment levels, labour market reforms, social inclusion and social protection reforms (pensions, health care), and its various OMCs inspired by the previously existing process for employment issues (see the Amsterdam treaty – 1997), have meant major governance shifts for EU social policy making.

A first governance discontinuity with the traditional pattern is down to the fact that, with the Lisbon Strategy, the widening of the employment and social agenda has occurred on the basis of political commitments issued by European Councils outside the Inter-Governmental Conferences (IGCs); this is a break from the classical trend of social incrementalism through successive treaty reforms. Such a course of action is indeed a way to bypass unsuccessful IGCs and to set up appropriate institutions and procedures for dealing with urgent economic and social priorities.

Second, seen as an institutional design, the Lisbon Strategy grants a central role to the European Council of heads of state, national governments and numerous expert committees. If the setting up of a yearly Spring Council on the Lisbon Strategy has, on the one hand, granted higher political profile to employment and social protection issues on the EU agenda, the development of expert committees has, on the other hand, given a more elite-driven touch to public policy making – the latter indeed offering an alternative way to channel and solve increasing member state conflicts and diversity due to, among others things, enlargement. By 'expert driven committees' one must distinguish two types: i) those representing member state interests, such as the Employment Committee in charge of the European Employment Strategy (EES) and the Social Protection Committee dealing with the OMCs on social inclusion, pensions and health care – both bodies being support committees of the Council of Employment and Social Affairs and comprising top level civil servants, and ii) the numerous expert and advisory committees comprising more specifically of experts, academics and practitioners. If, on the one hand, the growing role of the European Council was meant to increase 'politicisation' of EU agenda matters, on the other hand, the important role of expert committees, added to new public management tools, meant their relative 'de-politicisation'.

As to the role of the Commission, it has become more complex since the 2000s: it has played a permanent initiating and steering function in the various OMCs, but also a slightly less active role in legislative initiatives compared to the past. Quality of implementation and less regulation have also been general key concepts of this period. The Commission has further pushed for the development of an autonomous dialogue among the EU social partners and encouraged them to draw up their own multi-annual programmes (Smismans 2012). It has also promoted social responsibility among private actors, that is, essentially large enterprises.

Regarding the European Parliament (EP), which had in the frame of the community method gained a co-decision role in social matters in the Amsterdam Treaty (1997), its role is limited to information and consultation to the Lisbon Strategy. The EP had to confront two developments during the same period, which weakened its role, that is, the concurrent co-regulator role of social partners stemming from the Maastricht Treaty (1992) and its rather weak involvement in the Lisbon Strategy and various OMC processes from 1997 onwards.

Concerning social partners, even if they have been regularly solicited to take part in the Tripartite Summit previous to the yearly Lisbon Strategy EU spring council (a tripartite summit which has become an official institution within the Lisbon Treaty), their role has been less emblematic in the 2000s than during the previous decade of the post-Maastricht social agreement (1992), in which many hopes were raised as to the social role for invigorating Social Europe. Their involvement in the various OMCs has been unequalled (more important in the EES than in the other OMCs), depending on the quality of the social dialogue in the various member states (De la Porte and Natali 2009).

Third, the Lisbon Strategy innovated on the issue of policy coordination, whereby a newly broadened set of employment and social policy objectives have been linked closely with objectives of other policy fields (economic, environmental, education and training, research and development) both at the

EU and national levels. The benefits to be drawn from policy coordination were twofold: the setting up of a vast EU socio-economic project had to embody a new step in EU economic integration (previously the common market, internal market, monetary union), and more coherence and linkages among policy objectives were considered to be a good governance asset. Later on in 2009, the Eurozone crisis showed clearly that the EU needed more macro-economic coordination, as well as more EU surveillance in regard to competitiveness and the financial sector than had been foreseen in the Lisbon Strategy.

With the policy coordination objectives of the Lisbon Strategy and the widening of the social agenda, the traditionally fairly fragmented Social Europe grew in coherence. The risk of such policy interweaving – despite the concomitant political upgrading of employment/social issues – remains through the development of a hierarchy of policies where economic matters continue to override employment matters, the latter tending to have precedence over social issues (such as social inclusion). Moreover, the Lisbon Strategy had to acknowledge and to be in line with 'framing policies' such as the Stability and Growth Pact (SGP) and the EU Monetary Policy.

Fourth, what is interesting about the various OMCs of the Lisbon Strategy is the vast set of new public management tools put in place, which are meant to foster policy evaluation through benchmarking, reporting, monitoring, mutual reviewing, naming and shaming and so forth – tools that were supposed to make member states (MS) more responsible and accountable for their policy outcomes. All those comparison exercises took place – although they were not very visible in the public opinion arena and were 'captured' by meso-level committees. They entailed decisive policy changes (Hemerijck 2011).

3. Social Europe and the Crisis

What role has Social Europe been playing in the crisis period from 2008 onwards, to resolve problems linked to growing unemployment (especially long term and youth unemployment), poverty (number of homeless, child poverty), the working poor and increasing inequalities? Recent EU assessments witness worrying results, confirming the deepening of such trends. The Commission's annual review of Employment and Social Developments in Europe in 2011 shows how the economic crisis has aggravated Europe's structural weaknesses, like income inequality and the decrease in middle-paid jobs; poverty remains high with 23 per cent of the population at risk of poverty (European Commission 2012c); 8 per cent of the employed are classified as working poor; unemployment has grown to 10.5 per cent with youth unemployment mounting to 22.7 per cent. Despite a great disparity among MS, with the Mediterranean countries being particularly hit, the situation has also been deteriorating in all these aspects in traditionally more well-off countries (European Commission 2012c).

Social Europe Achievements from 2008 Onwards: A Clear Governance Shift Towards the National Level

A first assessment is that social and employment answers to the successive crises from 2008 onwards came essentially from the national level. In the immediate aftermath of the 2008 crisis, beside the financial amounts devoted to national recovery plans and to the rescue of banks, most EU member states and the variety of stakeholders (governments, employers, unions) have been searching for national solutions and company devices to preserve employment, to avoid massive lay-offs and to deploy social protection measures, so as to protect the most vulnerable. This trend illustrates the importance granted to the national level rather than the EU level under the pressure of this urgency. However, following the Greek crisis in 2010 when severe austerity plans were adopted, it rapidly appeared that those costly national measures of 2009 were not sustainable, given increasing budgetary deficits and competitiveness difficulties among member states (for a detailed analysis of national responses to the crisis as regards social protection and employment issues see European Commission 2013a).

As to Social Europe (at EU level), its answers to the crisis were very scarce, though not completely absent. In the legislative field, three social directives were adopted and somehow speeded up by the crisis: the directive on temporary agency work in 2008, the revised directive on European Works Council in 2009 and the revision of the parental leave directive in 2010 (resulting from a social partner framework agreement). After many years of discussions, MS did not manage to find agreement on the revision of the working time directive, and the issue was then taken over by social partner negotiations which lasted for a year until the end of 2012, but did not end successfully.

The EU level cross-sectoral social dialogue had mixed results, as it failed to agree a joint declaration on behalf of social partners on the solutions to the crisis and was not successful in reaching an agreement either on company restructuring or on the revision of the working time directive. More positively though, an agreement on the revision of the parental leave directive (2009), a joint declaration on Europe 2020 (in 2010), and an autonomous agreement on inclusive labour markets (2010) was reached. In contrast, the EU level sectoral social dialogue saw many joint texts adopted after the 2008 crisis across a number of sectors (chemicals, building trade, transports, commerce, catering, local authorities, audiovisual) albeit with little national impact. Their issues concerned re-launching measures, and labour market issues, such as qualifications, training and restructuring. Such declarations were linked both to the crisis and to ongoing EU liberalisation processes.

As to the role of European Works Councils in the crisis, it is often reported that their activities relative to restructuring matters has been increasing, but that in numerous cases they had difficulties in obtaining information in due time from companies. By 2010, the number was 953, covering 17. 3 million wage-earners in 40 per cent of multinationals regulated by the directive.

Regarding company restructuring (a subject which has for many years been conflict-prone at EU level and has not led to successful outcomes, either on the EU institutions side or on the social partners side), the EP has (on the basis of Article 225 in the Lisbon Treaty) adopted a resolution on company restructuring on 15 January 2013 with 14 recommendations to better anticipate and manage such situations to which the Commission has to provide an answer.

Besides, in 2008 the EU undertook the adaptation of both the European Globalisation Adjustment Fund introduced in 2006 and the European Social Fund, to face urgent financial needs due to the crisis, by relaxing some of their conditional criteria. In 2013, with its social investment package and youth package, the EU acknowledged the severe and lasting character of the crisis.

Europe 2020: Its Social Policy Agenda

Though there was great continuity of the policy agenda between the Lisbon Strategy and Europe 2020, the 2008 crisis had influenced its economic and social objectives.[1] On the social policy side, this was most clearly shown by including among its five main quantified objectives the adoption of a quantified objective for the fight against poverty and social exclusion (with the aim to reduce the poverty level by 25 per cent, which means getting 20 million persons out of poverty by 2020). On the employment policy side, more traditional issues, such as the fight against youth unemployment and long-term unemployment of specific groups (the low qualified, immigrants) surfaced again even though more innovative devices around flexicurity and transitional labour markets also remained high on the agenda, all the more so because the crisis had led to new experimental devices in many countries, combining, for instance, short-term employment and training. In a more novel vein, in Europe 2020, employment policies were also more closely linked to sustainable development with the hope of more 'green' job creation and with the KBS priority calling for a more prospective view of the labour market and its required skills (European Commission 2010e).

Though Social Europe's agenda was fairly deficient in its legislative and contractual outcomes, the OMC processes entailed in Europe 2020, on the contrary kept their full weight.

---

1   The five targets for the EU in 2020 are:
   • employment rate of 75 per cent;
   • R&D/innovation: to invest 3 per cent of the EU's Gross Domestic Product;
   • climate change/energy: to reduce by 20 per cent gas emissions (even 30 per cent if the conditions are right), 20 per cent of energy to come from renewables, 20 per cent increase in energy efficiency;
   • education: to reduce drop-out rate to below 10 per cent; at least 40 per cent of 30–34-year-olds to have tertiary education;
   • poverty/social exclusion: at least 20 million fewer people at risk of poverty.

What About Governance?

Europe 2020 inaugurated important governance changes aiming at greater stability of objectives, better policy coordination, improved implementation, more *ex ante* and *ex post* EU control, and new distribution of roles among actors involved in the process through new sequencing. Those changes were as follows:

- The integrated guidelines were reduced from 24 to 10 and were supposed to remain stable until 2014 (European Commission 2010f).
- Temporalities between the national reform plans (coordination of economic and socio-economic policies), the stability and convergence programmes (budgetary control), and preventive recommendations (macro-economic imbalances) were coordinated and gave birth to the so-called 'European Semester process'.
- More efficient procedures were planned for a better involvement of the EP, national parliaments and social partners.
- The Commission's Annual Growth Survey was to frame the European Semester process and to prepare for the decisions of the European Spring Council. The Semester process meant much closer intertwining between budgetary, economic and employment/social policies at EU level, as well as closer budgetary intertwining between the EU and the national level previous to MS national budgetary decision-making.
- Further, the national reporting exercises have also been more closely framed by the Commission (compare with the code of conduct of 2012 for the stability and convergence programmes and detailed methods for Europe 2020 national reporting), so as to improve implementation. For each of the five quantified targets to be reached by 2020, the Commission will cooperate with each individual member state setting up specific national targets.

Seen from a multi-governance perspective, those governance changes at the same time meant a strengthening of the centre, in the sense of an increased role of the Commission and the Council in the European Semester, as well as a greater consideration for national contingencies. This, for instance, includes the five negotiated national targets between the Commission and the MS, although it appears already that the sum of nationally negotiated targets will not be able to reach the official Europe 2020 targets except on climate change issues (European Commission 2012d).

The Other EU Level Macro-economic Governance Reforms

Beside Europe 2020, among the vast array of macro-economic governance reforms undertaken since 2008, two further MS engagements were adopted in 2011 and 2012 in order to promote growth and employment. With the 'Euro-plus pact' in March 2011 (signed by 23 member states), which tackles issues linked to MS competitiveness, debates on the comparisons of *wage policies* have become central at EU level. The pact aims at wage moderation both in the public and private sectors (a view also defended by the ECB) and thus at reducing competitiveness differences among MS; it intends to examine national wage systems, their structure and degree of centralisation. This Pact is not formally compulsory and relies on 100 concrete measures to stimulate employment, budgetary sustainability and financial stability.

In June 2012, the European Council adopted yet another 'Pact for growth and employment' as a 'pendant' of the Treaty on Stability Coordination and Governance (TSCG), consisting in a political catalogue of European and national growth measures.

At the same time, in order to secure the survival of the Eurozone, this period has seen the adoption of a whole set of macro-economic reforms which aim primarily at reducing and controlling budgetary and macro-economic imbalances and which bear heavy and direct consequences for national social protection and employment policy expenses. Among them, we can mention the new rulings on the growth and stability pact, the Treaty on Stability Coordination and Governance (November 2012, agreed by 25 members), the six-pack legislation (November 2011) and the two-pack legislation (2013).

In addition to this, the EU level financial solidarity instruments (in case the stability of the Eurozone is put at risk by a country) and in particular the European Stability Mechanism set up in 2012, which will replace the two previously existing solidarity mechanisms, entail conditional factors which concern labour market and social policy structural reforms.

The last set of economic reforms relates to financial regulation and devices for a banking union – but those elements are less directly crucial for our subject. Beside their highly intrusive impact content-wise on national employment and social policies, those EU budgetary and macro-economic reforms also contain major governance changes as to the respective role of the EU and MS, which led to a debate on their democratic legitimacy (see conclusions). Broadly seen, they reflect a shift of sovereignty from the national to the European level.

The Lisbon Treaty (2009)

The Lisbon Treaty was to be implemented in 2009 in the midst of the crisis. It reinforced EU social objectives and integrated the Charter of Fundamental Rights, which became constraining. The latter concerns areas such as equality of treatment and non-discrimination, the right to information and consultation in companies, the right to collective bargaining and to strike, to protection devices in case of unemployment and access to placement services, to the protection of children and young people at work, to the conciliation of professional and family life, to social security and social help and to access to services of general interests etc. The Charter – initially adopted in 2000 on a non-compulsory basis – is legally binding for 25 member states, with Poland and the UK benefiting from derogation as to its implementation.

However, the treaty specifies that the course of the implementation of its social objectives cannot lead to increasing EU competences. Moreover, the balance to be found between economic and social rights will in practice remain a contentious issue, because the Lisbon Treaty puts them on an equal footing. This means that the tension between social rights and economic rights remains high, as was already the case in previous years with the Laval, Viking, Rüffert and Luxembourg cases which led to tough debates.

The Lisbon Treaty also requires social and environmental mainstreaming in all EU policies: new social objectives, such as full employment and social progress, the fight against social exclusion and discrimination, and solidarity between the generations, the member states and the regions, are to be integrated into all European policies. Internal market policies have thus to take into account a whole set of horizontal social and environmental clauses. The Treaty also recognises the essential role of public services as constituent parts of the European political project.

Regarding social competences *stricto sensu*, the treaty extends qualified majority to social benefits of migrant workers and introduces 'passerelle clauses' for third country residents. The qualified majority is also extended to dismissals concerning the representative institutions.

The Lisbon Treaty could potentially play a protection role for its citizens in a globalisation and crisis period. However, in practical terms, experience shows that citizens have great difficulties in mobilising such potential rights and getting access to the EU legal system which is perceived by them as complex and distant, without identifiable actors; it remains most often discouraging for them to envisage having recourse to legal courts on the basis of EU rights (Barbier and Colomb 2012).

4. Conclusions

Where Does Social Europe Stand?

While not being a cohesive or comprehensive system, the EU social policy field does comprise several elements of what could be considered as a European social model, namely a) social values and principles enshrined in the Charter of Fundamental Rights integrated into the Lisbon Treaty; b) a fragmentary legislative set of numerous directives, as well as a set of EU collective agreements; c) the existence of diverse institutional procedures (legislation, collective bargaining and social dialogue, OMC, redistributive structural funds), on which Europe's political and social partners can draw whenever appropriate.

From 2008 onwards, a twofold *development* took place at EU level with regard to social and employment matters: on the one side, the increasing weight of more stringent economic reforms around budgetary policies with direct impact for national budgets (that is, social and employment expenses), and on the other, a relative absence of EU social policy devices to deal with the consequences of the crisis (an issue left essentially to the national level), both trends leading to growing euro-scepticism among citizens (Vandenbroucke 2012).

The EU has been stigmatised with regard to the EU troïka memoranda linked to the Greek rescue plan in 2011; indeed, the Council of Europe (2012) as well as ILO (2012) have been denouncing certain of their labour market reforms for infringing the European Social Charter (not to be confused with the EU Charter of Fundamental Rights) and certain ILO conventions. Besides, it has also been argued that certain elements relative to wages, collective bargaining, social security and public sector, of recent EU level economic reforms went beyond EU existing treaty competences on those social matters.

Moreover, the various contradictions inherent to the plurality of EU social and economic policy objectives became blatant. On the one hand, new rights for citizens and proactive social objectives have been introduced in the Lisbon Treaty (with sometimes ambivalent meaning though), and on the other hand, a set of economic reforms aiming at budgetary and wage rigour – not always compatible with those new rights – has been disclosed. One must add the various ongoing OMC processes within the frame of Europe 2020, which often also entail ambivalent aims.

What About Governance Shifts in EU Socio-Economic Proposals in the Last Decade?

The EU governance shifts which occurred with the Lisbon Strategy in the 2000s taught us two things: a) that there existed a broad consensus among MS on the necessity to reform national social and employment systems and a wish to vest the EU level with enabling powers as to such a task; b) that the Europeanization of national employment and social policies through soft devices rather than constraining EU policies was the only acceptable path for MS (Goetschy 2013).

The Lisbon Strategy implied a growing role of the European Council and the Commission in EU decision-making to the detriment of the EP role. Member states too were pro-eminent in this process. This trend was accentuated with Europe 2020, the European Semester and the set of other economic governance reforms after 2008. The EP was unevenly involved (although the six-pack entailed economic dialogue for the EP with four of the regulations adopted on a co-decision basis, and the TSCG is planning for a joint conference on behalf of the EP and national parliaments) and national parliaments rather little solicited (at least *ex ante*) (de Streel 2011).

After 2008, variable geometry was gaining ground. If the Lisbon Strategy and Europe 2020 concern the 27 member states, the other economic reforms imply a 'variable geometry' – the TSCG gathers 25 MS, the Euro-plus pact 23 MS, most of the sanctions apply to 17 Eurozone MS. This situation grants all its importance to Europe 2020 which remains the most integrative and federative project and process in relation to its geographic and policy scope, even if subject to a slow implementation tempo given the lack of sanctions (Marzinotto et al. 2012).

The whole set of economic reforms including the European Semester have been criticised concerning their content (not enough growth oriented) and lack of legitimacy. Many authors have reckoned that those reforms are too complex, overlapping, decided by too many central actors (Commission, Council, ECB) and not bearing sufficient democratic legitimacy. Not only did the policy centre shift from the national to the EU level, but at EU level it favoured executive over elected actors (de Streel 2011).

But other quarters rejoice over the fact that under pressure of the crisis, the EU managed to adopt European governance instruments (budgetary, macro-economic) of a quasi-federal orientation (some speak of a 'silent revolution'), especially if one adds the financial solidarity mechanisms – difficult to imagine a few years ago – though the origin of many of those after crisis economic reforms was intergovernmental.

What About the Links Between Economic and Social EU Policies?

To level up social policy to the higher governance level of economic policies has not, until 2014, represented a central issue for policy makers. Historically, new steps in social policy developments – be it through treaty changes or through more ad hoc arrangements – have generally followed EU economic integration developments in a compensatory and ancillary capacity. With the Lisbon Strategy in 2000, there was a tendency to put social priorities on a similar level as economic policies (structural economic and macro-economic policies), but such an endeavour was not really successful due to policy hierarchies, especially after 2005, and to a lack of institutional treaty support. At that time a group of Left-wing economists even argued that, given that negative externalities between EU economies were not an issue in the case of social/employment policies, the latter should not be a subject for EU level governance, unlike economic policies which required urgent EU central governance devices (Collignon et al. 2005).

Since 2008, very little attention has been paid to the need for more EU central coordination and new devices between economic and social policies within the frame of ongoing EU economic reforms, apart from some Europe 2020 declarations of intent. Despite the fact that EU budgetary restraint policies on the one hand, and new solidarity mechanisms with regard to the management of MS public debts on the other hand, bear consequences for national social policies, one must reckon that the search for stricter EU level policy coordination mechanisms between social and economic issues does not yet represent an essential preoccupation of the EU agenda. The main reason for such a standstill since 2008 resides, among others, in the political attention requested primarily by difficult EU economic reforms, in the growing diversity of EU social systems since the crisis[2] and in the additional conflicts such a debate would lead to among MS.

---

2   With the crisis, at least six social models can be identified within the EU: (a) Nordic; (b) Belgium, France; (c) Germany; (d) Mediterranean countries; (e) UK; (f) Eastern and Central Europe.

Chapter 9

The Euro-Crisis – Welfare State Conundrum

Anton Hemerijck

1. Introduction

The welfare state and the European Union (EU), two of the most important feats of mid-twentieth-century European social engineering, find themselves at a crossroads amidst the turmoil of the Euro-crisis and in the aftermath of the global credit crunch of 2008. The good news is that by 2013 economic growth returned to Europe, five years after the fall of the New York based Lehman Brothers investment bank. While the emergence from the double-dip Great Recession is surely welcome, many leading economists believe Europe's nascent recovery to be far too feeble to overcome the dramatic social crisis that Europe is confronted with since the beginning of the crisis. Unemployment is at an historic high of 24 million out-of-work EU citizens and this number is likely to continue to rise. Truly catastrophic levels of youth unemployment – far above 50 per cent in countries like Greece and Spain – are threatening the fabric of European societies as adverse growth and employment prospects will imply rising poverty and social exclusion for many years to come.

The Euro-crisis clearly marks a serious 'stress test' for twenty-first-century European cooperation and national welfare provision. Will its aftermath, like the Great Depression and 'great inflation' predecessors, mark a new opportunity to reconfigure and perhaps re-legitimise social policy and the European project? Or are European welfare states, the Single Market and the European Monetary Union (EMU) in danger of becoming 'crisis casualties' in the cascade of violent economic, social and political aftershocks across Europe, unleashed by the global financial crisis?

From 1945 to the mid-1970s European economic integration and the expansion of comprehensive systems of social protection were extremely successful in fostering economic and social progress. From the 1980s onwards, a more complex relationship emerged of mutual support, but so did strains between the 'market opening' logic of the deepening of European market integration and the 'social protection' logic of national welfare states (Ferrera 2005). Because of greater capital mobility, fiscal pressures mounted with the introduction of the EMU. In parallel, important social trends altered the endogenous policy environment of European welfare states. Population ageing and declining fertility rates, together with a trend towards early retirement of baby boomers, pressed social policy makers to update pension systems. In addition, rapid technological change triggered falling demand for low and medium-skilled work across advanced European political economies. The shift towards post-industrial labour markets, on the one hand, opened up job opportunities for women, but, on the other hand, de-industrialisation came along with declining levels of steady lifetime jobs and rising job precariousness, especially for women and young people. Changing family structures and gender roles – with longer education spells, later child-birth and lone parenthood – meanwhile created new tensions between work and family life and raised new demands for the provision of social care, especially for young children and the elderly.

Although the drivers of intensified European integration and social transformation are common, the pressures they create for different welfare regimes and the policy responses they trigger vary from country to country. While the Nordic welfare systems, together with the Netherlands, Germany and the UK, have been quite successful in *updating* their policy repertoires in light of the social transformations preceding the global financial crisis, others, especially the welfare states of Southern Europe, fared less well for various economic, political and institutional reasons (Hemerijck 2013). Add to this the differential impact of the Euro-crisis and it is easy to see that European welfare states and the EU have entered a new era of flux that will see major reform, transformation and adaptation to short and medium-term financial crisis aftershocks and long-term social change.

In times of deep economic crisis, politics and economics become inseparably linked. High unemployment, strained pensions, social distress, and public debt and deficits put enormous pressure on elected politicians, especially across Europe where citizens hold high expectations of social protection from economic uncertainty. Social retrenchment and incisive labour market reform have already been met with a wave of strikes, walkouts, and demonstrations in many EU member states. Sometimes, however, deep economic crises *can* provide important political windows for transformative policy redirection. This we know from the Great Recession of the 1930s and the experience of the Great Stagflation crisis of the 1970s and 1980s. At such critical junctures, policy change is guided by important changes in expert economic policy analysis, coupled with significant shift in the overall balance of political power, required to institutionalise novel policy paradigms.

To say that the Euro-crisis has brought European welfare states and European integration to a new crossroads, however, is not to suggest that a benign novel 'elective affinity' between innovative economic policy analysis and supranational political consensus will come forth easily. Protracted failures to resolve the Euro-crisis at the supranational level are increasingly mirrored by domestic political pressures to water down ruling governments' commitment to European solutions. Although financial markets seemed to have calmed down somewhat, in the expectation of a protracted period of low growth at levels of unemployment not seen since the 1930s, 2013's capital market acquiescence, I believe, could be deceiving. In this contribution, I argue for room for a more realistic and slower pace of fiscal adjustment, coupled with long-term productivity enhancing domestic social (investment) reforms, informed by readily available evidence about the new efficiency–equity frontier. In so doing, I hope to challenge, on economic, institutional and political grounds, the false 'necessity' of the prevailing *pensée unique* of social austerity.

For the rest of the chapter, in Section 2 I first review the wave of social reforms that has swept across the European Union over the past two decades. The available quantitative evidence over this period, presented in Section 3, reveals that generous welfare provision is no anathema to economic competitiveness and macroeconomic stability. 'Pareto-optimal' social investments can bolster the fiscal capacities of mature welfare states by raising employment participation while contributing to long-term productivity growth. Next, Section 4 surveys the EU's crisis management endeavour since 2008. After a short intermezzo of firefighting Keynesianism, of fiscal stimulus, bank bailouts and flanking social spending increases, the Greek sovereign debt crisis pushed policy elites to embrace strategies of intrusive austerity in order to strategise the contagious Euro-crisis – albeit to little avail. In Section 5, I analyse the Eurozone predicament as a crisis of economic policy regime, resulting from a deep intellectual inertia in policy analysis and practice, which theoretically rules out the importance of social investment in times of demand-deficient slump. Building on recent publications together with Frank Vandenbroucke and Bruno Palier (Vandenbroucke et al. 2011; Hemerijck and Vandenbroucke 2012), Section 6 is devoted to anchoring a social investment perspective in EU macroeconomic governance as an institutional device for economic and social policy reconciliation. Without a more overarching paradigm shift, reconciling a stronger economic with an more ambitious social Europe, the EU is likely to remain trapped in self-defeating policy indecision, conjuring up a spectre of a long lost decade for Europe, worse than that experienced by Japan since the early 1990s.

2. Changing Welfare States

The welfare state of mid-twentieth-century Europe emerged from the economic and political lessons of the war and depression years. In the 1950s and 1960s it proved highly successful in protecting workers and families from the vagaries of the market through comprehensive social insurance, without undermining the *modus operandi* of the free market economy. After the advanced Western economies ran into the crisis of stagflation in the 1970s, academic observers, policymakers, and opinion leaders have been permanently engaged in a highly politicised debate over the welfare state in crisis. Ridiculing the so-called 'European Social Model' became a particularly favourite pastime of international business elites, political leaders, and economic experts in the 1990s. The European welfare model system took the blame for the region's slow economic growth and lagging competitiveness and technological innovation, as a consequence of overprotective job security, rigid wages, expensive social insurance, and employer-unfriendly collective bargaining that developed over the post-war period. However, the crisis of stagflation did not invoke the welfare state's demise. On the contrary, the remarkable stability of social spending in rich democracies, at about 20–30 per cent of GDP, over past decades of neoliberal austerity is testimony to the staying power of modern welfare state policies across the advanced EU countries (Pierson 2011). The popular claim that stable levels of social spending are representative of welfare states as an *immovable object*, is, I argue, a misnomer. Irrespective of constant social spending, all welfare states of the European Union, in the shadow of the Single Market project and the introduction of the rule based fiscal and monetary framework of EMU, have been recasting the basic functional, normative, distributive and institutional underpinnings, upon which they were once based, across a wide array of policy areas (Hemerijck 2013).

As macroeconomic policy gave way to low inflation and budget consolidation, in the field of *wage policy*, a reorientation followed in favour of market-based wage restraint in order to facilitate competitiveness, profitability, and employment growth, prompted by the new rule-based macroeconomic policy prescriptions. Wage moderation in many countries was pursued through social pacts between trade unions, employer associations, and government, often linked with wider packages of negotiated welfare reforms that made tax policy, social insurance, and pension and labour market regulation more 'employment friendly' (Avdagic et al. 2011).

Old age pensions are often seen as the most resilient artefacts of the post-war 'old risk' mitigating welfare state, and a least likely case to confront profound reform. Yet, financing problems due to population ageing and lower growth have prompted widespread reform. Steps have been taken to reverse the trend towards early retirement policies, together with initiatives to promote longer and healthier working lives. A string of adjustments, however, have fundamentally altered retirement welfare over the past two decades (Bonoli and Palier 2008; Häusermann 2010). A key shift has been the growth of (compulsory) occupational and private pensions and the development of multi-pillar systems, combining pay-as-you-go and fully funded methods, with relatively tight (actuarial) links between the pension benefits and contributions, with strong incentives to delay early exit from the labour market and reward those working longer (Clark and Whiteside 2003; Ebbinghaus 2011).

In the area of *labour market policy*, in the 1990s the new objective became maximising employment. Spending on active labour market policies across OECD countries increased considerably from the 1990s and the mid-2000s, in the context of falling unemployment rates, the mobilisation of women, youth, older workers, and less productive workers through early intervention, case management and conditional benefits, gained sway. With respect to *labour market regulation*, several European countries have moved towards greater acceptance of flexible labour markets. It was the introduction of these active elements into the Danish and Dutch labour markets that gave rise to the European 'flexicurity' model (Schmid 2008; Bonoli 2011).

In terms of *social insurance* and *assistance*, the generosity of benefits has been curtailed through reductions in benefit levels, eligibility criteria and duration. Through this weakening, especially of earnings-related benefit provision and by harmonising benefits across different risk categories, social insurance provision has become less status confirming (Clasen and Clegg 2011). At the same time, conditionality and job search requirements have been made more 'demanding', targeting labour market 'outsiders' such as young, female or low-skilled workers, supported also by the universalisation of minimum income protection and minimum wage legislation (Bonoli 2012).

Social services have significantly expanded, especially in the 2000s, to especially boost female participation though family policy (Lewis 2006; Mahon 2006; Orloff 2009, 2010). Spending on family services, childcare, education, health, and care for the elderly, as well as training and employment services, has increased as a percentage of GDP practically everywhere in the EU. Leave arrangements have been expanded, in terms of both time and scope of coverage, including the frail elderly. Pioneers in such work and family reconciliation policies include the Nordic countries, followed by the 'path-shifters' of Germany, the Netherlands, and the UK.

An overarching reform concerns the changes in the territorial organisation of social policies and the related *administrative reforms*, or the 'rescaling' of social policies (Kazepov 2010). Most important has been the attempt to bring social insurance and assistance and labour market policies institutionally under one roof in so-called one-stop centres, thus ending previous separation of social security and public employment administration. Ideas of New Public Management and novel concepts of *purchaser-provider* models within public welfare services have been especially instructive in respect of the restructuring of Public Employment Services (PES) (Weishaupt 2011).

The final important trend is the overall shift in *welfare financing* from social contributions to general taxation. In general the continental welfare states are largely financed through social contributions from workers and employers, following their Bismarckian policy legacy, whereas the Scandinavian and Anglo-Irish social security systems are largely financed out of taxes, consistent with the Beveredgean tradition. Over the past two decades the source of social protections expenditure financing has shifted from social contribution to fiscal financing. The shift to tax financing represents a shift from earnings-related employment-based social protection towards more universal provision (Eichhorst and Hemerijck 2010).

In the shadow of the incisive shift to the supply-side economics and the stricter rule-based fiscal and monetary policy framework, most European welfare states have become more efficient. Especially the introduction of EMU ignited the wave of social reform across Europe. National social policy reformers were far from the blind followers of the competitive retrenchment-deregulatory adjustment strategy espoused by simpleminded supply-side economists. The overall scope of change varied widely across the member states of the European Union. With their tradition of high quality child care and high employment rates for older workers, the Scandinavian countries performed particularly well throughout the past quarter century, both in terms of efficiency and equity, but we also observe reconstructive change in countries like the Netherlands (social activation), Germany (support for dual earner families), France (minimum income protection for labour market outsiders), the United Kingdom (fighting child poverty), Ireland (much improved education) and Spain (negotiated pension recalibration) in the period leading up to the financial crisis. In the process, European welfare states did not become the lean and mean welfare states that European central bankers and fiscal policy authorities in Frankfurt and Brussels hoped for; they became 'active welfare states'!

3. Social Investment Dividends

Over the past two decades, some countries, notably the Nordics, have been able to re-establish new virtuous mixes of equity and efficiency by enlarging scope for markets in the sphere of production, on the one hand supported by more active and capacitating social policy provisions, and on the other, anchored in rule-based macroeconomic policy. Elsewhere, notably in a number of continental welfare regimes and the Anglo-Saxon countries, labour markets have been reconfigured and social spending reoriented towards active labour market policy and capacitating family services, with higher levels of employment for both men and women as a result. In more than a handful of countries, the reform momentum was critically informed by 'social investment' policy prescriptions, bent on increasing labour supply and productivity through 'capacitating' family, training and employment services (Ferrera et al. 2000; Esping-Andersen et al. 2002; Morel et al. 2012). Only a minority of countries, notably Greece and Italy, has continued to resemble the popular caricature of change-resistant welfare states. The abortion of the 1990s reform momentum in the pension-heavy and segmented welfare systems of Southern Europe, after their successful entry into EMU, should be associated with too low real interest rates – a financial market failure *par excellence*. This policy mistake, inherently bound up with the incomplete architecture of EMU (see below), gives reason to believe that the poorly performing – economically uncompetitive and socially deficient – Greek, Italian, Portuguese and Spanish welfare states, facing extremely high levels of youth and long term unemployment, are not per se structurally incapable of effective welfare recalibration.

The social investment perspective is essentially based on three central tenets: the easing of the 'flow' of contemporary labour market transitions and the development of human capital 'stock', undergirded by strong minimum-income universal safety nets as social protection buffers. Both labour market transition flow and human capital stock have to be viewed interactively through the lens of the life-course contingencies of modern families and how to utilise labour inputs most efficiently thoughout working lives. The social investment approach in essence rests on policies to raise the human capital stock (from early childhood education and care, vocational training, education, and lifelong learning) on the one hand, and labour market flow policies, serving to make the most efficient use of human capital across the life course, on the other. This is to be achieved through policies supporting women and lone-parent employment, through active labour market and other activation policies, and facilitating access of the labour market also for vulnerable groups, and social protection buffers that promote flexible security across the life-course bridges between: (1) training and employment; (2) full and part-time employment; (3) the raising of family and the caring of the frail and elderly; and (4) the passage between employment and (flexible) retirement.

Can the social investment turn be associated with key measures of welfare performance, such as output growth, macroeconomic stability, job creation and relative poverty declines? Figure 9.1 portrays the employment/population ratios among people in the working age population over time. First, what is striking is the long-term increase in employment in most countries. Both the Anglo-Saxon and the Scandinavian countries had about 75 to 80 per cent of the working-age population in employment before the global financial crisis. Apart from the Netherlands, most other continental and Mediterranean European countries lag behind with employment rates of 60 per cent to 70 per cent, but even there we can see some progress, also in Spain.

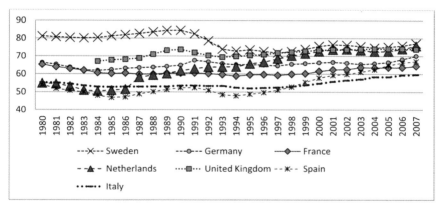

Figure 9.1   Employment/population ratio, 1980–2007
Adapted from Hemerijck, 2013, fig. 7.16, p. 244.
Source: OECD, labour force statistics, extracted February 2012.

Positive employment growth is strongly correlated with the steep rise in female labour market participation. Over the past quarter century, female employment increased by about 20 per cent. Female employment rates vary between 52 per cent in Italy and 73 per cent in Sweden (see Figure 9.2).

The main drivers of the increased female labour force participation are feminist emancipation, educational expansion, and the shift to the service economy and its associated demand for labour market flexibility, supported by augmented possibilities of reconciling work and family care responsibilities (Jaumotte 2003).

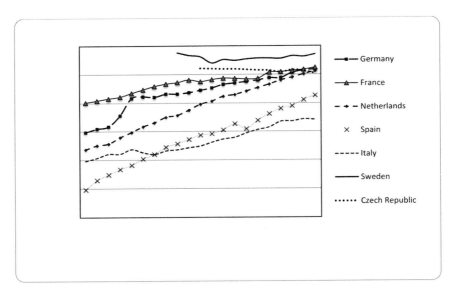

Figure 9.2   Activity rates of women (1987–2007)
Adapted from Hemerijck, 2013, fig. 7.18, p. 247.
Source: OECD, labour force statistics.

Since the late 1990s, the employment rate among older workers has also been rising, most strongly in Sweden, but also in some continental welfare states, with the Netherlands taking the lead (see Figure 9.3). This is consistent with the recent pension reform momentum and rising expenditures of lifelong learning/(re) training programmes.

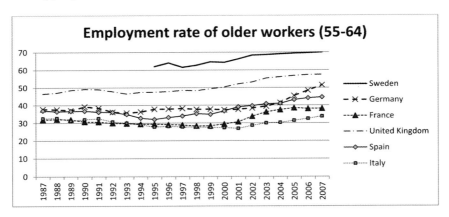

Figure 9.3   Employment rates of older workers (55–64), 1987–2007
Adapted from Hemerijck, 2013, fig. 7.23, p. 252.
Source: Eurostat

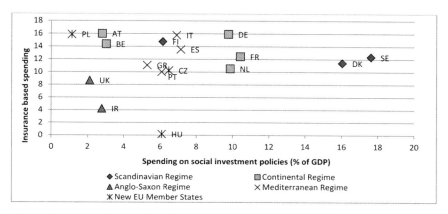

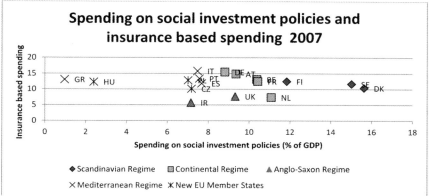

Figure 9.4   Social investment spending and social (insurance) protection based spending in 1997 (top panel) and 2007 (bottom panel), per cent of GDP

Adapted from Hemerijck, 2013, fig. 7.38, p. 266.

Source: Own calculations using OECD Social Expenditure Database (SOCX), extracted October 2011.

Notes: Spending on social investment policies include childcare, elderly care, education, active labour market policies, and maternal and parental leave; Spending on social insurance based spending includes old-age, survivors, disability pensions, excluding the rehabilitation expenses, and unemployment spending excluding expenses on active labour market programmes.

Loosely aligned with the shift towards active labour market policy, the development of capacitating social services for dual-earner families marks a distinct departure from the longstanding male-breadwinner/female-homemaker legacy, especially in continental Europe. Building on earlier work (Hemerijck 2013), I have tried to relate 'capacitating' social investment and more 'compensating' social protection categories of spending to one another. The social investment category includes active labour market programmes, childcare, education, research and rehabilitation policies, as these items contribute to employability and human capital development. The remaining social protection categories combine old age and survivor benefits, unemployment-related benefits and disability benefits, as well as healthcare and housing and are gathered under the second category of social protection spending, which aims at mitigating periods of inactivity. By comparing spending on capacitating social investments and compensating social insurance spending across European welfare states in 1997 and 2007 (Figure 9.4), we are able to observe that several countries have increased their spending on social investment policies. No country has shifted emphasis away from social investment by privileging social protection.

What is particularly interesting to observe is that higher total budgets for social policy are both associated with better outcomes in terms of poverty and employment. Countries with relatively higher budgets for capacitating social investment policies fare particularly well in terms of employment, suggesting that social investments are especially effective in raising employment. By contrast, budgets spent on social protection (narrowly understood) are much less effective (only 0.25 per cent higher).

Aggregate socio-economic performance speaks to important accomplishments of the social investment turn, before the onslaught of the global financial crisis. Employment levels have improved for all age groups and gender groups, but significant differences persist between welfare states, in the degree to which they are able to integrate youth, women and older workers into the labour market. The new role of women, especially, has critically altered the character of social risks in fundamental ways (Esping-Andersen 2009). Women no longer enter the job market 'unencumbered' by the burden of caring for dependents. Ambitious social investments and higher budgets for social policies are generally associated with better performance outcome in terms of employment, fiscal balance, gender equality, relative poverty, rates on return on education, early childcare and lifelong learning, suggesting that more investment-oriented social policies may be particularly efficient in raising employment levels and competitiveness, without necessarily producing higher levels of poverty (OECD 2008; 2011).

In the decade leading up to the 2008 credit crunch, it became evident that the high tax-high spend economies in Northern Europe outperform most other welfare states on EMU and Stability Pact indicators. Therefore, the generous Scandinavian welfare systems were able to create budget surpluses during most of the 2000s, thereby expanding the policy space for automatic stabilisation in hard times later on. By contrast, the Mediterranean regimes show lower levels on practically all relevant social indicators, displaying high levels of inequality, low levels of employment for women and older men and high long-term and youth unemployment, most notably in Italy and Greece. Tragically, in the aftermath of the global financial crunch, these countries are the ones most in fiscal dire straits. What went wrong?

4. Euro-Crisis Management Flaws and EMU Governance Deficits

Will the social investment paradigm that emerged in the shadow of shift to supply side economic policy carry the day, or will it revert to marginality and be left orphaned in the new epoch of reinforced fiscal austerity since 2010? Between 2008 and 2010, automatic stabilisers were initially allowed to cushion the recession. National economies were also granted, by Brussels, to temporarily deviate from the Stability Pact benchmark indicators on deficits and debt. The swift Keynesian response was complemented, in a fair number of Eurozone economies, by measures to extend short-term working arrangements, often linked to training and activation incentives, consistent with social investment policy prescriptions. But the main impetus for firefighting Keynesianism was to stabilise the financial system by bailing out banks and other financial institutions.

By December 2009 a second wave of crisis management took shape, punctuated by the Greek sovereign debt predicament. After European governments were pushed to bail out systemic national banks, the financial crisis was redefined from a global banking crisis to one of fiscal profligacy, requiring tough and prolonged public austerity. Within the span of a single year, policymakers forgot that the credit crunch originated in behavioural excesses in financial markets and not in excess public spending, except for the outlier Greek case. Greece and other besieged countries like Ireland, Portugal, and Spain immediately enacted bold social retrenchment programmes, including labour market deregulation, civil servant salary cuts and pension benefit freezes. In this context, it is important to emphasise that the vulnerabilities of the Irish and Spanish economies after 2008 find their root cause in high private, rather than public debt. Historically low real interest rates, following the introduction of EMU in 1999, in effect triggered reckless and unsustainable construction sprees, thus contributing to the long-term erosion of competitiveness in more peripheral Eurozone economies.

As the sovereign debt crisis turned systemic, the original EMU regime was revamped with a vengeance, through the so-called 'Six-pack' and 'Two-pack' new regulatory 'European semester' framework, with the clear aim of fostering fiscal balance in just a few years, as laid down in the December 2011 'fiscal compact' (see Rodrigues, this volume). Ever since, recovery has been weak, and many expert observers belief that the Eurozone's austerity politics set the stage for a double-dip economic recession for 2012 and 2013.

The Euro-crisis – or welfare state conundrum, as I see it – is beset by three critical institutional fault lines. The first fault line concerns deep-seated intellectual inertia in social and economic policy analysis. After a brief interlude of firefighting Keynesianism in 2008 and 2009, the Euro-crisis after 2010 came to be (re) interpreted as mainly a question of regaining competitiveness through country-specific wage-price devaluation, and through welfare state retrenchment and labour market deregulation, directed very much at restoring and reinforcing the macroeconomic policy regime *ex ante*. In retrospect, the 'one-size-fits-all' interest rate policy seemed to have created two groups of countries, one 'periphery' group with stronger output growth and inflationary pressures, resulting from low real interest rates, and the other 'core' group seemingly confronted with stagnation as a consequence of high real interest rates. This eventually resulted in an ever widening productivity gap between Italy, Portugal, and Spain and the rest of the Eurozone.

European policymakers are not merely locked into a revamped EMU and Stability and Growth Pact monetary and fiscal regime, because of ideational stasis. Equally important, in second place, is that, institutionally, it has become practically impossible to modify EU rules and their associated fiscal constraints, as these are hard-won quasi-constitutional instruments that emerged from lengthy treaty negotiations among 18 Eurozone and 28 internal market member states. Any crisis-induced changing of the rules thus requires broad intergovernmental consent, which by definition cannot be achieved overnight. Especially in times of crisis, when intellectual disagreement over crisis management touches deep beliefs about appropriate politics and economics, policy consensus is surely hard to come by, because of practically unmanageable collective action problems. This problem arises in particular when asymmetric shocks have to be dealt with by national government with large debts that have little policy discretion to use automatic stabilisers. Institutionally, the Eurozone's capacity of policy-coordination and steering is weak and the Treaty basis for negotiating important changes in institutional relations is extremely inflexible (see Fabbrini, this volume). The Treaty on European Union did not give the European Central Bank (ECB) serious competences in banking supervision and stabilisation responsibilities in the financial system beyond inflation targeting. The option of the ECB acting as a 'lender of last resort', moreover, was intentially ruled out. Hereby the architects of EMU hoped to forestall problems of 'moral hazard' and fiscal profligacy. Also, the 'no-bail out' clause in the Treaty deliberately served the purpose of not having to compromise on the key responsibility of the ECB for price stability.

The third fault line concerns the domestic politics of the Euro-crisis (Martin and Ross 2004). It is fair to say that European welfare states have become ever more 'semi-sovereign' with the progressive deepening of the internal market and monetary union. By centralising monetary policy and monitoring fiscal discipline, EMU has been a radical step, with important implications for (domestic) political craftsmanship. Irrespective of the loss of nation-based fiscal and monetary policy autonomy, political identification, mobilisation and accountability have remained overwhelmingly national. Electorates continue to hold national leaders accountable for their real and perceived socio-economic fortune and misfortune. High and rising youth and long-term unemployment, strained pensions and fiscal consolidation packages, resulting from important agreements reached at the level of the EU and the Eurozone, put enormous pressure on nationally elected politicians in EU member states, where citizens continue to hold high expectations of social protection from economic uncertainty. Protracted failures to resolve the Euro-crisis at the supranational level, as a consequence, are increasingly mirrored by domestic political pressures to water down ruling governments' commitment to European solutions.

Democratic governments are thus caught between Scylla and Charybdis. On the one hand, pressures for deficit reduction, coming from the EU and the ECB, constrain domestic social policy space. On the other hand, disenchanted electorates are increasingly unwilling to continue to abide by the austerity promises of national political leaders through supranational rescue agreements and reinforced EU fiscal rules. Betwixt rising anti-austerity popular sentiments and the EU's inquisitive expert calls for overnight fiscal consolidation, a 'political vacuum' emerged at the heart of the European integration project, reinforced by widening competitive divergences and social imbalance between the prosperous north and vulnerable south. The more the EU institutions step up austerity measures, the more European voters, from Finland to Greece, seek refuge with extreme anti-EU left and right populist parties.

Dyson (2000) underscores the extent to which the ECB lacks a secure base of political legitimacy outside of the technocratic realm of output-legitimacy of depoliticised monetary policy. The ECB must therefore associate its pursuit of economic stabilisation with a position of neutrality between different national conceptions of the public good. Technocratic supranational rationales in hard economic times, incurring significant social costs in different states, regions, families, and citizens, are difficult to sustain. When push comes to shove, national political parties and governments will be increasingly hesitant to defend European crisis resolution strategies, which trump the pro-welfare values shared by most Europeans. Particularly harmful is for the leadership of the ECB to take a deliberate stance on welfare reform imperatives. Statements like 'the European social model is dead', as exclaimed by Mario Draghi in the *Wall Street Journal* in February 2012, sets the stage for an anti-EU political boomerang effect in the member states at a time of escalating unemployment.

5. Competing Social and Economic Policy Paradigms

The tragedy of the Euro-crisis is that EU institutions and national governments were confronted with the aftershock of a huge global financial crisis, for which EMU was not designed. EMU was brought into being to help mitigate inflation and more serious stagflation problems. Problems of deflation do not appear in the EMU economics textbook. The Euro-crisis thus conjures up a paradigmatic crisis in economic policy paradigm. This is best seen as a coherent causal framework for understanding (macro-) economic trends, from which fairly stable economic and social policy choices naturally follow (Hall 1993; Temin 1989). As policy makers weigh alternative policy options, they do so within the boundaries of the prevailing paradigm. Over the evolution of global financial crisis since 2007, European fiscal and monetary policy authorities have been forced to advance a whole series of seemingly important deviations for standard operating procedures in monetary and fiscal policy. Most of these measures, except for the firefighting Keynesian interlude of 2008 and 2009, have been enacted to revitalise and restore the original sound money and sound budget EMU policy paradigm.

Each macroeconomic policy paradigm is based on some kind of explicit or implicit understanding of the role of the state and related social policy functions. In this respect, the EMU architecture was firmly grounded in the belief that redistributive welfare provision 'crowds out' private economic initiative, consumption and investment. Generous welfare provision, alongside employment protection legislation, are believed to act as disincentives to employment participation and cost competitiveness. More social spending thus means lower output and job growth. EMU's insistence on the reduction of public sector debt and deficits is part and parcel of the supply-side economics' larger rejection of the Keynesian argument that deficit public (especially social) expenditures over long and deep recessions constitute important investments from which economic demand be sustained and thus social progress will follow.

The Maastricht Treaty was benignly anchored in the assumption that the ECB's strong mandate on price stability, together with the strong commitment to fiscal consolidation by member state governments and enforced by the Stability and Growth Pact, would raise competitive pressures among the member state economies. Enhanced competitiveness in financial and product markets would subsequently translate into greater tax and cross-border labour markets competition. This, in turn, would force democratic governments to launch incisive reforms in their welfare states and labour markets, if need be, by blaming the EU for their inevitability. With respect to welfare provision and labour market structures, there is then a distinct retrenchment-deregulation bias in the original EMU policy regime, whereby long-term unemployment is primarily seen as the consequence of poor motivation and low search intensity resulting from welfare state generosity, creating negative 'moral hazard' and 'adverse selection' externalities (see Addison and Siebert 1997; Bertola, Boeri, and Nicoletti 2001, and for a critique Esping-Andersen 2001). The 1980s and 1990s problems of fiscally overburdened welfare states and labour market 'hysteresis', from this perspective, was essentially a problem of institutional inertia best tackled by fierce social retrenchment and labour market deregulation, providing employers with much freedom to 'hire and fire', minimal restrictions on working hours, reductions of trade union influence in wage setting and employment relations, and low taxes and less regulation.

Since the onslaught of the global financial crisis, the Euro, a collective good without precedent, has been confronted with destabilising macro imbalances. As the European single currency never lived up to the criteria of an Optimum Currency Area (OCA), because of low regional labour mobility and the lack of a central fiscal authority (Eichengreen 2007; De Grauwe 2009), no happy equilibrium has been forthcoming. The importance of domestic structural reform took pride of place, based on the belief in markets as the most efficient mechanism for the allocation of scarce resources and the desire of a non-interventionist role of the state.

Instead, we have been confronted with high current account deficits in Greece, Spain, Portugal, Ireland, and Italy, housing bubbles in Ireland, the Netherlands, and Spain, and current account surpluses in Germany and the Scandinavian countries. Therefore, the low interests that came along with the introduction of EMU slowed down the proactive welfare reform momentum in the Mediterranean countries, with traditionally passive and insider-biased welfare systems and labour markets. Paradoxically, it was the current account surplus countries, more concerned with global competitiveness, such as Germany and the Nordic countries, which intensified the social (investment) reform momentum after 1990s. As the EMU and Stability and Growth Pact (SGP) policy regime singularly focused on inflation and public deficit ratios, they completely ignored how in the aggregate the sum total of public and private debt levels deepened Europe's sovereign debt and banking crises. Further divergence between the competitive North, paying close to zero interest rates on moderate levels of public debt and government deficits, at manageable rates of unemployment, and the uncompetitive South, facing exceedingly high spreads on high debt and deficits and two-digit levels of unemployment and politically unmanageable rates of catastrophic youth unemployment, further destabilised the Eurozone economy. Belated 'structural reforms' in besieged countries offer no relief at distressed macroeconomic conditions. In the absence of fiscal room, economies with unsustainably high interest rates are trapped in a vicious cycle of semi-permanent economic decline. Under the weight of fiscal consolidation and private sector debt deleveraging, the Euro-crisis is rapidly turning into a deep underinvestment crisis across the region.

Just as generals are said to be ready to fight previous rather than current wars, it may well be that EMU has armed policy makers with the wrong material, well-equipped to resolve another stagflation crisis, but ill-disposed to foster long-run recovery in the face of demand-deficient decline. But as the Euro-crisis further unfolded, policy alternatives outside of the reinforced Stability Pact regime have not really been taken seriously. This surely applies to the overwhelming evidence that social investment reforms come with important social and economic returns, in terms of gender and family-sensitive labour market 'flow' and human capital 'stock', in line with the EU's long-term commitment to foster more inclusive growth, laid down in the Europe 2020 Strategy. The recent successes of sustaining a capitalism with a human face in the Nordic countries, Germany and the Netherlands, before and after the credit crunch of 2008, continue to be interpreted as either fully consistent with the espoused 'structural reform' imperative, or as spurious exceptions to the otherwise stable and effective EMU macro-policy regime. In my view, Pareto-optimal social investment dividends press us to rethink the larger Single Market, EMU and SGP order away from austerity. To the extent that capacitating welfare provision adds to economic competitiveness and social progress, it needs to have a place of pride in macroeconomic policy analysis and coordination, to support domestic social policy makers to maximise the returns on social investments. Structural reforms are needed to enhance competitiveness in many EU economies to foster convergence. But there is more to Pareto-optimal welfare recalibration than lowering wages, deregulating labour markets, eradicating dismissal protection and privatising welfare provision.

Table 9.1   Core differences between EMU's social retrenchment policy regime and social investment policy

	Social retrenchment *Axiomatic-deductive*	Social investment *Empirical-inductive*
Policy problem	Cost containment	Revenue raising
Core policy imperative	Engineer 'risk shift' to the private spheres/deregulation	Maximise employment in open economy
Policy theory	Trade-off 'equity and efficiency', 'crowding out' private economic initiative	'Crowding in' social investment economic synergies (participation / skill) across life course (devil in the detail)
Policy instruments	Targeted minimum poverty provision *ex post* (inequality inevitable and fair in new global economy)	Mitigate life cycle contingencies *ex ante* (skills / gender / family / children). Optimise life chances ('stock' and 'flow' over the life course) with strong safety net 'buffers'
Macro-Policy	Fiscal (procyclical_ consolidation SGP, inflation targeting EMU, Six-Pack, Two-Pack, Fiscal Compact, Troika, MoU	Macroeconomic stabilisation more than fighting inflation (sailing – anti-cyclically – against wind) focus on long-term growth
Institutional capacities Positive/negative State theory	Take out market barriers through NPM (contracting out) while disciplining low-trust 'rent-seeking' distributive coalitions (especially trade unions)	Institutions as both *constraints* and *resources* (high-trust public regarding social partnerships), 'productive coaltions' and key quality public service professionals
Political discourse	There is No Alternative (TINA) ('European social model is dead' – Mario Draghi 2012)	Capitalising and caring solidarity (recalibration ESM)

Cumulative social investment evidence suggests that a stable Euro currency can be made compatible with strong welfare provision, also in line with a positive conception of the state's role in defending, promoting and recalibrating social justice and giving the EU a 'human face' in hard economic times, by raising revenue rather than focusing narrowly on costs. Table 9.1 summarises the core differences between EMU's social retrenchment policy regime and the more benign social investment policy perspective.

In principle a common currency can be made compatible with generous welfare provision. A single currency can act as a collective insurance device against destabilising asymmetric shocks and slumps in times of intense economic interdependence. A stable supranational monetary and fiscal policy environment also suggests greater national autonomy over other politically salient policy areas. Despite important efforts at attaching a 'social dimension' to EMU by Jacques Delors in the late 1980s (Dyson and Featherstone 1999), issues of social justice have largely been ignored in the establishment of a technocratic and depoliticised EMU policy regime. On the eve of the outburst of the global financial crisis, it was possible to observe an emergent, albeit fragile, European consensus about social investment supply-side welfare provision, consistent with EMU fiscal criteria. It could even be argued that the introduction of EMU in 1999 was functional in the development of the social investment perspective, by unleashing the dynamic of cross-national social and economic policy learning and lesson drawing based on comparisons of national social policy best practices within EU-forums, setting the stage of 'supply-side' reforms and restructuring welfare states, under the Lisbon Agenda (Zeitlin 2010; Zeitlin and Heidenreich 2009).

6. Anchoring Social Investment in Euro Macroeconomic Coordination

The Euro-crisis teaches us, economically, institutionally and politically, that the implicit long-term consensus that macroeconomic policy can be determined at the supranational level in a currency union, in accordance with the efficient market hypothesis, while social policy is best left to the policy space of the national state, is both naïve and wrong.

Can European policy makers free themselves from the fiscal compact–social retrenchment straitjacket? Incremental but transformative policy change, I believe, is not inconceivable. At the intellectual level, authoritative expert supranational institutions, such as the International Monetary Fund (IMF) and the Organisation for Economic Co-operation and Development (OECD), are increasingly critical of Europe's hard currency and balanced budgets policy orthodoxy, suggesting that austerity politics is particularly self-defeating against the background of a contracting world economy. Ideas become powerful when they can be associated with empirical successes. *Ex negativo*, they fall from grace, when their continued pursuance becomes counterproductive. Important changes have already been implemented in monetary and fiscal policy and financial regulation. A banking union is no longer a political taboo and fiscal solidarity and discipline, essential for the survival of EMU, are taken ever more seriously. On the other hand, countering worrying economic divergences and social imbalances, through stronger countercyclical risk mutualisation, guaranteed by Eurobonds, have yet to receive critical attention. All in all, the deeper intellectual assumptions of the EMU and Stability Pact policy paradigm have not really been challenged.

Existing ideas and rules, even when they are under siege, precondition the pace and direction of consequent policy change, especially when potentially distributive conflict looms large, as in the case of the Euro-crisis. The institutional viability of a new policy regime is surely not self-evident, and not very likely to come from the inner technocratic circle of the ECB, the Commission and national finance ministries. If transformative policy change is to come about, it is more likely to emerge out of domestic political struggles over fiscal austerity. In 2013 austerity politics is increasingly becoming a recipe for losing elections, as the returns to power of the centre-left in Denmark in 2011, France and the Netherlands in 2012, and Italy and Germany in 2013, seem to suggest. For the majority of European citizens, European policy remains a matter of domestic politics. Electorates do not blame policy paradigms, supported by supranational institutions. Instead, they reward or punish their government for the health of their national economies, irrespective of EMU policy virtue or failure.

The EU requires a fairly dramatic and highly visible change in policy regime, based on a robust political exchange between countries that are in better shape and countries experiencing dire budgetary conditions, which have been less able (and willing) to pursue social investment reforms. Room must be created for a more realistic pace of fiscal adjustment (more symmetrical, and for some countries slower than first foreseen), associated with a reform-oriented social investment strategy and anchored in an improved EU financial, budgetary and macroeconomic policy framework (Eichengreen 2010). The New Deal that is required is one wherein *all* governments pursue budgetary discipline and social investment over the medium and long run, and are effectively supported therein (Vandenbroucke et al. 2011; Hemerijck and Vandenbroucke 2012).

Already the Treaty of Lisbon stipulates in Article 2, paragraph 3, that '[T]he Union shall work for the sustainable development of Europe on balanced economic growth and price stability, a highly competitive social market economy, aiming at full employment and social progress, and a high level of protection and improvement of the quality of the environment'; EU institutions are to play a complementary role in sustaining a social market economy, compatible with protecting and enabling the state's role in protecting and promoting social justice. This surely requires additional agreements on minimum standards of working conditions and social protection against unruly tax competition combined with measures to encourage credible budgetary consolidation policies that enable national automatic stabilisers to operate more effectively.

Endogenous social changes that prompted many welfare states to turn towards the promotion of investment-oriented social policy will not go away. If anything, they have become more pressing. Demographic headwind will bring social contracts under further duress, especially in countries facing high unemployment and the most daunting budgetary pressures, where long-run population ageing and the feminisation of the workforce have not been adequately dealt with before the crisis.

Social investment can no longer be dismissed as a 'fair weather' policy when times get rough. In the years ahead, intensifying fiscal pressures will lead many finance ministers to demand scrutiny on social spending. In both employment and social policy, there is a strong urge to do more with fewer resources. At the same time, the aftermath of the financial crisis will also reinforce the need for human capital investment and the importance of poverty relief and social protection. The Social Investment Package launched by the European Commission on 20 February 2013 (European Commission 2013b) suggests that after a decade of benign neglect or mere lip service to active welfare provision, the idea that social investments 'crowd in' private economy initiative through high long-term employment and productivity returns has finally been understood. This is a significant change, away from the hegemonic economic policy proposition that inevitably there is a 'trade-off' between social equity and economic efficiency. A second silver lining concerns the rekindling of the debate over a genuine 'social dimension' to EMU, pushed onto the European agenda by Council President Herman van Rompuy. The Social Investment package, the new debate on EMU's social dimension, together with associated proposals on new 'contractual arrangements', conjures up an attempt to 'socialize' the European semester. I hasten to emphasise that these 'silver linings' should not to be mistaken for 'silver bullets' in tackling the deeply embedded fault lines in the European architecture. The silver linings I see as important 'openings' in a policy debate about competing economic paradigms which has so far remained trapped in a moral tale of 'profligate' countries having to redo their structural reform 'homework', anchored in a highly veto-prone institutional setting, which under recessionary conditions only serves to fuel populist nationalism, making European solutions for obvious EMU design mistakes ever more difficult to breach. Without a more solidaristic fiscal union or some other counter-cyclical stabilisation capacity, based on a much stronger normative social (investment) compass, the co-dependent EU – welfare state architecture remains inadequate for promoting economic prosperity and social progress in twenty-first-century global capitalism. To convince the larger European democratic publics, in terms of political legitimacy, the EU social investment turn should be tangibly based on a well-articulated vision of a 'caring Europe', caring about people's daily lives and future social well-being.

Chapter 10

Game Change in EU Social Policy: Towards More European Integration[1]

Caroline de la Porte and Elke Heins

1. Introduction

Welfare states have been under pressure during recent decades, in the wake of challenges such as ageing populations and changing family patterns. To support member states in their welfare and labour market reforms in the context of Economic and Monetary Union (EMU), the European Union (EU) developed soft policy advice and comparative knowledge through various open methods of coordination (OMC). While there is dispute about the OMCs' impact (de la Porte and Pochet 2012), it is an ideational tool that is not intrusive, since member states (MS) can voluntarily use ideas or knowledge emanating from the EU. In the context of the ongoing global financial crisis and the sovereign debt crisis which followed in Europe, EU actors have sought to increase coherence between economic and fiscal policies in an attempt to restore financial stability in the Eurozone. This involves altered and new instruments for social and labour market policy governance being determined almost entirely by economically oriented actors. Also the socially oriented actors are considering new ideas around social and labour market policy coordination, but through less powerful instruments. Thus far, no systematic comparison has been made of these instruments, which is necessary in view of their potential impact on welfare states.

This chapter provides a comparison of selected EU instruments for economic and social policy coordination before and after the onset of the sovereign debt crisis. It analyses the direct and indirect effects that selected instruments may have on national welfare reforms by developing a typology to capture their type and degree of 'integration' effect. The analysis of integration of various EU instruments on national social and labour market policy is important, since these are areas where MS are still formally sovereign, or at least semi-sovereign (Ferrera 2005)

1   Special thanks to the editors Eleni Xiarchogiannopoulou and Maria Rodrigues for very helpful comments. Thanks also to participants of the workshop 'The Transformation of EU Governance and Its International Implications' held in Brussels in April 2013 and to the participants of the seminar 'The Sovereign Debt Crisis, the EU and Welfare State Reform' held in Odense in May 2013 for constructive comments on an earlier draft. We would like to thank Jochen Clasen for detailed suggestions.

and intrusion (through increased integration effects) into these areas would raise questions of democratic legitimacy (Scharpf 2011; Streeck 2011). We argue in this chapter that the altered and new instruments potentially have a more integrative effect (and potentially also more intrusive in extreme cases) on national welfare states and labour markets than the pre-crisis instruments.

2. Conceptualisation of Integration

We develop a typology of 'integration' along three dimensions (interference, surveillance, coercion) to capture how a particular instrument may affect national policy, directly or indirectly. In our typology (Table 10.1), four degrees of integration (from low to very high) are suggested for each dimension. In the empirical analysis that follows, we consider the balance of actors involved in each instrument along our three dimensions, that is, in devising policy aims (which could involve more or less interference in MS policies), in the surveillance process and/or in ensuring coercion. Based on our insights into the different processes, we argue that including employment and social policy actors (or other issue-specific actors) within a policy process provides a more comprehensive approach, compared to processes driven exclusively or mainly by actors in economic and financial affairs.

The first dimension of integration is interference in national policy, that is, the extent to which the EU interferes in MS sovereignty in labour market and social policy – where EU competencies are marginal – by requiring policy changes in these areas. This may lead to controversy about, or resistance against, the EU policy intervention at national level among populations and/or among political elites. In other words, interference assesses the extent to which an EU measure meddles with existing welfare state arrangements. There are some areas which all MS would regard as interference, such as EU intervention in taxation or wage policy. Other issues, e.g. childcare policies, may be considered to be interfering in some MS, such as the familialistic southern European welfare states.

The second dimension of integration is the surveillance of national policy by EU actors (Rodrigues 2002), which addresses the extent to which the EU is endowed with power to control whether MS are implementing the agreed policies and respecting or moving towards EU benchmarks and/or national targets. The strength of surveillance is, on the one hand, indicated by the frequency of surveillance as a marker of the genuine level of policy monitoring. On the other hand, it is also important which EU actors are involved in a particular surveillance process. Some EU actors, namely economic and financial actors, operate in areas where the EU has strong jurisdiction, in particular policy coordination around the Maastricht criteria (3% budget deficit and 60% public debt), so that surveillance is based on hard law. These actors have more power than others, such as employment and social affairs actors, where the EU has only weak legislative competence. Contingent factors like exogenous shocks or political party majorities in the Council may also influence the involvement of various EU actors. Social policy,

Table 10.1   Typology of 'integration'

Dimension of integration	Degree of integration			
	Low	Medium	High	Very high
Interference NB. This may differ according to the type of welfare state (and policy area)	Uncontroversial objectives, not challenging existent MS policies or institutional arrangements, merely suggesting some minor adjustments in a particular policy area.	Objectives challenging some existing policies, but not the underlying institutional structure of a policy area.	Objectives requiring comprehensive policy reform with the potential for undermining the existing institutional structure and fundamental principles of a policy area.	Objectives requiring far-reaching structural policy reform with a high potential for undermining the existing institutional structure and for changing the fundamental principles of a policy area.
Surveillance	Infrequent *ex-post* EU surveillance of national policy reports.	Frequent *ex-post* surveillance of national reports that specify policy which should meet common benchmarks and/ or own national targets.	Regular *ex-ante* and *ex-post* EU surveillance of national policy reports. MS are held accountable to EU benchmarks and are required to specify national targets and action plan to meet these.	Frequent *ex-ante* and *ex-post* EU surveillance of national policy reports. MS are held accountable to their own policies (which must aim to meet European targets and/or policy).
Coercion	'Naming and shaming' and/ or soft recommendations (with a weak treaty base).	Strong treaty-based recommendations, but no sanctions.	Treaty-based recommendations and ultimately financial sanctions in the case of non-compliance.	Treaty-based corrective action and/or conditionality in order to receive financial assistance.

Source: Own conceptualisation

social cohesion and quality in work were high on the agenda when there were a majority of left-leaning governments in the EU (see de la Porte 2011).

The third dimension of integration is coercion, referring to the type of measures EU actors have at their disposal to ensure corrective action in the case of non-compliance or deviation from EU policy. The strongest form of coercion is financial conditionality, such as in a Memorandum of Understanding. Other forms include political sanctions, which could in the most extreme cases refer to exclusion from particular aspects of EU integration, such as EMU. This option, however, is not seen as viable among the European elites, due to the fear that it would lead to a domino effect and ultimately the dismantling of EMU (Scharpf 2011). Softer forms of political sanctioning may involve brandishing of a MS as a bad performer in a benchmarking process. Depending on political culture, some countries may be more sensitive to such 'naming and shaming' than others (Barbier 2008). Other types of coercion include country-specific policy recommendations or softer policy advice in overall performance assessments. In assessing coercion, it is important to take account of the institutional power balance between European institutions and MS. For example, if a Qualified Majority Vote (QMV) in the Council is necessary to impose a sanction, this means that MS have more leverage than European actors. By contrast, a Reverse Qualified Majority Vote (RQMV) gives more power to the European Commission, because a qualified majority of MS would need to agree not to implement a sanction.

This typology is used to analyse EU governance instruments affecting social and labour market policy before and after the onset of the 2008 financial crisis. We distinguish between two types of instruments affecting social and labour market policy. These are firstly, instruments aimed at the sustainability of public finances, but which put indirect pressure on welfare state policies, and secondly, instruments that aim at re-calibrating social and labour market policy. Recalibration refers, firstly, to developing new policies in line with new circumstances, such as childcare institutions to ensure cognitive development of children and to facilitate female labour market participation, central in the social investment paradigm. Social investment refers to investment in the capabilities of individuals throughout the life-course to have high rates of labour market participation, and in order to ensure that welfare states are socially and economically sustainable (Morel et al. 2012). Secondly, it refers to adapting existing arrangements in order for particular programmes to meet their original aims, such as sickness insurance (Pierson 2001).

3. The Stability and Growth Pact (SGP) for Fiscal Consolidation

The SGP Before the Crisis

European Integration took on an entirely new turn with the Maastricht Treaty (1991), which institutionalised EMU. Monetary policy was pooled at EU level, with the independent ECB as the key player, setting the interest rate based on the average performance of EMU economies. EMU also deprived MS of the ability to adjust exchange rates in response to economic problems. The belief was that a common monetarist policy would have an integrative effect with positive spill-over effects from monetary to economic policy and eventually to other areas, such as social policy (Scharpf 2002, 2011; Degryse 2012).

The micro-foundations of monetarism lie in neo-classical economic theory and are associated with various supply-side policy solutions, such as tax cuts, privatisation, liberalisation and de-regulation. Formally, the ECB does not have the power to propose such policies (Scharpf 2011). Nevertheless, social policy came under pressure via the fiscal consolidation aims, necessary for the establishment and functioning of the the the EMU. As a consequence, public expenditure – of which pensions and health care are important components – became the object of close European scrutiny.

EMU governance pre-crisis consisted of strict legally binding fiscal monitoring of MS by the European Commission and the Council of Ministers through policy coordination in the SGP that stipulated a maximum limit for budget deficits of 3 per cent GDP, and public debt of maximum 60 per cent GDP (or falling). The 'preventative arm' of the SGP prescribes the measures for sound fiscal policies. Before the crisis, MS had to annually submit their medium-term budgetary plans in stability programmes (Eurozone members) or convergence programmes (members outside of the Eurozone), to illustrate their efforts with regard to the objectives of the SGP.

A second 'corrective arm' of the SGP prescribed 'hard' remedial action through an 'Excessive Deficit Procedure' (EDP) in case the 3 per cent budget deficit criterion was violated. The public debt level – at maximum 60 per cent GDP or falling – was 'unavoidably imprecise' and thereby non-sanctionable (Hodson and Maher 2004: 801). If corrective action under the EDP remained absent after multiple warnings, the Commission and the Council could issue a pecuniary fine for Eurozone members and, for all countries, the possible suspension of support from the Cohesion Fund until the excessive deficit was corrected (Degryse 2012).

The *interference* of the SGP with MS policies was *high* – sound fiscal policies were a pre-condition for EMU membership, which required strict discipline with regard to the set ceiling for government deficit that had to be respected permanently among Eurozone members. For some countries, such as Germany, this initially posed only little pressure, since the EMU was developed on the basis of the German model, consisting of a centralised monetary policy and with it, a central bank. In other countries eager to join the EMU from the outset, such as Spain, Portugal or Italy, a series of reforms was undertaken to meet the entry criteria of the SGP. In particular, tri-partite social pacts were agreed on fiscal and labour market policy to enhance competitiveness (Fajertag and Pochet 2000).

EU *surveillance* via the SGP was *medium* – fiscal surveillance took place annually and was overseen by the Directorate-General for Economic and Financial Affairs (DG ECFIN) and the Economic and Financial Affairs Council (Ecofin), with a treaty base for their activity. *Coercion* was formally high, as non-compliance with the budget deficit criterion could lead to an EDP that required corrective action and in the event of continued non-compliance, the Council could impose financial sanctions. However, in order to issue country-specific recommendations or an EDP, a qualified majority of MS needed to be in favour of this. In practice, the SGP has proven to be non-enforceable against big MS such as Germany and France, which were drivers of its creation, yet both ran excessive deficits after the SGP came into force and were under the EDP for some years (Howarth 2007). In fact, of the then 27 EU members, 13 have been under the EDP before the onset of the crisis in 2008 (Table 10.2).

Table 10.2   Excessive Deficit Procedures starting before 2008

MS	EDP period
Czech Republic	2004–2008
Cyprus	2004–2006
France	2003–2007
Germany	2002–2007
Greece	2004–2007
Hungary	2004–2013
Italy	2005–2008
Malta	2004–2007
Netherlands	2004–2005
Poland	2004–2008
Portugal	2002– 2004; 2005–2008
Slovakia	2004–2008
United Kingdom	2004 and 2005–2007

Source: http://ec.europa.eu/economy_finance/economic_governance/sgp/deficit/index_en. htm (last accessed 30 May 2013)

The members aiming to be members of EMU show efforts to meet convergence criteria in their convergence programmes, while full EMU members show how they continue to meet the criteria or in the case of an EDP, how they plan to correct the breach of the deficit criterion to meet the deadline set by the Commission for this. Most countries then adopted policies to reconsolidate public finances, which the European Commission closely monitored, in collaboration with Finance Ministries (see de la Porte and Natali 2014 for a recent case study). In some cases, more time was given to consolidate public finances, so the period for surveillance was extended. In yet other cases, policies required to comply with the convergence criteria were not adopted and the fiscal situation did not improve. But even when that was the case, financial sanctions were not levied. The Ecofin Council was reluctant to trigger sanctions against MS, but at the time, markets did not react adversely to the inaction of Ecofin.

There were limitations to SGP since the bigger Member States had some political room for manouevure: when Germany and France, did not fulfill their obligations under their respective EDPs, the Commisison's recommendations to step up the EDPs were vetoed in the Council. Following pressure from Germany and France, in 2005 the SGP was altered, to take due account of public investments that would bear success in the future. The SGP had thus been criticised for its weak enforcement of the deficit rule, as well as the neglect of the debt criterion (de Haan et al. 2004). Hodson and Maher (2004: 809) argued that the SGP has from the outset been a highly discretionary instrument in the realm of soft law. On the basis of the capability of some member states to negotiate whether and if so when and how to meet the excessive deficit criterion, we assess that *coercion* was *de facto* only *medium*.

The SGP Since the Crisis

Since the 2008 global financial crisis and the sovereign debt crisis which followed in Europe, EU actors (especially the ECB, DG ECFIN and the Ecofin Council) have sought to increase coherence between economic, financial and fiscal policies, in an attempt to restore financial stability in the Eurozone. In addition, efforts have been made to enhance both *ex-ante* and *ex-post* surveillance of policies and to increase coercion, especially increasing possibilities for sanctions in case of deviation from agreed policies or benchmarks. The revised SGP and new instruments are coordinated jointly in the 'European Semester', which includes first and foremost policies of fiscal consolidation and, at the very end of the list, policies for social sustainability of European welfare states. In the following, we present the core features of the European Semester and central instruments – the Fiscal Compact (FC) and the six-pack – within it. Thereafter, we present the Europe 2020 strategy – also integrated into the European Semester – with an emphasis on its social policy aims.

Instruments for Sustainability of Public Finances (2008–Present)

In 2010, the European Semester was developed in order to coordinate *ex ante* the budgetary and economic policies of MS and to increase coherence among different policies. More specifically, EU-level discussions take place prior to MS drawing up their annual draft budgets *and* on a broader palette of policy areas (with accompanying indicators), including macroeconomic imbalances, financial sector issues, and structural reforms. The European Semester is launched by the European Commission (DG ECFIN) via an Annual Growth Survey (AGS) (European Commission 2013d). The 2011 AGS, for example, focused on fiscal consolidation, labour market reforms, and 'growth enhancing measures' (European Commission 2010g). Following the AGS, country-specific recommendations are made to MS on the basis of a DG ECFIN proposal that must be approved by Ecofin through QMV and is then to be endorsed by the European Council. The AGS explicitly includes policy advice on 'social consequences of the crisis', with a focus on how to deal with the citizens hit by the crisis, in particular young people. In this regard, the AGS promotes active labour market policies, such as job search or training, as a way back to employment, with social protection systems as a last resort. In addition, the AGS promotes business creation and self-employment, although in particular the latter can be very precarious in a crisis context. The policy priorities decided in the AGS should be included in MS Stability or Convergence programmes (concerning monetary policy) devised within the SGP and in NRPs (concerning economic, employment and social policies) devised within Europe 2020. The European Semester and the AGS are therefore very powerful for the agenda-setting process.

The six-pack and the FC aim to reinforce the policy aims of the European Semester and to enhance EU surveillance of MS policies and coercion in the case of non-compliance. Both initiatives provide the European institutions with more surveillance power vis-à-vis the national budgets of MS compared to pre-crisis and are designed to reinforce the implementation of the SGP and the European Semester within which they are embedded.

The six-pack came into force in December 2011 (consisting of five Regulations and one Directive)[2] and applies to all 27 MS, but with some specific rules for Eurozone members, especially regarding financial sanctions. The six-pack covers not only fiscal, but also macroeconomic surveillance under the new 'Macroeconomic Imbalance Procedure' (MIP), which aims to be more broad-ranging than the former SGP which focused only on public finances. Under the six-pack, member states' budget balance should converge towards country-specific Medium-Term Objectives (MTOs) (relating to the SGP's preventative arm). Stricter application of fiscal rules should be ensured by defining quantitatively what a 'significant deviation' from the MTO, or the adjustment path towards it, means. The six-pack also reinforces the corrective arm of the SGP, that is, the EDP, which applies to MS that have breached either the deficit *or* the debt criterion (the latter not being operational before the six-pack). Another important novelty is that the six-pack introduces RQMV for deciding on sanctions. This means that a qualified majority of MS (in Ecofin) must be against a Commission (DG ECFIN) proposal for an EDP, or for a sanction to be overturned. This constitutes a very clear increase in power for the European Commission, especially DG ECFIN.

The FC, signed in March 2012 by all EU members except the Czech Republic and the United Kingdom, applies to all Eurozone members and, upon their discretion, also to non-Eurozone countries. It further strengthens the balanced budget rules

---

2   The six parts are the: (1) strengthening surveillance of budgetary positions and coordination of economic policies, (2) acceleration and clarification of the EDP through a Council regulation, (3) enforcement of budgetary surveillance in the Eurozone through a regulation, (4) definition of a budgetary framework of the MS through a Directive, (5) prevention and correction of macroeconomic imbalances through a regulation, (6) enforcement of measures for correcting excessive macroeconomic imbalances in the Eurozone.

of the SGP, with an additional limit of 0.5 per cent of GDP on structural deficits (that can be extended to 1 per cent in exceptional circumstances). The FC requires these budget rules to be integrated in national law, preferably at constitutional level. Corrective mechanisms at national level will be triggered automatically in case of deviation from the MTO or the adjustment path towards it. Likewise, the automatism of the EDP has been strengthened. Should a country fail to transpose the budget rules and the correction mechanism on time, the European Court of Justice has the jurisdiction to take a decision on the matter, including the imposition of a financial sanction (up to 0.1 per cent of GDP) (European Central Bank 2012: 83).

Contrasting with the pre-crisis period, the European Semester takes account of the whole economy via the MIP, and not just budget deficits and public debt. This is because it became clear to European actors that taking account of budgetary discipline alone would not suffice for economic growth or crisis prevention. The MIP thus focuses on total (public and private) debt, current account balances, unit labour costs, real effective exchange rates and other indicators that cover overall national economic performance. While this is designed to ensure early intervention in economies which are overheating, most of the indicators of the MIP are not under direct control of governments (Scharpf 2011: 33). Since the MIP is the central instrument on which European actors formulate national recommendations and, more crucially, launch an EDP in the case of non-compliance, *interference* in MS policies is *high*, as controversial structural adjustments are suggested following the MIP, including the privatisation of public services, labour market flexibilisation, tax reforms, liberalisation of product and service markets as well as social spending cuts (DG ECFIN 2012).

Surveillance is also reinforced – it is very frequent when a country is under EDP – and coercion is high – an interest-bearing deposit of 0.2 per cent of GDP may be imposed if insufficient progress is made towards the MTOs of Eurozone MS (European Parliament and European Council 2011). Thus sanctions can be implemented quite early on if certain targets are missed.

Table 10.3 shows a notable increase in the number of countries under an EDP since the financial and economic crisis set in (from 13 to 24). At the time of writing, it remains to be seen to what extent this is followed by stricter action than in the pre-crisis period. It has to be noted, however, that the if economic circumstances are adverse, recommendation to reduce the deficit are prolonged or even stopped temporarily, as long as effective action (recommended policies) has been taken. On this basis, in May 2013 six countries were granted an extension to rectify their deficits (European Commission 2013e: 6–7).

There is no doubt that for countries which are under special EU-IMF financial rescue packages (Greece, Ireland, Portugal and Cyprus) EU integration, through conditional financial support (EU-IMF loans) in exchange for structural reform, has increased to very high levels. Memoranda of Understanding (MoUs) specify in detail the policy measures that have to be implemented, often highly interfering with existing institutional designs. Monitoring takes place very frequently under MoUs.

Table 10.3   Excessive Deficit Procedures started after 2008

MS	EDP period
Austria	2009–ongoing
Belgium	2009–ongoing (EDP recommended to be stepped up in 05/2013)
Bulgaria	2010–2012
Czech Republic	2009–recommended to be abrogated in 05/2013
Cyprus	2010–ongoing (under MoU)
Denmark	2010–ongoing
Finland	2010–2011
France	2009–ongoing
Germany	2009–2012
Greece	2009–ongoing (under MoU)
Ireland	2009-ongoing (under MoU)
Italy	2009–2013
Latvia	2009–2013
Lithuania	2009–2013
Luxembourg	2010
Malta	2009–2012; new EDP recommended in 05/2013
Netherlands	2009–ongoing
Poland	2009–ongoing
Portugal	2009–ongoing (under MoU)
Romania	2009–2013
Slovakia	2009–ongoing
Slovenia	2009–ongoing
Spain	2009–ongoing
United Kingdom	2008–ongoing

Source: http://ec.europa.eu/economy_finance/economic_governance/sgp/deficit/index_en.htm.

4. Instruments for Re-calibrating Social and Labour Market Policy

Before the Crisis: The European Employment Strategy (EES) and the Lisbon Strategy

The policy coordination stipulated by the SGP gave rise to concerns about the limitations to MS autonomy in core redistributive areas. A political consensus among left parties in the Council in the mid-1990s led to an agreement on supplementing monetary and economic policy coordination with a similar, albeit softer, coordination procedure for social and labour market policies: the European Employment Strategy (EES), the first 'Open Method of Coordination' (OMC) (de la Porte 2011). The OMC became an important instrument to support MS in welfare state reform, in the view of common challenges, such as population ageing (Jæger and Kvist 2003) and built on ideas of 'social investment' (Morel et al. 2012).

The aim of the EES – integrated in the Amsterdam Treaty of 1997 – was to develop a highly skilled labour force and to achieve high levels of employment. The ambition was to create 'more and better jobs', hence not only boosting employment growth, but also maximising its quality with a view to shaping a competitive, knowledge-based economy. The policies initially promoted in the EES (and later in other social OMCs) resonate with the normative notion of a 'European Social Model' (Jepsen and Serrano Pascual 2005), associated with a high level of social protection and high rates of labour market participation. Activation, 'making work pay', and quality of work were key notions. The promotion of equal opportunities between men and women was also central, including the aim to develop childcare institutions. The EES was, however, subordinate to the monetarist policy framework established via the EMU. Since the EES – requiring considerable financial investments – was to be implemented in the context of the EMU – requiring fiscal consolidation – the inherent risk was that comprehensive social investment would not materialise (de la Porte and Jacobsson 2012).

The EES was nevertheless considered an appropriate way to address common challenges, while being adaptable to different welfare state types. On this basis, the Lisbon European Council in 2000 institutionalised the OMC as a voluntary non-treaty based mechanism for MS to confront common challenges in sensitive areas. The codified 'Lisbon Strategy' aimed to put economic policy and competitiveness on an equal footing with employment and social policy (European Council 2000). This included the EU benchmark of reaching an average employment rate of 70 per cent for the EU by 2010 (and 60 per cent for women as well as 50 per cent for older workers) (European Council 2000, 2001). There were high hopes that the Lisbon Strategy – strengthened with quantitative benchmarks – would be an effective vehicle for achieving activation, training, and high levels of (quality) employment.

The EES represented a *medium* degree of *interference* into national policies because of its promotion of high employment rates as well as family-friendly and activation policies. Particular pressure was put on countries with low rates of female and older worker participation. Furthermore, it also included more sensitive issues, such as the reduction of non-wage labour costs, and flexicurity – the combination of flexible labour markets, activation and social security – which was resisted by many unions who feared that it would be interpreted exclusively as labour market flexibility (Viebrock and Clasen 2009). Indeed, empirical evidence suggests that in countries that have caught on to the flexicurity buzzword, there has been most focus on labour market de-regulation. After 2005, the EES became more narrowly focused on boosting labour supply, skills enhancement and the improvement of education systems. The aims relating to gender equality and reconciling work and family life were put in the background. Impact analyses of the EES have revealed that activation as conceived in the EES has been influential discursively, but has only marginally been used as a resource through which to develop a comprehensive social investment policy, albeit with important cross-regime variation (de la Porte and Jacobsson 2012).

The *surveillance* in the EES was *low* for several reasons. First, although the EES has a treaty base, it is a voluntary policy coordination process. All MS participate in the process, but the extent to which they actually meet EES objectives is, ultimately, voluntary. The iterative policy cycle consists of setting common EU objectives (further specified by common benchmarks and EU indicators); regular National Action Plans (NAPs), designed to show what MS had done to meet employment policy objectives and to present their future plans in light of EES objectives; and monitoring and evaluation of these strategies jointly by the European Commission and the MS. The process was yearly until 2005, after which NAPs became more closely integrated with economic policy coordination in three-yearly National Reform Programmes (NRPs).

The Lisbon European Council strengthened the Employment and Social Affairs Council, since it aimed to put various Council formations on an equal footing with the Ecofin Council. This equally implied that the Directorate-General Employment, Social Affairs and Inclusion (DG EMPL) was strengthened vis-à-vis DG ECFIN (Rodrigues 2002). After 2005, however, when the EES became more strongly integrated with economic policy coordination (de Roose et al. 2008), the influence of DG ECFIN and the Ecofin Council increased. At the same time, a 'Mr. or Mrs. Lisbon' – often a Prime Minister or Finance Minister – was designated in each MS to ensure that the objectives of the Lisbon Strategy were integrated in national political processes, with mixed results (Borras and Peters 2011). Although economic and employment policy were coordinated jointly after 2005, surveillance remained low (de Roose et al. 2008).

Coercion of the EES was also *low*. Since 1998, the EES has involved country-specific recommendations, to be approved via QMV in the Council. However, compliance with the policy objectives, highlighted in country recommendations, was encouraged, but could not be enforced (de la Porte 2011). Indeed, the thought behind the social OMCs was that they should prompt transnational discussions and propose interesting ideas in a context where MS would be required to reform their welfare states due to common challenges. There is evidence that the ideas developed through the OMCs, and especially via the country-specific recommendations have at times been sources of inspiration for reforms (de la Porte and Jacobsson 2012). Yet, the EES only provided a legally non-binding framework of political coordination, leaving responsibility for reforms with MS.

Instruments for Re-calibrating Social Policy Since the Crisis: Europe 2020

In 2010, a new strategy coined 'Europe 2020' replaced the Lisbon Strategy, within which the instruments for re-calibrating social policy – in particular the EES – are embedded. In the EU's revamped strategy to deliver 'smart, sustainable and inclusive' growth, the aim to increase labour market participation – to 75 per cent by 2020 – stands stronger than ever (EU Commission 2010b). The link with the

SGP is much closer as well, since Europe 2020 is integrated into the European Semester. The assessment of the cause of the crisis by European economic elites and technocrats is that some countries have not paid sufficient attention to structural reforms. The main aim stipulated is therefore to undertake structural reforms 'of pensions, health care, social protection and education systems ... in order to achieve fiscal consolidation and long-term financial sustainability' (European Commission 2010h: 26).

Also, Europe 2020 is dominated by DG ECFIN and the Ecofin Council with a very marginal role for the European social policy actors (Pochet 2010). Europe 2020 is, aside re-iterating core aims of fiscal consolidation as stated in the SGP, designed to deliver growth, if possible, socially sustainable growth. However, as noted by Barnard (2012), this strategy is dependent on significant government expenditure, which governments encumbered by sovereign debt are hardly able to provide.

Although there have been remarkable increases in employment rates since the launch of the Lisbon Strategy, this was for the most part achieved through atypical contracts, providing little security for workers (Emmenegger et al. 2012). Unsurprisingly, atypical workers have been hit first by the crisis. Where employment has started to pick up again, we find a remarkably high proportion of non-standard contracts (Leschke 2012). Contrary to the optimistic social agenda that characterised the original Lisbon Strategy, Europe 2020 is silent on the previously prominent issue of quality of work. However, on a more positive note, the European Commission has launched a Social Investment Package, aimed at investing in individuals throughout the lifecourse, particularly focused on human capital development (European Commission, 2013f).

The potential integrative effect of Europe 2020 is the same as under the EES and much weaker as regards all three dimensions than the new fiscal policy instruments (Table 10.4). Only where Europe 2020 overlaps with the revised SGP is EU integration enhanced, as the FC and the six-pack clearly strengthens the European actors (especially DG ECFIN) to survey MS policies and economic indicators, as well as ensure coercion, since an EDP is easier to launch and sanctions are easier to impose through RQMV in the case of non-compliance.

Table 10.4   Integration effects of main EU fiscal and social instruments before and after the crisis

	Interference	Surveillance	Coercion
SGP (pre-crisis)	High	Medium	Medium
EES	Medium	Low	Low
Six-pack and FC	High	High	High
Europe 2020	Medium	Low	Low

In sum, the European Semester and the instruments designed to reinforce it are highly intrusive on the dimensions of policy interference, surveillance and coercion. Both the six-pack and the FC really give the European Semester and the SGP bite, which was not the case before the crisis. It is also to be noted that in the context of the crisis, it is mainly the actors in economic and financial affairs that set the agenda, while the labour market and social policy actors have less voice. However, there are attempts to develop a social investment policy approach among the socially oriented actors in the Commission (Kvist 2013; European Commission 2013).

5. Conclusion

Our analysis has shown that in the perpetuation of economic difficulties in the EU, European leaders have strengthened the existing European instruments and developed new ones to enhance compliance with EU economic and financial aims, which also affect welfare states indirectly. In the context of the crisis, it is along the dimensions of surveillance and coercion that integration effects of EU instruments for economic and financial policy coordination – European Semester, Stability and Growth Pack, the six-pack and the fiscal compact - has increased. The sharpened old and new instruments have increased the power of the EU, especially the economically oriented actors, to insist on national fiscal discipline, a necessary condition for the Eurozone to function. Indeed, if the instruments are applied correctly, then European economies should beome more competitive and welfare states would be reformed around social investment. But there are risks that tough austerity and the cost containment that has accompanied this undermines European welfare states.

The instruments designed to coordinate employment, social and labour market policy – that is Europe 2020 and especially the European employment strategy - are not sharper compared to before the crisis. While there are attempts to tackle youth unemployment and to encourage social investment policies, particularly in DG employment and the social affairs and employment Council, the available instruments are unlikely to have much impact on MS. This is particularly the case where most governments are still struggling to cope with recession, public debt and budget deficits and thus lacking the resources to develop comprehensive social investment policies.

PART IV
The International Dimension of the Transformation of EU Governance

Chapter 11

The Eurozone Crisis and the Transformation of EU Economic Governance: From Internal Policies to External Action

Maria João Rodrigues

European Union economic governance is being transformed by the combined effects of a sequence of different crises:

- the limits of a growth model which is no longer sustainable in the present context of globalisation;
- the financial crisis which started in 2008;
- the economic and social crises which have followed;
- the Eurozone crisis combining sovereign debt with bank debt and exposing the imbalances in the Eurozone and the flaws of the European Monetary Union (EMU) architecture;
- the crisis of EU integration triggered by the need for major reforms in the Economic and Monetary Union.

This transformation of the European Union governance can also have very relevant consequences for:

- its external action;
- its external role as a laboratory for multilateralism.

This chapter will focus on the implications of the Eurozone crisis for the reshaping of EU economic governance. It will elaborate on the possible choices for pursuing this process in the larger framework of the European Union as a laboratory for multilateralism and supra-national governance. Some lessons from the available international experience will also be drawn. The impact of the Eurozone crisis on the EU external action will also be analysed.

1. The Transformation of the EU Economic Governance: A New Framework for Economic Governance

Over three years of intensive political creativity, a new framework for the EU economic governance was developed to address the key problems of the EMU. This new framework can be summed up as follows:

Regarding *fiscal discipline* (with new legislation to reform the Stability and Growth Pact/SGP, and the new Intergovernmental Treaty on Stability, Coordination and Governance):

- a commitment to balanced budgets;
- a new focus on public debt and not only on deficits;
- a reference to the structural deficit complementing the usual reference to the nominal deficit;
- more automatic and tougher sanctions;
- closer monitoring of the Member States (MS) under financial assistance;
- many new commitments to structural reforms and spending cuts made by the MS.

Regarding *financial stability*:

- new regulations for financial systems concerning capital requirements, hedge and equity funds, some derivatives and bonuses;
- new European supervisory bodies and regular stress tests on banks;
- instruments to respond to sovereign debt crisis – European Financial Stability Facility (EFSF) and European Stability Mechanism (ESM);
- new roles for the European Central Bank (ECB).

Regarding *growth* (Europe 2020 Strategy):

- a long-term strategic commitment for smarter, greener and inclusive growth;
- European flagship initiatives;
- national reform programmes;
- an Annual Growth Survey and recommendations for the MS.

Regarding *macroeconomic imbalances* (with new legislation):

- A new process of macroeconomic surveillance, to monitor major problems of external and internal economic and social imbalances, with a more symmetrical approach.

Regarding *governance* (with legislation and a new Treaty):

- reorganisation of the annual cycle to prepare national budgets and national reform programmes with *ex-ante* European coordination, meaning more shared sovereignty (European Semester);
- regular Eurozone summits with a permanent President and leading team, including the President of the European Commission and the President of the Eurogroup; an inclusive approach regarding the MS willing to join;
- involvement of the national parliaments and the European Parliament (EP) in the discussion of Eurozone issues;
- more systematic coordination of the EU with its international partners (the International Monetary Fund (IMF) and the G20).

But There Are Still Many Problems...

Despite these important policy developments, the Eurozone crisis is still going on. The problems include:

- unsustainable debt levels in some countries;
- diverging levels of borrowing costs between countries;
- diverging growth trends, in several instances negative;
- a general trend towards recession and rising unemployment;
- increasing spill-over effects for the global economy: the Eurozone crisis has become a global problem;
- political opposition to further European solidarity in some MS;
- political opposition to more structural reforms, taxes and spending cuts in other MS;
- a widespread sense of a loss of democratic control over general living conditions. Europe is perceived by many as strongly shaping their lives, but not susceptible to democratic influence at national level.

In fact, these problems are so deep and central in many MS that the exit from this crisis can shape the future not only of the EMU, but also of European integration and Europe's position and role in the world.

... and Two Different Narratives

Furthermore, there are currently two very different narratives about the ongoing Eurozone crisis: a crisis *in* the Eurozone or a crisis *of* the Eurozone. According to the first version, the main problem is to do with the lack of fiscal discipline in some peripheral countries which led to unsustainable public debts damaging the credibility of the Euro. Hence, the logical solution should be to strengthen fiscal discipline and to impose austerity, even at the cost of recession in these countries.

According to the second version, the need to strengthen fiscal responsibility is also accepted, but a more comprehensive diagnosis is proposed. Some fiscal and macro-imbalances were already at work before the financial crisis, but they were worsened by this crisis which led to a deep recession and high unemployment. Special public stimulus packages were necessary to avoid depression and to rescue failing banks, but they increased public deficits and debts. This shock has hit the Eurozone as a whole, but the recovery process became more difficult for the MS with less fiscal space and/or less reliance on exports, outside of Europe. In this second version of what is happening, there are two reasons to consider why we are facing a systemic crisis of the Eurozone:

1. While some differences in the spreads across MS can be accepted as normal, the wide divergences are worrying, because they are also turning into divergences of their investment conditions, their growth and employment rates, as well as their public deficits and debts.
2. These cumulative divergences are magnified by the interaction between sovereign debts and banks' debts and the risks of contagion. This has led to a fragmentation of the European banking system, hindering the normal circulation of capital and the access to credit in the Eurozone.

Behind this systemic crisis, it is possible to identify some important flaws in the architecture of the Economic and Monetary Union. That is why a comparison with the available experience of monetary zones can be relevant.

2. Comparing the EMU with the International Experience

Can a monetary union survive without a fiscal union, and can this work without a political union? Furthermore, can an economic union be sustainable without a social dimension? The EMU and, more generally, the process of European integration is confronted with crucial choices. This chapter will also draw on some lessons of existing monetary, fiscal and political unions, to debate on the ways to complete the EMU.

Can Monetary Integration Work Without Fiscal Integration?

What are the basic conditions for a monetary zone to work and survive? A rich and long international experience tells us two basic conditions are required (Castells and EuropeG 2012: 1):

1. sufficiently integrated markets and mobility of factors to facilitate a certain degree of convergence between the competitiveness of the MS;
2. monetary integration must be coupled with a considerable degree of fiscal integration.

The European debate recognises these two conditions, but is divided about the importance to be given to the convergence objective, as well as the meaning to be given to fiscal integration: for some, this is just about defining and enforcing a common fiscal discipline, while for others, it is also about coupling this common fiscal discipline with a common budget, based on some common taxes and with better instruments to issue and manage public debt.

The available international experience shows that fiscal unions with shared currency have a basic set of similar features:

- common principles of fiscal discipline in the sub-central governments;
- in this common framework, sub-central governments enjoy different degrees of fiscal autonomy to meet their financial obligations with their own fiscal resources;
- a central government with a relevant budget based on own tax resources and a Treasury responsible to issue common debt.

The roles of this central government budget are usually the following:

- a macroeconomic stabilisation and anti-cyclical function to protect regions under asymmetric shock, whatever their relative level of wealth (richer or poorer regions);
- a mutualisation of risks if there is mutualisation of the decision-making, notably on issuing public debt;
- a redistributive function, involving a transfer of resources from more competitive and wealthy regions to less competitive and wealthy ones. A Vertical Fiscal Imbalance (VFI) between income and spending is accepted to enable this redistribution, provided free rider and moral hazard are prevented (Hueglin and Fenna 2006).

The fiscal union in the European Economic and Monetary Union has precise principles of a common fiscal discipline, but:

- its macroeconomic stabilisation function remains very weak, because its instruments at national level are reduced to very a tight fiscal room for manoeuvre and they are not complemented by instruments at European level;
- it is silent about the need for a Eurozone budget and its possible roles. The discussion about equipping the Eurozone with some kind of 'fiscal capacity' has just started;
- it is still incipient about the possible ways to mutualise risks and decision-making about debt issuance. The ESM is used to issuing Eurobonds on a small scale but the discussion of conditions to issue Eurobonds on a larger scale is being postponed;

- The EU Community budget plays a redistributive role but only on a small scale.

The Sequencing Between Monetary, Fiscal and Political Union

It is also important to analyse the sequence of steps in building this combination between monetary union, fiscal union and political union, according to available international experience. This sequence starts with political union first, fiscal union after and monetary union only after that.

The sequencing depends of course on concrete historical circumstances. In the American case or Canadian case, political union was a normal consequence of the Wars of Independence and fiscal union was first necessary to meet the costs of these wars. In the case of European integration, the predominant dimension which was chosen to consolidate peace after World War Two was the economic one with the single market leading and the need to adopt a single currency coming afterwards.

This was probably the only possible way to start European integration, but the problem is that the political and fiscal dimensions, which have been considered since the beginning, have always remained at an embryonic level. This is particularly clear in the Maastricht Treaty, where the Economic and Monetary Union was enshrined but coupled with limited concepts of fiscal union and of political union. The votes of European citizens can only influence a tiny Community budget (1 per cent of EU Gross Domestic Product – GDP), with even fewer own resources, which is used to support some European programmes and make some regional redistribution in the European Union.

Choosing Between Different Types of Fiscal Union

There are different types of fiscal union. It is also particularly relevant to compare the European and the international experiences regarding the political deal which was historically forged to underpin each type of fiscal union. In the typical American case, the Hamiltonian deal involved two crucial points which have equipped the federal government with a budget, own taxes and a Treasury:

- The American states accepted to transfer part of their tax collection power in exchange for the Federation assuming their excessive debts (due to the Independence War effort);
- The American states accepted rules of fiscal discipline and no federal bail-out in the future in exchange for counting on the role of a federal budget (which became bigger particularly after the New Deal in 1930).

Therefore, in the American type of fiscal union, the states have a relative fiscal autonomy, but they need to ensure their credibility because they are exposed to market pressure and they cannot count on bail-out mechanisms.

Nevertheless, there is another type of fiscal federalism where states need, on the one hand, to comply with the strict fiscal rules and decisions taken at federal level but, on the other hand, they can count on a federal budget and bail-out mechanisms in case of difficulty.

The European case so far is a hybrid one, combining the decreasing fiscal autonomy of MS with the building up of a last resort mechanism for bail-out with a strong conditionality for fiscal discipline. However, the Community budget remains very limited and without capacity for macroeconomic stabilisation. Furthermore, both the bail-out mechanism and the Community budget are mainly based on national guarantees and contributions.

Choosing Between Different Types of Political Union

That is why we also need to compare the European and the international experience regarding political union. First of all there are two different kinds of federalisation processes (Croisat and Quermonne 1996), through dis-aggregation, as in Belgium in 2013, or through aggregation, as in the United States of America (USA) or Germany. We will focus on the second type. The building up of a federation needs to be analysed as a process which can produce a continuum of constitutional arrangements from an alliance, a league and a confederation to a federation. Beyond the socio-economic federalism proposed by Proudhon in the nineteenth century, there are two main historical traditions of bringing together difficult entities (Hueglin and Fenna 2006):

- 'republican federalism' forged by Hamilton, based on citizens' rights and duties, elected federal government and parliament, and check and power balances between the three powers;
- 'consociational federalism' forged by Althusius in Germany in the seventeenth century, based on the principle of subsidiarity and a governance by a council of state representatives.

These two traditions have led to two basic different types of federalism and political union (Hueglin and Fenna 2006: 51, 60, 63, 162):

- divided federalism (as in the USA), where the states have full competences in some policy fields, but are complemented by the full competences of the federal level in other policy fields; and
- integrated or cooperative federalism (as in Germany), where states participate in the federal policy-decision and implementation in most of the policy fields and therefore, where the federal level depends on the state level to implement most of its decisions.

The European Union is not a federation for many reasons, including one basic one: the MS and not the European citizens remain masters of the EU Treaties

(Boerzel 2008). But against this comparative background we can conclude that the European Union, as it is defined by the Lisbon Treaty, is closer to the German type of political union because:

- in most of the policy fields, the competences are shared between the Union and the MS and the implementation of the EU decisions depend on the MS means of implementation.
- MS have an even stronger influence on European level decision-making – when compared with the German Länder in the Bundesrat – because the European Council and the Council of Ministers remain the central decision-making bodies in the European Union.

In fact, the EU offers a unique type of government, which is mainly council based, whereas the German or the Canadian models are more parliamentary based and the American more president based (Hueglin and Fenna 2006). Nevertheless, the Lisbon Treaty has also extended the policy areas covered by the so-called 'normal legislative procedure', where the proposition role by the European Commission and, most of all, the legislative role of the EP are stronger. Moreover, the Lisbon Treaty has also included a Charter of the European Citizens Fundamental Rights. In addition, the Lisbon Treaty has explicitly introduced the election of the President of the European Commission by the EP after being proposed by the European Council. The Lisbon Treaty is even admitting that the same person can be elected for the posts of President of the European Commission and President of the European Council. In any case, this gives European citizens a stronger role in the election of the EU executive power. We should also bear in mind that the territorial representation in the European Council, the Council and the EP is completed by the Committee of Regions and complemented by the socio-economic representation in the European Economic and Social Committee.

Hence, the European Union is a complex and dynamic construction driven by:

- centripetal forces shaped by the EP and the European Commission which are supposed to represent the 'Community interest';
- *more* centrifugal forces driven by the Council (an implicit second chamber), where national interests are more formally represented (Ricard-Nihoul 2012).

That is why the concept of 'Federation of Nation States' coined by the former President Jacques Delors seems particularly suggestive and appropriate (Delors and Vitorino 2012). New challenges and particularly the need to overcome the Eurozone crisis are pushing this construction to new developments and recognition of the following:

- the need to strengthen instruments at a European level in different policy fields – financial supervision and regulation debt management, investment, energy, trade and external action;
- the need to create a clearer chain of command in the executive power and particularly in the Eurozone;
- the need to politicise the choices for European citizens, and hence for a stronger role to be given to European political parties in shaping the executive and legislative powers;
- the need to empower and engage European citizens about these political choices.

3. Completing the EMU Architecture: The Key Issues

Against this comparative background we can better highlight the rationale behind the debate on how to complete the EMU, which was introduced on the European Council table by the document 'Towards a Genuine EMU' coordinated by President Van Rompuy and involving the Presidents of the European Commission, the Eurogroup and the European Central Bank. Four basic frameworks were identified to complete the EMU: financial, economic, budgetary and political.

In the financial framework, what is fundamentally at stake is to complete the monetary union, with more European integration regarding financial supervision and regulation, in order to restore the conditions for normal circulation of capital and cross-national investment in the Eurozone and for more responsible lending and borrowing. In the economic framework, the European strategy for a new growth model – greener, smarter and more inclusive – should be translated into a more effective coordination of national policies involving reforms and investments. A better follow-up and correction of the macroeconomic imbalances between MS should be also included. And another central objective for deepening the economic union should be to improve economic, environmental and social performance with more convergences rather than divergences between MS.

This will be impossible to achieve if in the budgetary framework the rules for common fiscal discipline are not complemented with a Eurozone budget, based on European taxes and providing the conditions for macroeconomic stabilisation and for a Eurozone Treasury to issue common debt via Eurobonds.

Why Impossible?

This is impossible because different specialisation patterns will expose the Eurozone MS to different asymmetric shocks, which can no longer be overcome by national instruments alone, and because the investment needs to ensure catching up and a certain level of convergence are different between MS. Therefore, national resources for public investment need to be complemented by some European resources in order to enable more real and structural convergence in the

Eurozone. The other – alternative or complementary – possibility would be to use this European Treasury to issue national debt via Eurobonds.

In any case, the legitimacy to decide on a Eurozone budget, European taxes and European debt issuance can only come from a European democratic body representing European citizens and electing a European executive body. These are new tasks for the EP and the European Commission. Nevertheless, the way to combine these new tasks with the European Council and Council of Ministers in their legislative and executive roles, and particularly, the way to develop a European government, will define whether the current Federation of Nation States will evolve to (a) a more federal architecture or (b) a more intergovernmental one.

4. The New Instruments of the EMU: A Critical Assessment

So far, the instruments which have been developed to cope with the Eurozone crisis have been designed more in the intergovernmental direction. Even when setting a new balance between national responsibility and European solidarity, the European dimension has mainly been understood as just a sum of the national dimensions. A paradigm of 'mutual insurance' has been preferred to a more federal or 'Community' paradigm:

- in the European instruments to rescue MS in risk of sovereign default. When the Greek crisis irrupted in 2010 an already existing instrument was considered: the European Financial Stability Mechanism (EFSM), which had been created to deal with the balance of payment problems of the non-Eurozone EU MS, but which could be easily adapted to the Eurozone members. This mechanism is managed by the European Commission and can make loans to the MS with the new resources it can mobilise in the markets by issuing Eurobonds with a guarantee provided by the Community budget.

This typically 'Community' solution remains active (in 2014 for Ireland and Portugal) but is kept small in size. A new instrument was instead built from scratch, starting with EFSF and enshrined as permanent in the Lisbon Treaty: the ESM. It is based on national financial guarantees to be authorised by the national parliaments each time a new loan needs to be decided, and to be attached to tough conditionality.

- in the European mechanism to rescue banks, as this will also depend on this ESM.
- in national fiscal policies, which are being framed with tighter rules by the new regulations to reform the SGP ('six-pack' and 'two-pack') and particularly with the new Intergovernmental Treaty on Stability,

Coordination and Governance. Nevertheless, the coordination of spill-over effects of the national fiscal policies remains very weak, and an aggregate fiscal policy for the Eurozone is not even conceptualised.

• in the new process of macroeconomic surveillance, this one is mainly focused on the macroeconomic imbalances of each national case, implicitly assuming that the ideal situation would be for each Member State to have a surplus in the current account and even in the balance of payments as a whole. This, if at all possible, would make Europe a very competitive economy but also a worrying factor of global imbalances. This new process of macroeconomic surveillance is certainly very useful in identifying national problems to be addressed, but should also consider the spill-over effects, notably between deficit countries and surplus countries in the Eurozone, as well as being used to discuss the most appropriated policy-mix for the Eurozone as a whole.

The economic implications of this new architecture are the following: it is possible to reduce the spreads of sovereign debt and private credit, but it is not possible to reduce the divergences between MS regarding investment rates, growth rates and unemployment. The final economic outcome of this situation is that some MS have lost the basic conditions to implement the common EU strategy for a new growth model (Europe 2020 Strategy), replacing it with an organised destruction of viable companies and viable jobs triggering a dis-organised emigration flow and associated 'brain-drain'. And the final political outcome of this situation is that national policies of some MS are more shaped by the national parliaments and governments of other countries (the creditor ones). One can naturally ask for how long this situation can be sustainable in economic, social and political terms – the nature of European integration seems to be changing.

5. Redesigning the Instruments for a Sustainable EMU

The new instruments were forged in extreme situations, where the choice was between a collective abyss and a patch-worked solidarity. As the risk of Eurozone break-up seems less dramatic but the crisis is far from over, it is time to consider a more systemic and Community approach for a crisis which *is* systemic. Against the previous background, this approach can be logically developed according to the following steps and by building on the existing instruments:

1. All EU MS and therefore all Eurozone members should have the conditions to implement the EU strategy for a new and more sustainable growth model which is greener, smarter and inclusive. This requires a particular combination of investments and reforms which should be coordinated at European level according to the new schedule defined by the so-called

European semester. This means that the consistency of national policies with European policies is to be checked at European level before final adoption by national governments and parliaments. This should also be used to identify the kind of European support which should be provided to complement the national effort.

2. The same should happen with the solutions to address the macroeconomic imbalances, and should combine national efforts with support by a Eurozone budget, in case of asymmetric shocks. On top of this surveillance of national imbalances, a more general macroeconomic coordination should take place in order to define the better policy-mix for the Eurozone as a whole.

3. Fiscal coordination should supervise the national efforts for fiscal consolidation as well as identify the needs for complementary European support.

4. The European support for investment and structural convergence should be provided by the EU Community budget via the Community programmes or the structural funds, to be aligned with the Europe 2020 Strategy.

5. The European support for macroeconomic stabilisation which is required to address specific problems of the Eurozone should be provided by a complementary Eurozone *budget* based on Eurozone taxes and borrowing in the markets via Eurobonds issuance.

6. The European support via the Community budget or via the Eurozone budget should be attached to a conditionality to be aligned with the EU priorities – assuming they are defined in a balanced way.

7. The ESM should focus its activity on a rescuing role regarding sovereigns. When requested by a Eurozone Member State, and under conditionality, it should also use its capacity of issuing Eurobonds to buy in the public debt on the primary markets.

8. The European Council, the Council, the European Commission and the EP should organise themselves internally to deal with the Eurozone issues more effectively. The national parliaments should also be better involved insofar as they frame the national governments' positions at European level.

We also assume that the ongoing process to build up a banking union with a single supervisory system, a bank resolution mechanism and a harmonised deposit guarantee will be completed soon, as this is a crucial pillar in overcoming the Eurozone crisis. This means that throughout this process, the ECB will build up a new role dealing more specifically with financial stability.

6. Including a Social Dimension

Another controversial issue is emerging: what kind of social dimension is necessary to ensure the long-term sustainability of the EMU?

When the EMU was defined in the EU Treaties, it was assumed the basic conditions for its sustainability would be a monetary zone coupled with stronger common fiscal discipline which would be combined with other already existing Community instruments, notably:

- A single market with more mobility of factors pushing for real convergence on competitiveness;
- A set of some common basic social standards defined by Community law;
- A Community policy for social and economic cohesion;
- A Community budget financing this policy;
- The support to social dialogue at European and national level.

Hence, it is important to underline that the original EMU was already counting on some instruments with a social purpose.

Nevertheless, we should ask if these existing instruments are sufficient to ensure the EMU's long-term sustainability in economic, social and political terms. This assessment should be based on the EMU's capacity to keep its internal consistency by responding to different types of challenges. The first challenge: cyclical divergences created by asymmetric shocks hitting particular regions or counties due to their pattern of productive specialisation. This kind of cyclical divergence of growth and employment will always exist due to a natural – and desirable – variety of productive specialisations. In other monetary zones, these divergences are reduced by federal instruments for macroeconomic stabilisation. In the EMU, the national instruments with this purpose were reduced to having only a small amount of room to manoeuvre in the budgetary policy and there are no instruments at European level. This means that if a Eurozone MS is hit by an asymmetric shock, there are few means to avoid the social impact in terms of wage and benefit cuts and job losses.

The second challenge: the higher pressure of globalisation and the need to move to a new growth model that is more knowledge-intensive and less carbon-intensive, with adapting structures and to prepare people for new jobs. This transition requires an important amount of new investments and structural reforms – in business framework conditions, labour markets, social protection, education, and innovation systems which should be better coordinated at European level, because they have many spill-over effects. So far, the divergences between the Eurozone MS have increased due to lack of investment means and coordinated reforms. These structural divergences in competitiveness have led to macroeconomic imbalances which were not identified and corrected in time.

The third challenge: the recent financial crisis leading to a general credit crunch and magnifying the macroeconomic imbalances which were already building up in the Eurozone. The crisis of the Eurozone interconnecting high sovereign debt with high bank debt has created cumulative divergences between MS regarding financing conditions, investment rate, growth rate, unemployment rate and sustainability of welfare systems. The instruments which were created so far, notably the ESM and the new ECB instruments, are able to reduce the divergences regarding financial conditions, but not the other divergences regarding growth and social indicators.

If these EMU flaws are not addressed, the most likely sequence of events will be:

- In the most vulnerable Eurozone countries: first will be a significant reduction of wages and social benefits, followed by significant jobs losses triggering a recessive spiral and uncontrolled emigration;
- In the other Eurozone countries: increasing pressure on their social standards and risks of social dumping;
- In the EU as a whole: erosion of the existing instruments to provide a social dimension, reduction of the aggregate internal demand, shrinking of the internal market, and systemic pressure towards lower growth or recession.

In order to reverse these trends, the EMU should be completed in regard to its missing instruments in the financial, fiscal, economic, and social dimension. It can certainly be useful to make full use of the previous social instruments already referred to. But the financial and economic pressure is so high that they will be eroded if they are not complemented by some stronger instruments for a social dimension in the EMU, such as:

- Refocusing on the social objectives defined by the Europe 2020 Strategy and to be implemented by the European Semester;
- Defining a clear set of social standards;
- Introducing additional social indicators for macroeconomic surveillance;
- Developing a macroeconomic coordination to improve the overall policy-mix with a symmetric approach (deficit and surplus countries);
- Improving the coordination of the major structural reforms;
- Improving the coordination of main priorities of social policies (using the integrated guidelines);
- Improving the framework conditions for internal migrations with better social integration (portability of rights, and so forth);
- Developing social investment, notably in training, active labour market policies, child care;
- Defining the room for manoeuvre for this social investment in the investment rules of the SGP;
- Creating a fiscal capacity with instruments for macroeconomic stabilisation in case of cyclical shock and with instruments to support priority reforms
- Creating a Eurogroup of Social Ministers.

Wage adjustments, job losses, migration, structural reforms but also investments, job creation and income transfers will also certainly be ingredients in the next stage of the EMU. But there is a big political choice to be made about the preferred axis:

- Either a Eurozone of internal divergences with deep internal contrasts regarding wages, social benefits, unemployment rates and migration flows; or
- A Eurozone of internal upward convergences, with more coordinated reforms and investments, and with upward trends in growth, employment, inclusion and social sustainability. Nevertheless, in the crisis this can only be possible if a banking union makes real progress and if some kind of Eurozone fiscal capacity is defined.

7. The Implications of the Crisis for the EU External Action

The economic and financial crisis was probably the first big test of the new framework of the EU's external action as defined by the Lisbon Treaty (which was only fully ratified in 2009). This new framework was one of the most relevant added values of the new EU Treaty, establishing a comprehensive concept of external action, giving a central guidance role to the European Council and creating the post of High Representative/Vice President of the European Commission to chair the Foreign Affairs Council of Ministers and to be support by a European External Action Service (EEAS). Two different questions should be addressed for policy assessment:

- How has the EU's external action responded to this crisis?
- How has this crisis shaped the EU's external action?

From this view point, it is possible to identify two quite different periods: the first, during the financial and economic crisis between 2008 and 2010, when the EU was a key-player; the second, during the Eurozone crisis after 2010, when the EU had also become a source of global problems.

During the financial and economic crisis between 2008 and 2009, the EU (and some of its MS in particular) played a relevant role in the creation of the G20, with a strong influence in its organisation, working methods and agenda setting. In parallel, the European Council has improved its internal methodology to improve the coordination of the EU MS in some strategic issues of external action, including G20 and the key-strategic partners. The specific roles of the President of the European Council, the President of the European Commission and the HR/VP were better defined. The EEAS was put in place to strengthen the coordination of the EU's external policies in Brussels, in the MS and in all capitals worldwide.

After 2010, with the Eurozone crisis unfolding, the EU also started to be perceived as a source of global problems as follows:

- Reducing trade opportunities in Europe for many EU international partners;
- Reducing the EU flow of foreign direct investment to many EU international partners;
- Creating financial instability due to the turmoil in the Eurozone and the risks of sovereign default or bank bankruptcy;
- Introducing a new factor, a political uncertainty: can the EU solve its own problems?

This new situation at home has damaged the potential of the EU external action thus, by:

- Weakening the EU focus on external challenges;
- Weakening the EU resources for a more consistent and coherent external action (for example defence or cooperation);
- Turning the EU situation into one of the main concerns of G20, regarding the risks of financial instability and double-dip recession;
- Reducing the EU influence in the reform of the IMF-World Bank (WB) governance;
- Reducing the EU negotiation leverage regarding its main strategic partners (countries and macro-regions).

Any progress which can be underlined in this period is related to bilateral trade agreements or negotiations, one way of responding to the ongoing stalemate in the World Trade Organisation (WTO) multilateral negotiations with the Doha Round.

Yet, the EU remains the most important economic and trade bloc, even if a relative decline is underway due to the general re-balancing of the world economy. Overcoming the Eurozone crisis with a credible solution will be crucial in resetting the potential of the EU external action in the following spheres:

- Trade policy;
- Development cooperation;
- External projection of EU internal policies;
- Agenda and standards setting at a global level;
- Foreign affairs and defence.

Against this background, some priorities for the next stage of the EU external role can be identified as follows:

- To overcome the Eurozone crisis with a credible solution in order to restore EU international influence and the main sources of its smart power: a new and successful growth model, green, smart and inclusive; an effective and democratic political system with supra-national governance; the diversity of economic competences, cultural backgrounds and international connections; a consistent preference for multilateralism. This credible solution will depend on how the EMU is completed;

- To recover a EU leading role in the G20, becoming a consistent driving force for the implementation of G20 strategic priorities: financial reform, sustainable growth, job creation, development support and better global economic governance;
- To clarify the EU strategy to reform the governance of IMF-WB, by adding a Eurozone seat as a central objective;
- To strengthen the financial and political means and EU consistency between European and national levels, as well as EU policy coherence in key external policies: trade, development cooperation and the external projection of EU internal policies, notably finance, macroeconomic policy, industrial, energy, research, education, employment and social policies;
- To deepen EU strategic partnerships with the global key-players;
- To encourage regional integration processes;
- To create a more comprehensive partnership for joint economic recovery with the accession countries and neighbourhood regions, notably the Balkans, Northern Africa and the Middle East;
- To coordinate and rationalise the resources for a more consistent and effective foreign affairs, security and defence policy.

Chapter 12

Assessing the EU's 'Social' Trade Policy from an External Europeanization Perspective: The Case of the Generalised System of Preferences

Eleni Xiarchogiannopoulou

1. Introduction

Trade policy is the most significant European Union (EU) policy area. Starting with the genesis of the European Communities in the 1950s, trade has been the stimulus of European integration. In 2013, the Single Market area has the biggest Gross Domestic Product (GDP) in the world, while the EU is the leading global exporter of goods and one of the biggest importers (European Commission 2013c). The EU also uses its trade policy to pursue social goals such as the promotion of human rights, core labour standards and environmental and good governance principles. It does so through its wide network of Preferential Trade Agreements (PTAs). A PTA is any trade agreement by which the EU offers trade preferences to countries outside its borders. The wide network of PTAs offers an international regulatory regime of trade that operates in parallel with the World Trade Organisation (WTO). This chapter focuses on a specific type of PTA, namely the EU's Generalised System of Preferences (GSP). The particularity of the GSP compared to the rest of the EU's PTAs is that the trade preferences it offers are non-reciprocal and that Social Conditionality (SC) governs the participation to the scheme. In other words, trade preferences are conditional to the adoption and implementation of a number of international human and labour rights, environmental and good governance conventions.

The aim of this chapter is to assess the effectiveness of SC, that is, its impact on the implementation of the social, environmental and good governance clauses in the GSP beneficiary countries. Theoretically, it focuses on the external dimension of Europeanization. According to Schimmelfennig, external Europeanization refers to 'the domestic adaptation to the impact of European governance (Schimmelfennig 2010: 3). Following Radaelli's definition, he clarifies that external, like internal Europeanization, is a process of the incorporation 'of formal and informal rules, procedures, policy paradigms, styles, 'ways of doing things', and shared beliefs and norms which are first defined and consolidated in the making of EU public policy and politics and then incorporated in the logic of domestic discourse, identities, political structures, and public policies' (Radaelli 2003b: 30, quoted in Schimmelfennig 2010: 3).

The external dimension of Europeanization has attracted intense academic interest. Building on the literature on the internal dimension of Europeanization, studies agree that the process is underpinned either by the logic of 'consequences', according to which the adoption of the EU rules of governance is the necessary solution to certain policy problems, or, the logic of 'appropriateness', according to which the adoption of the EU rules of governance is domestically the appropriate solution to certain policy problems (March and Olsen 1989). Europeanization occurs through direct or indirect mechanisms. The direct mechanisms include conditionality, socialisation (Schimmelfennig 2010: 8) and persuasion (Boerzel and Risse 2012: 5), and are those in which the EU intentionally promotes its rules of governance beyond its borders. The indirect mechanisms are externalisation and imitation, in which either non-EU actors 'shop around' for best practices or the mere presence of the EU is enough to instigate the adoption of EU rules (Schimmelfennig 2010: 8; Boerzel and Risse 2012: 5).

It can be argued that in the case of SC in the GSP the EU is not promoting its own rules but international ones and hence it is hard to associate this policy instrument with the process of external Europeanization. The assumption that underpins the chapter is that of 'domestic analogy' according to which countries (and in the case of the EU, polities) prefer to have an international environment that resembles their domestic principles and procedures. In the case of the EU this would be the principles that govern European integration and governance (Schimmelfennig 2010). This is because an environment with which EU political and economic actors are familiar offers a better context for them to operate, as it reduces the adaptation and information costs and gives them a competitive advantage over other international actors.

According to Schimmelfennig (2010: 6–7), the rules of external EU governance include: (a) regional integration as a means of promoting economic growth and peace in a similar way that its own model of intensive multilateralism does; (b) the creation and regulation of transnational markets, as a means of projecting globally its own 'neoliberal' economic model, and its commitment to market-building, market regulation and economic liberalisation; and (c) the promotion of human rights, and the rule of law and democracy, as a means of projecting the constitutional norms of its member states and its accession criteria to third countries. It is in the context of this last rule of external EU governance that the study of SC in EU's GSP from an external Europeanization perspective makes sense, as the 'external projection of internal solutions' (Lavenex 2004: 295).

The majority of the research on the external dimension of Europeanization so far deals with countries or regions that are proximate to the EU borders, such as the European Economic Area and neighbouring countries (Schimmelfennig 2010; Boerzel and Risse 2012; Lavenex and Schimmelfennig 2009). This chapter focuses on the EU's impact on developing countries. The following section will offer a short presentation of the EU's GSP. Sections 3 and 4 will focus on the impact of SC on the implementation of social, environmental and good governance principles in developing countries. Section 3 uses Boerzel's and Risse's (2012) typology of external Europeanization scope factors that determine final policy outcomes, while Section 4 focuses on policy coherence as an additional scope factor that is missing from the original typology. Finally, the last section offers an overview of the limitations of SC in the conclusions. It also discusses the implications of these limitations for the EU's role as an international actor within the context of the Eurozone crisis.

2. The Generalised System of Preferences and Social Conditionality

Since the first United Nations Conference on Trade and Development (UNCTAD) in 1964, developed countries have agreed that trade is the most effective route to economic growth. At the EU level such consensus had already been reached in 1957 when the European Economic Community Treaty provided that the EU was to act 'in association of the overseas countries and territories in order to increase trade and to promote jointly economic and social development' (Art. 3(k) EEC Treaty). The GSP is the product of this broad consensus. It is a trade policy programme that allows the exemption of developing countries from exports tariffs as a way of assisting their growth and development.

Under international trade law, the GSP exempts developing countries from the Most Favoured Nation (MFN) principle. The MFN principle is the cornerstone of the international legal order on international trade and it is an integral part of Article I of the General Agreement on Tariffs and Trade (GATT), the predecessor of the WTO. According to this, any country that offers preferential trade arrangements to another country must offer exactly the same treatment to all of the GATT/WTO member states. The exemption from the MFN principle allowed countries contracting to the GATT to establish systems of trade preferences with other countries on the condition that they are: (a) generalised, in the sense that they are offered to clusters of countries and not to individual ones; b) non-discriminatory between developing countries, with the exception of the least developed; c) non-reciprocal, in the sense that the granting countries cannot receive concessions from the beneficiary countries in return; and d) autonomous to the beneficiary countries, in the sense that they have to be part of a contractual agreement.

Since the early 1980s the GSP has also been a tool of exporting principles of democratic governance. By 1982 a small human and labour rights advocacy coalition emerged in the United States (US) that proposed to amend the country's GSP, so that trade preferences are made conditional with respect to labour rights (Compa and Vogt 2001). In 1984 a labour rights clause was incorporated at the US GSP Renewal Act. Copying the US example and in response to the EU failure to introduce a social clause at the WTO rules, and thus to connect social standards with hard law (Panagariya 2002), the EU incorporated SC in its GSP in 1996. In 2006, it broadened its SC to include the ratification and application of conventions on sustainable development and good governance standards (Orbie et al. 2009). SC is a 'hard' instrument in the sense that it consists of both a positive (carrots) and a negative aspect (sticks) (Panagariya 2002). With the positive aspect, trade preferences are allocated to the beneficiary countries provided that they adopt the social, environmental and good governance clauses. The negative aspect entails the withdrawal of the preferences when the beneficiary countries fail to incorporate or violate these clauses.

The new GSP scheme came into force in January 2014. The chapter focuses on the previous one that was renewed in 2005 and was applied until December 2013. In general, the GSP operates on three levels: the standard GSP, the GSP+ and the Everything But the Arms. Until 2013 the standard GSP scheme offered non-reciprocal trade preferences to 176 developing countries and territories (European Commission 2013c), whereas the new GSP scheme offers preferences to 90 countries. In both cases the trade preferences are offered on the premise of economic development. These are open to all countries, which are not classified as high income countries by the World Bank and are not sufficiently diversified in their exports. The countries participating in the standard GSP scheme are expected to avoid 'serious and systemic violations' of the 16 core human and labour rights (European Council 2005: Annex III part A and B; see Appendix I).

The GSP+ offers additional preferences to vulnerable developing countries in return for ratifying and effectively implementing 11 additional international environmental and good governance conventions (European Council 2005; see Appendix II). Vulnerability is defined in terms of poverty, non-diversification of exports, and share of EU GSP-covered imports (no more than 1 per cent of these imports) (European Council 2005). With the new GSP scheme the number of GPS+ beneficiary countries increased from 15 to 16 (see European Commission 2013c). Finally, the Everything But the Arms (EBA) scheme was introduced in March 2001. Since January 2014 it offers duty-free access on all products except guns and ammunition to 41 Least Developed Countries (LDC), while until the end of 2013 it benefited 50 LDC (European Commission 2013c; see Appendix III). According to the United Nations (UN), the LDCs are those that exhibit the lowest indicators of socio-economic development and the lowest human development index ratings of all countries in the world. It must be noted that there is a graduation mechanism in place that guarantees that countries do not receive trade preferences in trade sectors that have reached a certain level of competitiveness.

The impact of SC on the implementation of the social and environmental clauses has in general been contested. The 2011 EU GSP impact assessment showed that although the levels of ratification are satisfactory, the actual implementation of the conventions remains limited (European Commission 2011b). A number of external/international, internal/domestic and EU related factors contribute to this. The following two sections will focus on these factors and their implications under the lens of the theory on the external dimension of Europeanization.

3. The Impact of Social Conditionality on the Implementation of the Social and Environmental Clauses in the GSP: Progress, Limitations and Scope Factors

Boerzel and Risse (2012) identify a number of scope factors that determine the impact of external Europeanization on third countries. These include (a) the presence or absence of domestic incentives, (b) the degrees of statehood in the third country, (c) the quality of the democratic regime in the third country, and (d) the presence or absence of power asymmetries. This section will use their typology in order to assess the impact of SC on the implementation of the social, environmental and good governance clauses that are associated with the EU GSP.

Presence or Absence of Domestic Incentives

According to Boerzel and Risse (2012) the presence or absence of domestic incentives is crucial for institutional change. The domestic adoption of the EU rules of governance is more likely if the domestic political actors or society engage with them, either because EU policy demands facilitate their policy/political preferences (logic of consequences), or because they meet their policy goals (logic of appropriateness). In the case of SC in the GSP, evidence shows that the pressure coming from political actors, civil society or the informed general public have played an important role in the adoption of human rights conventions. For example, in Georgia the commitment of the political elites to EU membership and their European Neighbourhood Policy (ENP) action plan, facilitated the implementation of the conventions. Political actors tend to identify any policy commitments with the EU as an objective of meeting the standards of EU membership (Gasiorek 2010). Also, the pressure coming from domestic trade unions contributed to the country improving its relations with the International Labour Organisation (ILO) and to prolong the application of the GSP+ for the period after 2009.

Another example is the case of Nicaragua, where the implementation of the conventions was more successful when there was strong support from civil society. For example, the implementation of the conventions related to children's and women's rights has been successful due to the high levels of public awareness (Gasiorek 2010). Societal pressure resulted in policymakers being more supportive and committed to institutional change, and increased the interest amongst the donor community (Gasiorek 2010). In this context the policy makers were ready to invest resources in implementation, to develop the necessary regulatory and institutional frameworks and to increase the cooperation between central and regional agencies, which further increased public awareness (Gasiorek 2010). In contrast, the limited implementation of environmental conventions in Nicaragua is also linked to low levels of public interest and awareness.

The Degrees of Statehood

Another scope factor that influences the domestic impact of SC is, according to Boerzel and Risse, the *degrees of statehood*. This refers to the governmental/ statutory capacity to adopt and implement decisions. These could include the presence or absence of domestic governmental policymaking capacities, the governmental ability to implement and enforce law, as well as the presence or absence of influential non-state actors (such as civil society and business), who can exercise pressure on the government to reform or to provide them with additional resources. Again in the case of Nicaragua, the presence of a domestic institutional framework for implementation and inter-agency coordination with the local authorities contributed to the successful implementation of the conventions related to children's and women's rights (Gasiorek 2010). Similarly, compatibility with the existing regulatory framework and control mechanisms facilitated the implementation of the convention against illicit traffic in narcotic drugs and psychotropic substances. Likewise, in Peru the creation of the Ministry of Environment in 2008 and the decentralisation of certain environmental policies facilitated the implementation of environmental clauses (Gasiorek 2010). In the case of Peru, the pressure coming from international NGOs and other countries, with regard to respecting human rights, also influenced governmental decisions to improve their compliance with the conventions (Gasiorek 2010).

At the same time, the weakness of the government in both countries compromised the full compliance with international conventions. In Nicaragua, economic constraints and a complacency or even disregard for some of the conventions account for limited progress in their implementation. Also, although some conventions, such as the international convention on economic, social and cultural rights have been on the governmental agenda, they were overtaken by other structural factors, such as the prevalence of poverty (Gasiorek 2010). Widespread poverty, along with economic interests vested in crime and illegal activities, has also been a major impediment to progress in the case of Peru (Gasiorek 2010). Corruption has also been an obstacle to the implementation of conventions in Georgia.

The Quality of the Democratic Regime

A third domestic scope factor is the *quality of the democratic regime*, as it influences the willingness of governmental actors to adopt the EU rules of governance. It is shown, for instance, that democratic countries with market economies are more likely to adopt the EU rules of governance simply because the adaptational costs are lower (Boerzel and Risse 2012). In the case of Peru, for instance, the authoritarian regime and armed conflicts amplified the violation of human rights, despite international pressure to comply with international conventions (Gasiorek 2010). Similarly, in the case of Sri Lanka, the dependency of the garment sector on EU imports was not a strong enough incentive for the country to meet human rights obligations stemming from the GSP+. Indeed, 60 per cent of the sector's exports go to the EU, while the Sri Lankan garment industry itself accounts for 11 per cent of the GDP of the country, 33 per cent of industrial output, 45 per cent of total merchandise exports and occupies 6 per cent of the total workforce (Asian Development Bank 2009). Despite this, the deep-rooted culture of political violence that originates from the 26-year civil war remained intact even after the end of the conflict and in 2009 contributed to the continuation of civil tensions, political persecutions and the violation of basic human rights, which resulted in the withdrawal of EU preferences in 2010 (Yap 2013).

Power Asymmetries

Another factor that influences the impact of external Europeanization is that of *power asymmetries*. These may refer to the uneven distribution of material and/or ideational resources between the EU and the target countries/regions. They may also refer to the degree to which third countries are interdependent with the EU or to which they also have strong relationships with other international actors such as the US, Russia or China. Indicative of the influence of power asymmetries in the implementation of the international conventions are the cases of Myanmar and Belarus, both of which had their EU GSP preferences withdrawn in 1996 and 2006 respectively. The fact however that both of these countries have strong links with other economic partners compromised the impact of EU sanctions on their trade flows and the implementation of social, environmental and good governance clauses.

On one hand, Mayanmar/Burma has strong trade relations with China, which tolerates the violation of human rights and labour standards, and is considered to be the most important economic partner of the country (Zhou and Guyvers 2011). Mayanmar/Burma also has close economic and political relations with other ASEAN countries, as well as with most of its neighbouring countries. In fact Mayanmar/Burma was the largest trade partner of ASEAN in 2008, while the ASEAN-China Free Trade Agreement (FTA) covers almost 75 per cent of Mayanmar/Burma's total trade (Eurostat 2013). Similarly, Belarus has strong trade relations with Russia and the Commonwealth of Independent States (CIS), both of which import the majority of products produced in Belarus. In 2008 Russia was the largest trade partner of Belarus, accounting for 60 per cent of its total imports, while the total trade with CIS countries accounted for 56 per cent and that with the EU was 31.8 per cent (Eurostat 2013).

On top of this, EU trade sanctions had a positive instead of a negative impact on the trade flows of these countries with the EU. Indeed, during the period 2002–2006 Belarus's total exports to the EU grew by almost 30 per cent on an annual basis, increasing by almost 150 per cent. Similarly, the total exports of Mayanmar/ Burma to the EU during 1997–2002 increased from €141.90 thousand million in 1996, to 489.56 in 2001 (Eurostat 2013). The literature suggests that in order to understand this paradox we also need to look inside the EU, the governance of the GSP and its relation with the other trade policy instruments and EU policies. The following section will focus on this scope factor that evades the typology of Boerzel and Risse.

4. The Coherence of EU Policies and the Limitations of GSP Governance

Policy coherence is an integral element of the ongoing debate on the EU's international role in a multilateral, globalised world. The notion of coherence refers to the absence of contradiction (Hillion 2008) and the presence of positive synergies (Hoffmeister 2008) between EU policies. The literature distinguishes between three levels of coherence: (a) the *horizontal*, that refers to the absence of contradictions and presence of positive synergies between the policy objectives of different EU policy areas (Orbie and Tortell 2009), (b) the *external* level that refers to tensions or synergies between the EU and other international actors, such as the ILO (Gebhard 2011), (c) and the *internal* level that refers to the presence or absence of positive synergies between the policy instruments/initiatives used in the same policy area (Gebhard 2011). The remainder of this section will show the relevance of all three levels of coherence to the impact of SC on the implementation of the social, environmental and good governance clauses of the GSP.

The Horizontal Level of Coherence

According to various studies, the GSP social objectives are *horizontally* incoherent with other policy areas, either because they contradict their objectives or because there are no positive synergies between them. Huybrechts and Peels (2009) find that the despite the EU commitment to fortify the social dimension in its external policies towards developing countries, social, trade and development policies are still not mutually reinforcing. Even more interestingly Novitz (2009) thinks that the EU's external policy priorities are subordinated to its market enhancing priorities and not the social ones. In other words, rather than exporting its social model, the EU primarily aims at exporting a market model that facilitates the roles that social norms play in the internal EU market. Similarly, Eichhorst et al. (2010) conclude that the social priorities in external trade policy are subservient to economic/trade priorities. In this context the EU has been criticised for being more concerned with increasing its imports through the GSP rather than with providing a coherent strategy for the improvement of social conditions in the beneficiary countries (Von Schöppenthau 1998).

The Internal Level of Coherence

At the *internal* level, studies highlight the lack of coherence between trade policy instruments. This stems from the fact that the GSP is not the only trade tool that offers preferential access to the EU market (European Commission 2011b).

In fact, Meunier and Nikolaïdis (2011) argue that the web of the EU's preferential trade agreements is so extensive that it undermines its preferential nature. In this context it is not surprising that the preferential exports of Mayanmar/Burma and Belarus to the EU increased during the withdrawal of their GSP preferences, as they are only a small fraction of their total exports to the EU.

In fact, many of these preferential agreements often offer more favourable market access to developing countries than the GSP, combined with a looser commitment to social and environmental clauses (Orbie and Babarinde 2008; Vandenberghe 2008). For instance, the EU cooperation agreements with countries such as Laos, Cambodia, Chile, Mexico and South Africa combine economic development with respect for human rights (Doumbia-Henry and Gravel 2006). Similarly, the ACP countries have committed to respecting labour rights and enhancing cooperation through the Lomé/Cotonou agreements. The EU has also included social clauses in the new generation of bilateral trade agreements, such as the Economic Partnership Agreements (EPAs) and Free Trade Agreements (FTAs) (Eichhorst et al. 2010). Nevertheless, none of these bilateral or multilateral agreements comprises any legal obligation for the beneficiary countries to adopt international conventions, nor do they entail any formal enforcement and monitoring mechanisms of their implementation (Vandenberghe 2008). Another example of the compromise of SC is the extension of the GSP drugs incentive scheme, from the Andean countries to the Central American Common Market area in 1998, and the Council's decision to unlink this from the application of the labour clauses, effectively making SC redundant (Orbie and Babarinde 2008).

Secondly, the EU is inconsistent regarding the application of SC in relation to withdrawing preferences. Indeed, the EU has withdrawn its preferences only in the cases of Mayanmar/Burma (in 1996), Burma (1997), Moldova (2000), Belarus (2006), El Salvador (2008), and Sri Lanka (2010). These countries however, are by no means exceptional cases, as in fact most of the countries participating to the GSP and GSP+ have a dubious record of respecting social and human rights. In other words, the number of cases the Commission investigates is limited. Moreover, the selection of the cases it chooses to investigate is arbitrary or at least unclear. It is indicative that in its 2008 report on the GSP+ status of ratification and recommendations the Commission concludes that although there are shortcomings to the implementation process according to the ILO and UN monitoring bodies, overall the level of progress made is considered to be satisfactory (European Commission 2008). Nevertheless, according to an Amnesty International report published in 2011 the violation of the right of association, opinion and press is present in most of the GSP beneficiary countries (Amnesty International 2011). In this context, it is not surprising that the EU has been accused of having a history of avoiding imposing GSP-related sanctions (Arnau 2002).

Thirdly, there are a number of factors that are related to the design of the policy itself, which also act as a counter-incentive, discouraging domestic stakeholders from participating in the GSP and from implementing international conventions. These include:

- Absence of compensation for the cost of implementing international conventions;
- Lack of a generally accepted definition of the 'effective implementation' of the conventions;
- Inadequate safeguard mechanism (unclear legal concepts, lack of information, unclear procedural framework);
- Suboptimal mechanism for withdrawal of preferences (lack of procedural rules, unclear investigation procedure, lack of procedure for the reinstatement of the preferences);
- Low level of tariffs that limits the size and scope of the preference margins and hence the potential impact of the GSP;
- Insufficient product coverage;
- Suboptimal graduation mechanism;
- Beneficiary countries not being properly targeted;
- Insufficient support for the diversification of exports;
- Low level of utilisation of preferences by the beneficiary countries (European Commission 2011).

The External Level of Coherence

Finally, the literature also points to limitations at the *external* level of coherence. More specifically, the lack of efficient monitoring procedures is a hindering factor in the ratification and the *de facto* implementation of international conventions (European Commission 2011b). The EU does not monitor the beneficiary countries itself, but instead monitoring is allocated to international bodies (mainly the United Nations/UN and the ILO) that report regularly on the implementation of the clauses. EU decisions on granting or withdrawing the GSP preference are based on these reports. In some exceptional cases, such as the withdrawal against Mayanmar/Burma and Belarus, the procedures are initiated after member states raise complaints about the violation of conventions. Although the cooperation between these bodies and the EU is smooth, the monitoring procedures themselves are limited. This is because not all of the conventions provide for a monitoring procedure. This is, for instance, the case with the convention on the prevention and punishment of crime and genocide, as well as the convention on the suppression and punishment of the crime of apartheid, for which a monitoring committee was never established.

Although Regulation 732/2008 allows for the consideration of reports from NGOs, in practice they do not play any role in the formal procedure. In fact, the same applies for the European Parliament (EP), which has criticised the Commission for avoiding cooperation (Bartels 2008: 10). As a result it remains unclear how the EU assesses the compliance of beneficiary countries with the conventions on apartheid and genocide, or even whether the assessment of these conventions plays any role in the allocation or withdrawal of trade preferences (Schneider 2012). Finally, another issue related to the external level of coherence is the timing of monitoring. This is particularly relevant regarding human rights conventions, whereby periodical assessments take place every two to five years, and as a result it is impossible to know whether any violations occurred in the allocating or withdrawing of preferences (European Commission 2011b: 6). According to Schneider (2012), NGOs could provide a valid alternative to the international monitoring bodies as they were able to provide reports more frequently.

5. Conclusions: The Limitations of Europeanization in the Era of the Eurozone Crisis

This chapter has offered an assessment of the impact of SC on the implementation of the social, environmental and governance clauses included in the EU's GSP during 2005–2013. Following the theory of the external dimension of Europeanization, it has shown that the impact of SC is compromised by a number of domestic and external factors, such as the presence or absence of domestic incentives, the degree of statehood, the quality of the democratic regime and the presence of power asymmetries. On top of these factors, the chapter identifies that policy coherence can also influence the impact of the external dimension of Europeanization. Indeed, the lack of coherence at the horizontal, internal and external levels also compromises the process of external Europeanization, as it hinders the implementation of international conventions.

The issue of policy coherence is particularly relevant to the future and the role of the EU in international affairs. In a recent study, Xiarchogiannopoulou and Tsarouhas (forthcoming) show that policy coherence was one of the crucial factors that enabled the EU to diffuse its policy idea of flexicurity to the International Labour Organisation (ILO) and eventually to upgrade itself to the leading international actor in this policy area. Similarly, the EU recognises the significance of policy coherence in its 2013 report on Policy Coherence for Development, where it stresses the need for a new policymaking style that builds positive synergies and cooperation between the different policies applied to developing counties, domestic and the EU actors, NGOs, civil society organisations, and international fora such as the OECD (European Commission 2013). Essentially, the chapter suggests that the external dimension of Europeanization depends not only on factors external to the EU, but also on its own policymaking. The subordination of EU social policy goals to its market goals, the lack of complementarity between the various preferential trade schemes and inefficient monitoring procedures compromise its capacity to project its rules of governance to the GSP beneficiary countries.

This is a crucial observation, given the existential dilemmas it has been facing since 2009 due to the Eurozone crisis that naturally cast doubts on its supremacy and created uncertainties about its future. Policy coherence seems indispensable for the EU to continue being the inspiration for other regionalisms around the world, and its external policy being regarded 'as unreflexive behavior mirroring the deeply ingrained belief that Europe's history is a lesson for everybody'

(Bicchi 2006: 287). One could assume that if the EU wants to be an influential global actor, then its policymaking style needs to become global as well, by cutting across the boundaries of the different policy areas, and promoting synergies between their objectives and their instruments. The practical implication of this observation is the advancement of policy coherence by the deepening of European integration and the strengthening of EU governance, both internally and externally. In terms of the Eurozone crisis, the ideal scenario would be the completion of the fiscal union or any other solution that would deepen European integration (see scenarios C and D in the Conclusion to this volume).

The revised GSP scheme that was introduced in January 2014 seems to acknowledge the necessity to improve policy coherence. At the internal level it excludes countries that have a Free Trade Agreement with the EU or a special autonomous trade regime. Moreover, it clarifies the conditions and administrative procedures for the withdrawal of the preferences, and strengthens the stability and predictability of the scheme for businesses in the sense that extends the life of the scheme from three to ten years and allows for longer transition periods. At the external level, it fortifies the monitoring mechanism in the sense that it includes local civil society organisations, social partners, the Council and the European Parliament that is also being involved in all changes affecting the GSP list of beneficiaries. Finally, at the horizontal level, it remains to be seen in the future if the positive synergies build horizontally between the GSP and development policy through the EU programme Policy Coherence with Development, as well as the new features of the revised GSP will have an impact on SC and the effective implementation of the international conventions.

Chapter 13

European Re-Regulation Meets Global Financial Governance: Constraint or Complement?

Daniel Mügge[1]

1. Introduction

Ever since the Asian financial crisis of the late 1990s, leading industrial countries around the world have been committed to support an integrated set of global financial rules. What was at the time dubbed the New International Financial Architecture (NIFA), lost steam after 2002 (Helleiner and Pagliari 2010). But since the credit crisis erupted, the G20 has reaffirmed its commitment to an integrated rule set, in the run-up to its summit in Saint Petersburg in September 2013.

At the same time, the crisis has made clear that faulty financial regulation can come at a substantial price, in the form of tax payer-funded bail-outs and wider, if indirect, economic consequences. The resulting fiscal implications of regulatory and supervisory policy are becoming ever more evident in Europe in particular, where the effects of the twin banking and sovereign debt crises linger. They imply that public authorities that regulate and supervise financial markets and institutions have to meet higher standards of accountability and that guaranteeing financial stability at home is not one policy goal among several – other goals could, for example, include the promotion of domestic financial sector competitiveness – but it is clearly the pre-eminent one.

This logic has consequences for international cooperation and harmonisation. An overriding concern with financial stability means that cooperation is welcome where it can boost domestic stability, but it will be met with scepticism where it cannot, for example, because of collective action problems or fundamental substantive disagreements, in particular across the Atlantic. In the past, both policymakers (Davies and Green 2008) and academics (Bryant 2003) assessed (and often championed) integrated global rules, primarily with an eye to the efficiency of cross-border markets (compare with the report of the Warwick Commission

1 This chapter has benefitted from the research assistance of Matthias Thiemann and helpful comments from the participants in the Visiting Scholars Seminar at the Center for European Studies of Harvard University.

on International Financial Reform (2009), which is a rare exception). From a European perspective, this chapter reassesses the case for or against global rules in light of the renewed emphasis on financial stability as the overriding policy goal. It asks: how strong is the case for a European commitment to global rule harmonisation in light of the EU-internal transformations of recent years?

This chapter compares the importance of various arguments across different policy areas – capital adequacy, executive compensation in the financial sector, structural reforms of banks, accounting rules, derivatives trading, and credit rating agencies – and shows that they weigh more heavily in some domains than in others. Only in two fields, capital adequacy rules and derivatives trading, is there a strong case for globally harmonised rules even in the face of substantive disagreement, with the USA in particular. In all other domains, the European Union (EU) is well-equipped to enhance financial stability through unilateral reforms, because the costs of internationally divergent rules are much lower than commonly assumed.

2. EU Financial Stability in a Globalised Economy

Before the financial crisis that started in 2007, financial stability's place in the range of policy goals to be achieved with financial regulation was different than it is during the crisis. Crucially, financial stability was not primarily seen as the alternative to a potentially catastrophic financial meltdown, but rather as a public good, which could be more or less on a sliding scale, such that a little less financial stability could conceivably be traded off against, for example, big efficiency gains in financial markets (Singer 2007).

Since the crisis set in, the relative importance of policy goals has shifted. International bodies, such as the G20, but also the various EU actors involved in financial regulation, emphasise that first and foremost, financial regulation needs to safeguard financial stability. From a normative perspective, other considerations, such as the promotion of the competitiveness of domestic firms, only have a place in regulatory considerations as long as financial stability is assured and mechanisms are in place to deal with financial emergencies. The remainder of this chapter will therefore ask how the case for or against global rule harmonisation looks when we assume that the central policy goal of financial governance is financial stability. It will only consider the competitiveness of domestic firms as a legitimate policy goal to the degree to which it contributes to that overarching goal.

3. Financial Globalisation as a Policy Constraint

From the perspective of the EU, capital is internationally mobile. Some jurisdictions, for example China, restrict the inflow of European capital. But owners of capital invested in Europe can chose from a wide range of alternative investment destinations should they wish to move funds out of the EU; these include many emerging markets, well-developed capital markets such as those in the United States of America (USA) and offshore financial centres around the world. Capital can exit the EU at little to no cost.

How does this capital mobility constrain the EU's capacity to regulate financial services with an eye to financial stability? The most prominent constraint is that domestic borrowers may face higher capital costs as a consequence of more onerous obligations on lenders active in the EU. The intensity of this effect will vary greatly between small and large and between emerging and well-developed capital markets. At the same time, if more stringent rules contribute to financial stability, the risk premium for loans would decrease, potentially offsetting higher funding costs. The net effect is open to question. In addition, domestic financial firms may operate in international market segments in which loosely regulated firms are also active. Financial instability abroad may introduce volatility in asset prices, for example because foreign firms face a funding squeeze and have to sell European debt or stocks rapidly. In short, capital mobility limits jurisdictions' ability to dampen volatility in funding costs and prices of internationally tradable assets. Beyond these factors, however, it does not in and of itself pose limits to the effectiveness of financial regulation.

Historically, capital mobility has co-evolved with the cross-border mobility of financial services, and many of the instability-effects associated with capital mobility are in fact related to service provision, not the mobility of capital itself. If a jurisdiction regulates, for example, domestic banks in line with what it considers necessary to safeguard financial stability, various sources of instability can still appear.

Consider a scenario in which financial firms, for example banks, operate across borders according to home-country rules and in which, in contrast to domestic rules, foreign rules are insufficiently stringent from a stability perspective. In that situation, soundly regulated domestic firms may interact in their home markets with lightly regulated foreign counterparties, who are a source of instability (counterparty risk), both because they may pursue overly risky strategies and because they may be rooted in markets that have a higher overall level of instability. Conversely, once domestic firms operate abroad, even the application of home-country rules cannot prevent a potential spill-over of loose regulation elsewhere, which may increase market volatility in foreign markets and so into home markets. In addition, foreign firms may capture a growing share of the domestic market because of their cost advantage and hence squeeze out sound domestic firms. In this scenario, a concern for domestic firms' competitiveness is warranted because domestic market dominance of foreign firms may undermine financial stability itself.

If foreign firms have to follow host-country rules for host-country activities, some sources of instability disappear. The issue is whether lightly regulated activities deployed abroad affect financial stability in the host country. For example, if an auditing firm sticks to tight auditing rules when auditing EU firms, it matters little to EU audit quality if that same firm follows lax standards when it audits a Japanese firm. On the contrary, a savings bank that acts carefully with its European customers might still endanger the latter if, for example, the Australian operations of that same firm were lightly regulated and undermined the whole bank. How host- and home-country regulations interact depends on the business sector in question.

The real public policy relevance of competitiveness, then, is not about competitiveness of domestic firms itself. Rather, it is an issue for public policy to the extent that a loss of competitiveness of domestic firms would imperil financial stability or the sustainable provision of credit to the economy, because these firms would see their market share fall. In contrast, neither job losses nor a higher cost of capital are problems in their own right. If regulation is sufficiently tight to ensure financial stability, but no higher, jobs would be lost mainly in activities that were deemed too risky in the first place and that are implicitly underwritten by society as a whole.

4. The Promises of Global Cooperation Re-examined

In financial markets, international harmonisation is commonly promoted on the basis of three arguments: decreased cross-border transaction costs and hence higher market efficiency, the emergence of international best practice, and the avoidance of regulatory competition.

Many scholars of international standardisation (mostly concerning product standards) acknowledge that it facilitates cross-border transactions, in particular trade and capital flows. The magnitude of any such effect is unclear, however. The lack of adherence to international financial standards across much of South-East Asia in the run-up to the financial crisis there in 1997 did not prevent enormous capital inflows. Both the USA and the EU have financial rules that are regarded as 'high quality' by financial market participants, so that it is not obvious that harmonisation itself would significantly alter the availability of capital on either side of the Atlantic.

Given the widespread perception that past financial regulation has been deficient, there is ample scope for regulators around the world to learn from turbulence-proof pre-crisis approaches (for example the Canadian experience) and each other's attempts to formulate new rules. An international dialogue to this end in the various standard-setting bodies, including the Financial Stability Board (FSB) in particular, is thus highly desirable. Such learning does not require, however, a commitment to harmonised international standards or even one recognised international best practice (compare with the Warwick Commission on International Financial Reform 2009). Indeed, from the perspective of learning from each other's approaches, international regulatory diversity is preferable to a global monoculture.

The Asian financial crisis of 1997/98 generated a strong push for what was then called a NIFA, centred on a comprehensive rule-book of financial standards and codes (Eichengreen 1999). But the Standards and Codes-agenda was not aimed primarily at overhauling or even harmonising standards globally. Rather, it concentrated on exporting regulatory best practice from the North-Atlantic region to Asia. Potential cross-border incompatibilities or gaps between the resulting regimes were of no major concern, just as input from emerging market economies into standard setting itself was hardly given serious thought.

Taken together, these arguments suggest that Singer's (2007) characterisation of global financial harmonisation does indeed capture the two most politically salient components: an effort to enhance financial stability through tight domestic rules on the one hand, and a worry about international competitiveness on the other. Rule harmonisation then is a negotiated truce in what would otherwise become a destructive regulatory race to the bottom – a dynamic that will be familiar to students of International Political Economy from many policy domains (harking back in important respects to Keohane 1984). It derives its usefulness from its ability to neutralise governments' deleterious concerns with banks' competitiveness. If we dismiss competitiveness as a legitimate policy goal in its own right, the case in favour of rule harmonisation is a lot weaker.

5. The Limits of Global Cooperation

What are the potential downsides of a commitment to global rule harmonisation? An agreement on global rules that are sufficiently tight to prevent what the regime-literature has thought of as 'cheating', prevents tailoring financial rules to domestic economic circumstances (for Europe, this case is strongly argued in Scharpf 2009) and 'constitutionalises' a single rules set instead (Best 2003). In addition, the lack of responsiveness to domestic views can undermine political legitimacy of the policy approach that is chosen. Financial deregulation is widely seen as having promoted widening income inequality, particularly in the USA (Hacker and Pierson 2010). Yet views on tolerable levels of inequality vary widely internationally, as do those on justifiable compensation in the financial sector and speculation. Given that also in Europe citizens have had to pay a high price for a crisis that was at least in part caused by misbehaviour of financial institutions, it is only reasonable for them to expect that their views on financial reform and the future shape of the financial sector be taken seriously (compare with Mügge 2011). A regulatory straitjacket that would prevent such accountability would count as a downside of a strong commitment to global rule harmonisation.

The most important downside of a commitment to global harmonisation, however, lies in regulatory preferences that differ across jurisdictions, sometimes substantially. In the classic prisoner's dilemma, which remains the cornerstone of the argument in favour of collective action, the individual actors have only two options – cooperating or defecting. The specific substance of what cooperation entails, is unproblematic. In financial regulation, in contrast, a willingness to cooperate does not necessarily mean that jurisdictions automatically get the standards they want. Neither the EU nor any other financial power around the globe has the means to force the USA into adopting rules not to its liking. Therefore, feasible transatlantic agreements may well fall short of substantive European preferences.

Compare regulatory harmonisation to international trade negotiations. The latter are tit-for-tat games in which trade concessions of one jurisdiction are offset by those of another. The logic of international financial regulation works differently. One country may have a preference for laxer standards across the board, and other jurisdictions have nothing to 'offer' to cajole it into ratcheting them up. It is therefore not obvious that global financial harmonisation actually solves collective action problems with respect to financial stability. Any jurisdiction can dig in its heels and refuse to tighten standards, and other than refusing market access, there is little that others can do to get it to move its position.

The – largely unacknowledged – crux of global financial harmonisation then, is that it does not contain any incentives for countries with a sizable financial market to go beyond what they consider an appropriate level of regulation. Such a country can undercut 'stability-optimal' rules in the name of competitiveness. Therefore, a jurisdiction that commits itself to global rule harmonisation effectively commits itself to the lowest level of regulation that another jurisdiction with effective veto-power considers optimal.

Three scenarios follow: the EU and the USA agree about what needs to be done and do it jointly to avoid unnecessary 'losses' due to unaligned standards. Or they disagree, but negative externalities from divergent rules are small enough to allow each jurisdiction simply to pursue its own policy preferences. In this scenario, disruptions to the flow of capital and services can often be limited through equivalence-arrangements that declare adherence to foreign standards to be sufficient for entry into domestic markets. Or there is disagreement, but negative externalities are so high that the jurisdiction aiming for higher standards has to consider the costs and benefits of applying host-country rules to foreign firms operating within its borders. In some cases, a foreign firm's conduct in the host country will be all that falls under host-country rules. In other cases, the firm's conduct in its home market (for example its capitalisation or the kinds of activities in which it engages) will also matter for access to the host market. In those cases, strict access rules are the only viable policy option.

How these different scenarios and the costs and benefits of each option play out depends not only on the shape and size of the jurisdiction in question – the EU in this case – but also on the stability relevance of a particular regulatory domain and the structure of the attendant market. The various considerations laid out above cannot be quantified, let alone put on a single scale. But they do offer a heuristic for assessing the strength or weakness of a case for global rule harmonisation in key regulatory domains. These considerations will be applied to six different regulatory domains in the following sections.

6. EU Embeddedness in Global Affairs Across Six Domains

This section applies these considerations to six regulatory domains to establish how effective unilateral action can be and, should it be rather ineffective, how well a commitment to global standards could remedy such ineffectiveness. The scenario to consider in each domain is one in which another major jurisdiction (in practice the USA) might apply less onerous rules and to ask what, with an eye to financial stability, a jurisdiction such as the EU should do about that (if anything).

Capital Adequacy Standards

Regarding capital requirements, consider first the activities of domestic firms in countries that have looser capital requirements. Even if home-country rules apply to these firms' activities around the globe, two problems can emerge: domestic firms may interact with lightly regulated foreign counterparties who are a source of instability (like through the Lehman Brothers collapse in 2008). And the foreign markets in which firms are active might see higher overall volatility, exposing domestic firms to market risk that cannot be eliminated simply through microprudential regulation (think, for example, of an inflated real estate market).

If significant differences on desirable tightness of prudential regulations remain and no global deal can be reached, other instruments remain available: domestic firms' supervisors could attach high capital charges to activities in the markets in question. They could also oblige domestic firms to operate through separately capitalised subsidiaries, without a claim to parent companies' capital, or forbid overly risky activities in lightly regulated markets for domestic firms.

A different set of issues arises with foreign firms active in domestic markets. If foreign firms can operate under their home-country rules, the key questions are to which degree their activities might generate unacceptable losses for domestic market participants and whether they pose systemic risks, for example through their interwovenness with domestic firms (counterparty risk). If either applies, host country rules will have to be imposed. The potential downside of erecting such barriers to market entry is limited. Indeed, jurisdictions such as the EU use them, but mostly invisibly because other major jurisdictions are all deemed to apply rules that are equivalent to European ones and are therefore exempted from host-country rules.

If strict application of host country rules can keep risky firms out of domestic markets, why would it be desirable to have globally harmonised rules for regulatory capital? Competitiveness issues only matter to a limited number of globally operating banks, but these firms are essential for cross-border financial flows. And to the degree that global financial intermediation requires competition between them, competitiveness issues cannot be entirely dismissed. If Deutsche Bank for example constitutes a crucial link between the European economies and global capital markets, it matters to Europe that 'its bank on Wall Street' is not disconnected from global financial flows, but also does not pose a systemic risk.

Hence, global agreements are desirable: if European banks faced much tighter rules than American ones, they might lose market share and be cut out of funding flows. But shared rules are only necessary for the most internationally active financial firms, such that they can act as intermediaries in global finance. It does not follow that the EU could not regulate its local savings banks more strictly than the US does without considerable negative externalities.

Executive Compensation for Banks

Compensation for bank employees follows a slightly different logic: the debate has centred not on the level of compensation per se but on the way in which remuneration structures in the past have constituted incentives for bankers to run excessive risks (Tabb 2012). If remuneration packages are readjusted such that the behaviour they encourage does not undermine financial stability, it is not obvious why rules need to be harmonised internationally. If firms abroad offer higher financial rewards than domestic firms that abide by strict compensation rules (for example, through deferring compensation), then those rewards also contain incentive structures for individuals that can undermine financial stability and are therefore undesirable. A unilateral rejigging of compensation structures will not necessarily lead to a 'flight of talent', but attract executives who see opportunities in long-term and sustainable business strategies – exactly the intended effect. If remuneration rules are applied as host-country rules, there is no pressing reason for these rules to be harmonised globally, or even across the Atlantic.

The EU has prominently addressed compensation in the Fourth Capital Requirements Directive (CRD4), whereas the USA has only adopted non-binding guidelines on bonuses. The Capital Requirements and Bonuses Package (CRBP) concentrates on capping the variable portion of pay and deferring its payout; the CRBP applies to EU firms, non-EU subsidiaries of EU firms, and the employees of non-EU firms in the EU. The British Bankers Association (BBA) has unsurprisingly complained about such moves and asked EU regulators and legislators to pressure the USA and Asian jurisdictions into adopting similarly tough conditions on pay (Ahuja and Chellel 2010). So far, however, the EU has rightly seen no need to deviate from its path because of international disparities.

Structural Reforms in the Banking Sector

One reform area that is directly tied to the backing of financial institutions with taxpayers' funds is structural reform in the banking sector. Which activities can be conducted by financial firms that enjoy de facto public guarantees? In the USA, the so-called Volcker Rule, included in the Dodd-Frank Act, has revived a divide between commercial and investment banking that the USA had pioneered with the Glass-Steagall Act in the 1930s. In the United Kingdom, the Vickers Commission has tabled its own proposals, and the EU has installed its own committee with the Liikanen Report as its set of recommendations.

In line with the preceding sections, the key question to ask is whether internationally divergent rules are sufficiently problematic to warrant global rule uniformity. The idea behind structural reforms is to ensure that depositor funds are not endangered through high-risk investments and that, by implication, public safety nets need not be activated. Given that such safety nets are national in nature, there is no reason why national arrangements could not differ. If one jurisdiction allows relatively risky banks to take retail deposits, that does not hinder another jurisdiction in the application of tighter standards. The link is simple: any institution that effectively relies on a sovereign's funds as a safety net must play by its rules. This principle swings free of what happens elsewhere and hence entails no incentive to harmonise regulation.

Accounting Standards

Accounting standards are a case apart because the relationship between key standards, such as those covering financial instruments and financial stability, is unclear. Twenty years of global efforts to devise a proper solution in this area have only produced a succession of temporary fixes (Mügge and Stellinga 2010). Any particular accounting methodology can both buttress and undermine financial stability, depending on market circumstances. Hence, it is difficult to argue that some standards are 'tighter' than others, and it makes little sense to build the case for or against global harmonisation on that basis. Instead, two other issues arise.

Accounting standards are wound up with banking rules as they inform how banks calculate their own equity and hence their capital buffers. If it is sensible to pursue a level playing field in capital adequacy standards, it is imperative that equity is calculated in comparable ways – otherwise, cross-border comparisons become meaningless. That does not imply *harmonised* standards; instead, *comparability* on stability-relevant measures is sufficient, which includes measures that affect the relative competitiveness of banks.

At the same time, the uncertainty surrounding accounting for financial instruments in particular has led standard setters to adapted accounting rules on several occasions. Also regulators recognise that in extreme situations, these rules may have to be adapted – as the EU has done repeatedly when it endorsed International Financial Reporting Standards (IFRS) in a customised version or refused endorsement altogether. This need for adaptation makes rigid global rules undesirable. Comparability between major rule sets is important, but it is potentially counterproductive to pursue to-the-letter harmonisation. The institutional set-up for the setting of International Financial Reporting Standards is appropriate in that respect: the IASB offers global templates, and the EU has strong incentives to endorse them, lest it stands accused of fudging standards in the interest of particular stakeholders. At the same time, the IASB will want to produce standards that major jurisdictions such as the EU find useful. Taken together, these incentives argue for a regime in which jurisdictions have the freedom to deviate from global templates but also have to explain their reasons for doing so.

The only domain in which an explicit commitment to globally harmonised accounting standards is sensible is in those areas that might, through their importance for the calculation of bank equity, otherwise undo any rule harmonisation achieved through the Basel agreements. Should that prove difficult, the relevant accounting rules should be incorporated in a revised future version of the Basel accord, such that the link between accounting standards as set by the IASB and banking rules would be severed. Then, there would be no strong reason to pursue global accounting standard harmonisation beyond the present level.

Credit Rating Agencies

Credit rating agencies (CRAs) have attracted substantial criticism (White 2009) for misleading investors with faulty triple-A ratings and, particularly in Europe, spooking sovereign debt investors. From a stability perspective, we can distinguish two different problems: the effects of ratings on rated entities (which can be self-fulfilling prophecies), and the effects of ratings on the (potentially risky) composition of investment portfolios. Are global rules necessary to tame these sources of instability?

Because the three dominant CRAs are incorporated in the USA, legislative attention to them, whether in the form of idiosyncratic EU rules or attempts to craft a set of global agreements, had long seemed a non-issue. In the wake of the scandals in the early 2000s surrounding Enron and Worldcom in the USA and Parmalat and Ahold in Europe, concern focused on the ability of faulty ratings to expose investors to huge losses. It was particularly worrying that the first Basel accord had 'hard-wired' ratings into capital adequacy rules. The revised version of the agreement (Basel II, of 2004) broke that link for the largest banks, which were allowed to use their internal ratings instead of those produced by the CRAs. The Dodd-Frank Act has gone further and removed hard-wiring of ratings in banking rules altogether; European rules in the co-decision procedure propose to achieve the same in Europe by 2020. While some reliance on CRAs, in particular by small banks and investors, will not disappear, previous automatisms will. How CRAs rate, for example, Latin American sovereign debt will have less direct consequences in Europe than before.

The second stability-issue concerns the rated entities themselves, in particular sovereign debtors who may see their debt become unsustainable as a consequence of adverse ratings. Here, the EU is in a much better position to impose its own rules with an eye to European financial stability, irrespective of steps taken elsewhere in the world. These rules specify, for example, the timing and frequency of ratings (thereby avoiding unexpected, ad hoc downgrades) and force CRAs to explain their decisions publicly, such that investors can themselves gauge the astuteness of CRAs' judgments.

These rated entity-specific rules can differ between jurisdictions without significant negative externalities. If the EU can, through regulatory reforms, prevent unexpected and undesirable gyrations in European sovereign debt markets, it matters very little to EU financial stability whether similar operational procedures are applied when CRAs rate entities elsewhere in the world. An obvious argument in favour of stronger global rules would have been a willingness to impose specific rating methodologies on CRAs, which would have to apply globally to preserve consistency. But both American and European authorities have stopped short of such a step – largely because they might appear to 'doctor' ratings to paper over financial troubles and, equally important, because it simply is unclear whether a fool-proof ratings methodology exists at all. Without an appetite to prescribe rating methodologies themselves, the absence of a global rule set for CRAs does not pose a problem from the perspective of safeguarding European financial stability.

Derivatives Trading

Derivatives vie with CRAs as the ultimate villain in narratives of the financial crisis, and many observers have demanded changes to the way in which they are regulated (Tabb 2012). Does it, from the perspective of the EU, take a global rule set to do so effectively?

In the case of derivatives, it is useful to distinguish three ways in which opaque and highly customised Over-The-Country (OTC) derivatives in particular can affect financial stability. First, firms may build up exposures that are too complex or opaque to be managed effectively, spawning major losses and potential bankruptcy, with attendant costs for taxpayers or retail-depositors. Second, in times of crisis, firms may doubt the viability of their counterparties, leading to a 'freeze' of financial flows. Third, derivatives may feed major asset bubbles, such as the real estate bubble in the USA, and thereby make the financial system as a whole vulnerable once the bubble bursts. At this point, policymakers intend to address this last problem mainly through macroeconomic tools (macroprudential policy), not financial regulation itself. The two former problems are regulatory challenges, however, requiring different answers and different degrees of international cooperation.

Tackling individual firms' exposures to potentially dangerous derivatives can be achieved unilaterally. Structural reforms in the banking sector can separate institutions that handle depositors' money from those that are effectively high-risk investment funds and explicitly come without a public safety net. The key is not to outlaw specific derivatives, but to prohibit their use for speculative purposes by institutions that are effectively backed by public funds. Initiatives to this end have been taken in different jurisdictions even in the absence of global agreements or rules.

The issue is very different once we consider counterparty risk. How can contagion between financial institutions be prevented? The answer, embraced on both sides of the Atlantic, is the installation of central counterparties – clearing houses of the complicated web of derivatives trades – which would act as firewalls should one market participant collapse. In order to intervene quickly if necessary, supervisory authorities want access to information that would allow them to gauge the size and importance of mutual exposures. Irrespective of questions that remain about the ultimate effectiveness of these measures, it is clear that their effective implementation requires intense global cooperation. A single trade between an American and a European bank cannot be cleared on two separate venues simultaneously. Hence, authorities will have to agree a regime in which central counterparties are able to satisfy both American and European concerns simultaneously (for example regarding collateral standards) and report relevant trade data to both American and European authorities. Even though the rules have not been finalised, it seems as though both European and US authorities are firmly moving in the direction of compatible, if not identical rules.

7. Conclusions

The financial crisis has clearly demonstrated the potential fiscal implications of faulty financial regulation. It has tied regulatory policy much closer to two policy areas that have traditionally been jealously defended against external interference – fiscal and monetary policy. This effect has been particularly important in the EU, both because of the severity of the sovereign debt crisis and because of the complicated distribution of policy competences between national and supranational bodies. Financial stability has become the pre-eminent legitimate policy goal of financial regulation; alternative goals, such as serving the competitive interests of financial firms, are clearly less legitimate should they contravene what financial stability demands. This chapter has asked how this shift in European financial governance has affected its international outlook, and in particular the rationale for a strong European commitment to harmonised global rules, for example through the G20.

An analysis of six different policy fields has shown that only in two of them – capital adequacy rules and derivatives trading – are there strong reasons to seek international agreement, even if other parties to such agreements prefer less stringent regulation than the EU. In all other fields, in contrast, the EU is well-equipped to regulate its own financial markets with an eye to financial stability irrespective of whether other jurisdictions, including the USA, apply standards of similar stringency. Truly global regulatory arrangements are desirable where they constitute pure coordination games – ironing out functionally equivalent differences. But in the face of divergent preferences concerning the stringency of financial re-regulation within the G20, there is no reason why the EU should not stick to its guns and implement the reforms it deems necessary to put financial markets on a stable footing once more.

Conclusion

Maria João Rodrigues

We hope that this overview of the economic, social, political and external implications of the Eurozone crisis for the transformation of European Union (EU) governance is relevant and inspiring to understand and assess what is still unfolding. New theoretical approaches and new concepts were suggested to cope with this extraordinary and complex process with its high level of uncertainty. This uncertainty is not only about the level of accomplishment to be achieved, but also about the overall direction of this process. That is why we propose to the reader a final element for consideration, which was also provided to the authors as background for inspiration.

This final piece identifies possible and contrasted scenarios for the evolution of the Economic Monetary Union (EMU) in financial, economic and social terms. These scenarios were developed to provide possible configurations of the EMU and of European integration taking 2020 as the horizon and stemming from the various policy choices that can be made in response to the central problems of the Eurozone. These crucial problems are indicated in the following table:

Table Conc.1   The central problems of the Eurozone

Areas described in each scenario	Central problems of the EMU
Financial stability	Credit shortage Inter-bank lending Widely diverging borrowing costs with regard to public debt issuance Risk of sovereign default
Fiscal discipline	High public debt High public deficits Little fiscal room to support public and private investment Tax divergences Social contributions and benefits divergences
Growth Sutainable development with its economic, social and environmental dimensions	Recession Low growth Unemployment Social inequalities Slow transition to green growth Slow transition to smart growth

Areas described in each scenario	Central problems of the EMU
Macroeconomic imbalances	Increasing divergences in growth, unemployment, investment rates High current account deficits and external indebtedness
Governance	Effectiveness Legitimacy

Scenario A – Muddling-through Scenario: European Hierarchy and Differentiation

The EMU remains incomplete, unable to ensure growth and employment and, even less, a transition to a new growth model that is greener, smarter and more inclusive. Access to financial resources remains unstable. Regulation of the financial system to reduce volatility and undue pressure is still not complete. For instance, rating agencies are still free to intervene in the political arena. The European financial system supervisory bodies remain weak and there are several bottlenecks in inter-bank lending across the MS. Such lending is constrained by hesitant last-resort provision of liquidity on the part of the European Central Bank (ECB). As a result, there is a chronic credit shortage.

As regards the issuance of public debt, differences in borrowing costs between MS remain too high. The resources of the European Stability Mechanism (ESM) are still inadequate and thus, there is always the possibility of sovereign default. Furthermore, the EU's dependence on financial support from external partners increases.

The revised Stability and Growth Pact (SGP) exerts pressure towards the regular reduction of the public debt and the structural public deficit and leaves little room for supporting public and private investment. Fiscal consolidation remains difficult in many MS because the growth rate is too low. The long-term sustainability of welfare systems is eroded. In parallel, the Euro Plus Pact committing MS to further convergence of corporate taxation and social contributions/benefits is difficult to implement for the same reason.

There are neither significant changes in the European instruments for supporting investment nor macroeconomic coordination for growth. Nor is there a European industrial policy to complement European trade policy. The European strategy for growth remains limited to completing the Single Market and structural reforms. In this context, the opportunities of the European Single Market and of external markets are falling in particular to the countries which have public and private financial resources to invest. As a consequence, the transition towards a greener and smarter economy is very uneven across MS. With these constraints on European aggregate demand, the average unemployment rate remains high, hitting particularly young people in many MS: social tensions will increase strongly in some European regions.

The new macroeconomic surveillance puts the focus on MS with low competitiveness and high external deficits and unemployment rates. It makes individualised recommendations on how they might reduce their problems. Nevertheless, against the background described above, it is difficult to reduce divergences between MS regarding growth, investment and employment rates, despite efforts to optimise use of the structural funds. Some regions are trapped in recession/stagnation, triggering emigration flows, including a 'brain drain', thus exacerbating the situation.

There are no fundamental changes in the budgetary process. The Community budget remains the same size and has few resources of its own. As a protectionist reaction, there is national resistance to closer coordination of national budgets and programmes at the European level. The new President of the European Commission might be elected by the European Parliament, but will remain constrained by weak financial and policy instruments in any efforts to prevent or solve problems. This, together with a lack of involvement by MS and citizens in decision-making, will lead to a weakening of popular support for European integration and to a strengthening of anti-European and populist parties.

Scenario B – Break-up Scenario: European Fragmentation and Disintegration

The EMU remains incomplete, unable to ensure growth and shaken by instances of sovereign default and exit, with uncontrolled contagion effects. Access to financial resources remains subject to constant uncertainty. Regulation of the financial system to reduce volatility and undue pressure is confronted with substantial resistance and disagreements. For example, rating agencies continue to play an active role in the political game. The European financial supervisory bodies are weak and there are a number of bottlenecks in inter-bank lending across the MS, which cannot be reduced by last-resort provisions of liquidity from the ECB. As a result, there is a chronic credit crunch, deepening the recession in several MS.

In the issuance of public debt, differences in borrowing costs across the MS are too high and, since the resources of the European Stability Mechanism are too low, the risk of sovereign default or of severe and disorderly debt restructuring becomes reality in some countries, with contagion effects on sovereign debt and banks.

A revised SGP puts pressure on MS to systematically reduce public debt and structural public deficits, leaving little room for promoting public and private investment. Fiscal consolidation becomes impossible in several MS because they have remained mired in recession over a longer period. Welfare systems are undermined and, in some MS, partially dismantled, leading to a major increase in poverty. In parallel, the Euro Plus Pact, involving commitments to further convergence of corporate taxation and social contributions/benefits, becomes impossible to implement.

There are neither significant changes in the European instruments for promoting investment, nor macroeconomic coordination for growth, nor European industrial policy in connection with European trade policy. The European strategy for growth remains focused on completing the Single Market and structural reforms, priorities that experience particular difficulties in countries in recession. In this context, the opportunities provided by the European Single Market and external markets benefit particularly those countries with public and private financial resources to invest. As a consequence, the transition towards a greener and smarter economy is blocked and even goes into reverse in several MS. With these constraints on European aggregate demand, the average unemployment rate and social inequalities increase to unprecedented levels. In the meantime, in the weakened economies, many strategic assets are bought up by non-European countries, reducing Europe's control over its own production chains.

The new macroeconomic surveillance puts the focus on MS with low competitiveness and high external deficits and unemployment rates, making individualised recommendations to help them to reduce their problem. Nevertheless, given the above-described circumstances, the divergences between MS regarding growth, investment and employment rates will increase, even with use of the structural funds. Some regions are devastated by deep recession with high unemployment triggering stronger emigration flows, including a strong brain drain element, which only worsens the situation. Hostility between European regions will increase, based on stereotypes, leading to a fragmentation of the European identity.

There are no fundamental changes in the budgetary process. The Community budget remains the same size, with inadequate resources of its own. As a protectionist reaction, some countries refuse to permit closer coordination of national budgets and programmes at European level. The new President of the European Commission might be elected by the European Parliament, but will remain limited by weak financial and political instruments for preventing or solving problems. This, together with opaque centralisation and a lack of participation by MS and European citizens in decision-making, will increase popular hostility towards Europe and strengthen anti-European and populist parties. Protectionist reactions will emerge everywhere pushing for a return to national borders and national currencies and paving the way for the breakdown and fragmentation of the Eurozone. The disintegration of the European Union will become a risk. A large global shock would follow, leading to a global recession.

Scenario C – Core Europe Scenario: Fiscal Union with a Smaller Group

The EMU is completed by a smaller core group of MS, which adopts a new full-fledged Treaty outside the EU Treaties and excludes the non-Eurozone Members and even some Eurozone Members (a 'two-tier Europe'). Regulation of the financial system is developed and provides more financial stability and focus on the needs of the real economy. Stronger European supervisory bodies ensure sounder banking with more responsible lending and borrowing but inter-bank lending between those inside and outside the core group remains difficult. Unconventional measures by the ECB are still necessary to provide better access to credit.

A European debt agency limited to the small core group ensures joint issuance of public bonds as a last resort, when issuance at national level becomes too difficult and borrowing costs become more reasonable in the core group. For nations in difficulty outside the core group, the European Stability Mechanism is equipped to provide financial assistance, albeit with strict conditionality.

A revised SGP applies towards the regular reduction of public debt and structural public deficits. Fiscal consolidation remains difficult in the MS outside the core group, because their growth is too low. The long-term sustainability of welfare systems is strengthened in the core group but weakened outside it. In parallel, the Euro Plus Pact, with its commitments to further convergence of corporate taxation and social contributions/benefits, is implemented, but only in the core group. It has to protect itself from increasing fiscal and social dumping from outside the core group.

New financial resources for investment, combined with a European industrial policy, the Single Market and appropriate structural reforms, foster the transition to a greener, smarter and more inclusive economy in the core group. More organised and competitive European production chains under the leadership of the core group are better able to reap the potential of the European Single Market and global markets.

The new macroeconomic surveillance puts the focus on MS with low competitiveness and high external deficits and unemployment rates, making individualised recommendations with a view to enabling them to address their problems. Nevertheless, in the circumstances we have described, the divergences across MS regarding growth, investment and employment rates will increase, even with the use of the structural funds. Some regions are trapped in a recession/ stagnation with high unemployment, triggering stronger emigration flows (including a brain drain), which only exacerbates the situation. Hostility between European regions will increase, based on stereotypes, leading to fragmentation of the European identity.

In the core group, the budgetary process is developed, so that there is better coordination of national budgets and a better interface with the Community budget. Outside the core group, there are no fundamental changes in the budgetary process. The Community budget remains the same size and has inadequate resources. As a protectionist reaction, there is national resistance to closer coordination of national budgets and programmes at European level. The European Commission will remain limited by weak financial and policy instruments for preventing and solving problems. This, together with a lack of participation of MS and European citizens in decision-making, will weaken popular support for European integration and strengthen anti-European and populist parties, both inside and outside the core group.

Scenario D – Completion Scenario: Fiscal Union in the EU

The EMU is completed in the EU, keeping membership open to all MS that want to join. A two-tier Europe will be avoided, but a two-speed Europe might be necessary, with a new Treaty for all MS that want to join. Regulation of the financial system is developed and provides more financial stability and focus on the needs of the real economy. Stronger European supervisory bodies ensure sounder banking activity with more responsible lending and borrowing and normal inter-bank lending across the EU. Hence, unconventional measures by the ECB are less necessary to provide normal access to credit.

A European debt agency ensures joint issuance of public bonds as a last resort, when issuance at national level reaches unreasonable levels. This favours lower and more reasonable borrowing costs in general. If certain countries encounter unusual difficulties, the European Stability Mechanism is equipped to provide financial assistance with a clear but balanced conditionality, deploying more effective and rapid rebalancing and recovery programmes.

A revised SGP applies pressure on MS to constantly reduce their public debt and structural public deficits, but leaves some room for promoting smart public and private investment. This smart culture of balanced budgets paves the way for more credible fiscal consolidation. The long-term sustainability of welfare systems is also strengthened. In parallel, the Euro Plus Pact, with its commitments to further convergence of corporate taxation and social contributions/benefits, becomes easier to implement.

Investment, growth and job creation are supported by stronger European instruments, notably Community Programmes, mobilising Community budget resources, EIB loans, guarantees and bonds, private project bonds and other available financing sources, such as pension funds, or taxation sources, such as a financial transaction tax. These new resources for investment, combined with a European industrial policy, the Single Market and appropriate structural reforms, foster the transition to a greener, smarter and more inclusive economy. More organised and competitive European production chains are able to better reap the potential of the European Single Market and global markets. The macroeconomic surveillance process is also used to improve macroeconomic coordination in the European economy, taking positive advantage of spill-over effects.

Macroeconomic surveillance is coupled with stronger resources for catching up, and not only swifter implementation of the structural funds, but also a European Fund for Economic Stabilisation to deal with asymmetric shocks. Social dialogue and bargaining are also encouraged at national and European level to better align wages and productivity. Under these framework conditions, differences with regard to investment, growth and employment rates decrease and regions lagging behind can more realistically catch up in terms of competitiveness, social and environmental standards, as well as reduce their external economic and financial deficits.

The budgetary process involves better coordination of national budgets and a better interface with the Community budget, which can also count on new resources of its own, notably based on VAT and a financial transaction tax. With these new financial and policy means, the European Commission, with a President elected by the European Parliament, can better energise the European institutions to prevent and respond to problems. Closer involvement of the MS and European citizens in decision-making also strengthens popular support of European integration, weakening the influence of anti-European and populist parties.

The Eurozone, building on a more consistent EMU, will coordinate its external position and there will be a single Eurozone representation in the Bretton Woods institutions. The Euro will become a reference reserve currency attracting financial resources from all over the world.

At the moment, as we are completing this book – May 2013 – these scenarios remain a possibility, but their relative probability will depend on the interplay of many actors, including those who propose and use new approaches and new concepts. We hope this book can be used to assess the consistency of such scenarios and to inspire some of these actors.

Appendix I

The 27 conventions related to political, human and labour rights, environment and good governance (European Council 2005: 42):

Core Human and Labour Rights UN/ILO Conventions

1. Convention on the Prevention and Punishment of the Crime of Genocide (1948).
2. International Convention on the Elimination of all Forms of Racial Discrimination (1965).
3. International Covenant on Civil and Political Rights (1966).
4. International Covenant on Economic, Social and Cultural Rights (1966).
5. International Convention on the Elimination of all Forms of Discrimination against Women (1979).
6. Convention against Torture and Other Cruel, Inhuman or Degrading Treatment or Punishment (1984).
7. Convention on the Rights of the Child (1989).
8. International Convention on the Suppression and Punishment of the Crime of Apartheid.
9. ILO Convention concerning Forced or Compulsory Labour, No 29 (1930).
10. ILO Convention on Freedom of Association and Protection of the Right to Organise, No 87 (1948).
11. ILO Convention concerning the Application of the Principles of the Right to Organise and Bargain Collectively, No 98 (1949).
12. ILO Convention concerning Equal Remuneration of Men and Women Workers for Work of Equal Value, No 100 (1951).
13. ILO Convention concerning the Abolition of Forced Labour, No 105 (1957).
14. ILO Convention concerning Discrimination in Respect of Employment and Occupation, No 111 (1958).
15. ILO Convention concerning Minimum Age for Admission to Employment, No 138 (1973).
16. ILO Convention concerning the Prohibition and Immediate Action for the Elimination of the Worst Forms of Child Labour, No 182 (1999).

*International Conventions Related to the Environment and the Good
Governance Principles*

17. Convention on International Trade of Endangered Species of Wild Fauna and Flora (1973).
18. Montreal Protocol on Substances that Deplete the Ozone Layer (1987).
19. Basel Convention on the Control of Transboundary Movements of Hazardous Wastes and their Disposal (1989).
20. Convention on Biological Diversity (1992).
21. Cartagena Protocol on Biosafety (2000).
22. Stockholm Convention on Persistent Organic Pollutants (2001).
23. Kyoto Protocol to the United Nations Framework Convention on Climate Change (1998).
24. United Nations Single Convention on Narcotic Drugs (1961).
25. United Nations Convention on Psychotropic Substances (1971).
26. United Nations Convention against Illicit Traffic in Narcotic Drugs and Psychotropic Substances (1988).
27. United Nations Convention against Corruption (2004).

Appendix II

List of GSP+ Beneficiary Countries

	Countries
1	Armenia
2	Azerbaijan
3	Bolivia
4	Cape Verde
5	Colombia (until December 2013)
6	Costa Rica
7	Ecuador
8	El Salvador
9	Georgia
10	Guatemala
11	Honduras (until December 2013)
12	Mongolia
13	Nicaragua
14	Pakistan (from January 2014)
15	Panama
16	Paraguay
17	Peru
18	Sri Lanka

Source: European Commission 2013c

Appendix III

Least Developed Countries that Benefit from the EBA Scheme

AFRICA

1. Angola
2. Benin
3. Burkina Faso
4. Burundi
5. Central African Rep.
6. Chad
7. Comoros
8. Congo, Dem. Rep.
9. Djibouti
10. Equatorial Guinea
11. Eritrea
12. Ethiopia
13. Gambia
14. Guinea
15. Guinea-Bissau
16. Lesotho
17. Liberia
18. Madagascar
19. Malawi
20. Mali
21. Mauritania
22. Mozambique
23. Niger
24. Rwanda
25. Sao Tome & Principe
26. Senegal
27. Sierra Leone
28. Somalia
29. South Sudan (from January 2014)
30. Sudan
31. Tanzania
32. Togo
33. Uganda
34. Zambia

ASIA
35. Afghanistan
36. Bangladesh
37. Bhutan
38. Cambodia
39. Lao PDR
40. Maldives (until December 2013)
41. Myanmar/Burma
42. Nepal
43. Timor-Leste
44. Yemen
AUSTRALIA & PACIFIC
45. Kiribati
46. Samoa
47. Solomon Islands
48. Tuvalu
49. Vanuatu
CARIBBEAN
50. Haiti

Source: European Commission 2013c

Bibliography

Addison, J.T. and W.S. Siebert (1997) *Labour Markets in Europe: Issues of Harmonization and Regulation*. London: Dryden Press.

Agence Europe (2011) 'Greece, Stability Pact, Stress Tests and Derivatives on Agenda', 18 June 2011.

Agence Europe (2012) 'Proposal on Single Banking Supervisor Expected on 11 September', 23 August 2012.

Ahuja, V. and K. Chellel (2010) 'CEBS Uses Final Bank Pay Guidelines', *eFinancialNews*, 10 December 2010, http://www.efinancialnews.com/story/2010-12-10/cebs-issues-bank-pay-guidelines, last accessed 20 February 2013.

Akbar, Y.H. and G.S.S. Suder (2006) 'The New EU Merger Regulation: Implications for EU-US Merger Strategies', *Thunderbird International Business Review*, 48(5): 667–85.

Allerkamp, D.K. (2009) 'Intergovernmentalism Reloaded: The Transformative Power of 'Intergovernmental' Council Policy-Making', mimeo.

Alternative Investment Expert Group (2006) *Report of the Alternative Investments Expert Group: Managing, Servicing and Marketing Hedge Funds in Europe*, Brussels, July 2006.

Amato, G. and Y. Mény, (with C. Barbier and D. Natali) (2012) 'Is the EU Becoming More Like the UN? Paradoxes Around Institutional Developments in 2011 and Risks for Future Integration', in D. Natali and B. Vanhercke (eds) *Social Developments in the European Union 2011*. Brussels: Etui Publishers.

Amnesty International Report (2011) http://www.amnesty.org/en/annual-report/2011/downloads#en, 5 September, accessed 20 May 2013.

Arnau, J.C.S. (2002) *The Generalised System of Preferences in the WTO*. London: Cameron.

Arnold, C., E.V. Sapir and G. Zapryanova (2012) 'Trust in the Institutions of the European Union: A Cross-country Examination', in Beaudonnet L. and D. Di Mauro (eds) *Beyond Euro-skepticism: Understanding Attitudes Towards the EU*. European Integration online Papers (EIoP), Special Mini-Issue, 16(2), http://eiop.or.at/eiop/index.php/eiop/issue/view/30, last accessed on 02 March 2013.

Asian Development Bank (2009) *Study on Intraregional Trade and Investment in South Asia*. Mandaluyong City, Philippines: Asian Development Bank.

Avdagic, S., M. Rhodes and J. Visser (2011) *Social Pacts in Europe: Emergence, Evolution and Institutionalization*. Oxford: Oxford University Press.

Aydin, U. (2012) 'Promoting competition: European Union and the Global Economic Order', *Journal of European Integration*, 36(6): 663–81.

Aydin, U. and K.P. Thomas (2012) 'The Challenges and Trajectories of EU Competition Policy in the Twenty-first Century', *Journal of European Integration*, 36(6): 531–47.

Bagehot, W. (1873) *Lombard Street: A Description of the Money Market*. King, London; reprinted Wiley, New York 1999.

Barbier, J.C. (2008) *La Longue Marche Vers l'Europe Sociale*. Paris: PUF.

Barbier J.C., and F. Colomb (2012) 'EU Law as Janus Bifrons – a Sociological Approach to Social Europe', *European Integration online Papers* (EIoP), Special mini issue, 16(1): 1–25.

Barnard, C. (2012) 'The Financial Crisis and the Euro Plus Pact: A Labour Lawyer's Perspective', *Industrial Law Journal*, 41(1): 98–114.

Barroso, J.M.D. (2012a) Speech at the European Parliament Plenary Debate on the European Council 28–29 June Plenary Session of the European Parliament, Strasbourg, 03 July 2012, European Commission SPEECH 12/518.

Barroso, J.M.D. (2012b) Speech by President Barroso to European Union Heads of Delegation Annual Conference of EU Heads of Delegation, EUSR and Chargés d'Affaires, Brussels, 04 September 2012, European Commission SPEECH/12/585.

Barroso, J.M.D. (2012c) State of the Union Address – Plenary Session of the European Parliament, Strasbourg, 12 September 2012, European Commission SPEECH 12/596.

Bartels, L. (2008) 'The Application of Human Rights Conditionality in the EU's Bilateral Trade Agreements and Other Trade Arrangements with Third Countries', Study Conducted for the European Parliament, EXPO-B-INTA-2008–57, PE 406.991, November, Brussels: European Parliament.

Baun, M.J. (1995) 'The Maastricht Treaty as High Politics', *Political Science Quarterly*, 110(4): 605–24.

Begg, I. (2009) 'Regulation and Supervision of Financial Intermediaries in the EU: The Aftermath of the Financial Crisis', *Journal of Common Market Studies*, 47(5): 1107–28.

Bellamy, R. (2010) 'Democracy Without Democracy? Can the EU's Democratic "Outputs" be Separated from the Democratic "Inputs" Provided by Competitive Parties and Majority Rule?', *Journal of European Public Policy*, 17(1): 2–19.

Bergsten, F.C. and J.F. Kirkegaard (2012) 'The Coming Resolution of the European Crisis: An Update', Petersen Institute, Policy Brief PB12–18.

Bertola, G., T. Boeri and G. Nicoletti (eds) (2001) *Welfare and Employment in a United Europe*. Cambridge MA: MIT Press.

Best, J. (2003) 'From the Top-Down: The New Financial Architecture and the Re-embedding of Global Finance', *New Political Economy*, 8(3): 363–84.

Bicchi, F. (2006) '"Our size fits all": Normative Power Europe and the Mediterranean', *Journal of European Public Policy*, 13(2): 286–303.

Boerzel, T. (2008) 'Der Schatten der Hierarchie. Ein Governance Paradox?, in G. Folke Schuppert and M. Zürn (eds) *Governance in Einer Sich Wandelnden Welt*. PVS-Sonderheft, Wiesbaden: VS Verlag für Sozialwissenschaften.

Boerzel, T. and Risse, T. (2012) 'From Europeanization to Diffusion: Introduction', *West European Politics*, 35(1): 1–19.

Bomhoff, A, A. Jarosz-Friis, N. Pesaresi (2009) 'Restructuring Banks in Crisis – Overview of the Applicable State Aid Rules', *Competition Policy Newsletter*, 3: 3–9.

Bonoli, G. (2011) 'Active Labour Market Policy in a Changing Economic Context', in J. Clasen and D. Clegg (eds), *Regulating the Risk of Unemployment*. Oxford: Oxford University Press.

Bonoli, G. (2012) 'Active Labour Market Policy and Social Investment: A Changing Relationship', in N. Morel, B. Palier, and J. Palme (eds), *Towards a Social Investment Welfare State? Ideas, Policies and Challenges*. Bristol: Policy Press.

Bonoli G. and B. Palier (2008) 'When Past Reforms Open New Opportunities: Comparing Old-Age Insurance Reforms in Bismarckian Welfare Systems', in B. Palier and C. Martin (eds), *Reforming the Bismarkian Welfare Systems*. Malden, Mass.: Blackwell.

Borrás, S. (2009) 'The Politics of the Lisbon Strategy: The Changing Role of the Commission', *West European Politics*, 32(1): 97–118.

Borrás, S. and K. Jacobsson (2004) 'The Open Method of Co-ordination and the New Patterns of EU Governance', *European Journal of Public Policy*, 11(2): 185–208.

Borras, S. and Peters, G. (2011) 'The Lisbon Strategy's Empowerment of Core Executives: Centralizing and Politicizing EU National Co-ordination', *Journal of European Public Policy*, 18(4): 525–45.

Borrás, S., Chaminade, C., and Edquist, C. (2009) 'The Challenges of Globalization: Strategic choices for Innovation Policy', in G. Marklund, S.N. Vonortas and C.W. Wessner, (eds) *The Innovation Imperative: National Innovation Strategies in the Global Economy*. Cheltenham: Edward Elgar.

Bräuninger, D. (2011) 'Labour Mobility in the Euro Area; Deutsche Bank Research', *EU Monitor*, September 20. http://www.dbresearch.com/PROD/DBR_INTERNET_EN-PROD/PROD0000000000278645.PDF.

Bryant, R. (2003) *Turbulent Waters: Cross-border Finance and International Governance*. Washington DC: The Brookings Institution.

Büchs, M. (2008) 'The Open Method of Coordination as a "Two-level Game"', *Policy and Politics*, 36(1): 21–37.

Buckley, J. and D. Howarth (2010) 'Internal Market: Gesture Politics? Explaining the EU's Response to the Financial Crisis', *Journal of Common Market Studies, Annual Review*, 48: 119–41.

Buckley, J. and D. Howarth (2011) 'Internal Market: Regulating the So-Called "Vultures of Capitalism"', *Journal of Common Market Studies, Annual Review*, 49: 123–43.

Caporaso, J.A. and J. Wittenbrinck (2006) 'The New Modes of Governance and Political Authority in Europe', *Journal of European Public Policy*, 13(4): 471–80.

Castells A. and EuropeG, Opinion and Discussion Group on Political Economy (2012) 'Is the European Union Really Moving Toward a Fiscal Union?', EuropeG, http://www.europeg.com, last accessed 14 August 2013.

CER (Centro Europa Ricerche) (2013) 'Europe's Choice: Austerity or Growth?' Rapporto Nr.1., Roma, www.stefancollignon.eu, last accessed 31 July 2013.

Chalk, N. and R. Hemming (2000) 'Assessing Fiscal Sustainability in Theory and Practice', IMF Working Paper WP 00/81.

Chwieroth, J. (2007) 'Neoliberal Economists and Capital Account Liberalization in Emerging Markets', *International Organization*, 61: 443–63.

Cini, M. and L. McGowan (2008) *Competition Policy in the European Union*. Basingstoke: Palgrave.

Clark, G.L. and N. Whiteside (2003) *Pension Security in the 21st Century*. Oxford: Oxford University Press.

Clasen, J. and D. Clegg (2011) *Regulating the Risk of Unemployment. National Adaptations to Post-Industrial Labour Markets in Europe*. Oxford: Oxford University Press.

Collignon, S. (2002a) *Monetary Stability in Europe*. London: Routledge.

Collignon, S. (2002b) 'The European Republic; Reflections on the Political Economy of a European Constitution'. The Federal Trust, London, England, www.stefancollignon.eu, last accessed 31 July 2013.

Collignon, S. (2011) 'The Governance of European Public Goods', in D. Tarschys (ed.) *The EU Budget. What Should Go In? What Should Go Out?*, Swedish Institute for European Policy Studies (SIEPS), 3.

Collignon, S. (2012) *Macroeconomic Imbalances and Comparative Advantages in the Euro Area*. Brussels: European Trade Union Institute (ETUI) with Bertelsmann Foundation.

Collignon, S. (2013a). 'European Wage Bargaining, Social Dialogue and Imbalances in the Euro Area. A Note to the Committee on Employment and Social Affairs of the European Parliament', 18 February, http://www.europarl. europa.eu/meetdocs/2009_2014/documents/empl/dv/european_wage_bargain ing_/european_wage_bargaining_en.pdf, last accessed 31 July 2013.

Collignon, S. (2013b) Implications of the Low Interest Rate Environment for the Real Economy. Note for the European Parliament's Committee on Economic and Monetary Affairs, February 2013. http://www.stefancollignon.de/PDF/ EP-Feb2013-draft.pdf, last accessed 31 July 2013.

Collignon, S. and D. Schwarzer (2003) *Private Sector Involvement in the Euro. The Power of Ideas*. London: Routledge.

Collignon, S. and P. Esposito (2014) 'Unit Labour Costs and Capital Efficiency in the Euro Area: A New Competitiveness Indicator', in S. Collignon and P. Esposito (eds), *Competitiveness in the European Economy*. London, Routledge.

Collignon, S., P. Esposito and H. Lierse (2013) 'European Sovereign Bailouts, Political Risk and the Economic Consequences of Mrs. Merkel', *Journal of International Commerce, Economics and Policy*, 4(2): 1–25.

Collignon, S., R. Dehousse, J. Gabolde, M. Jouen, P. Pochet, R. Salais, R.-U. Sprenger, and H. Zsolt De Sousa (2005) The Lisbon Strategy and the Open Method of Co-ordination. 12 Recommendations for an Effective Multi-level Strategy, Policy Paper 12, March. Paris: Notre Europe.

Commission of the European Communities (2008) 'Commission Staff Working Document Accompanying Document to the GSP+ Report on the Status of Ratification and Recommendations by Monitoring Bodies Concerning Conventions of Annex III of the Council Regulation (EC) No 980/2005 of 27 June 2005 Applying a Scheme of Generalised Tariff Preferences (the GSP regulation) in the Countries that were Granted the Special Incentive Arrangement for Sustainable Development and Good Governance (GSP+) by Commission Decision of 21 December 2005', SEC(2008) 2647, 21 October, Brussels.

Compa, L. and J. Vogt (2001) 'Labour Rights in the Generalized System of Preferences: A 20-year Review', *Comparative Labour Law and Policy Journal*, 22(2/3): 199–237.

Cooper, R. and A. John (1988) 'Coordinating Coordination Failures in a Keynesian Model', *The Quarterly Journal of Economics*, 103 (3): 441–63.

Croisat, M. and J.-L. Quermonne (1996). *L'Europe et le Fédéralisme*. Paris: Montchrestien.

Crum, B. (2012) 'The Democratic Dilemma of Monetary Union', paper submitted at the EUDO Dissemination Conference on 'The Euro Crisis and the State of European Democracy', EUI, Florence, 22–3 November.

Dabbah, M. N. (2003) *The Internationalisation of Antitrust Policy*. Cambridge: Cambridge University Press.

Dagens Nyheter, various dates.

Daily Telegraph, various dates.

Damro, C. (2006a) 'Transatlantic Competition Policy: Domestic and International Sources of EU-US Cooperation', *European Journal of International Relations*, 12(2): 171–96.

Damro, C. (2006b) 'The New Trade Politics and EU Competition Policy: Shopping for Convergence and Cooperation', *Journal of European Public Policy*, 13(6): 867–86.

Davies, H. and D. Green (2008) *Global Financial Regulation. The Essential Guide*. Cambridge: Polity Press.

De Grauwe, P. (2009) *Economics of Monetary Union*. 8th edition. Oxford: Oxford University Press.

De Grauwe, P. (2011) 'The Governance of a Fragile Eurozone', CEPS Working Document, 346, May.

De Haan, J., H. Berger, and D. Jansen, (2004) 'Why has the Stability and Growth Pact Failed?', *International Finance*, 7(2): 235–60.

De la Porte, C. (2011) 'Principal-agent Theory and the Open Method of Co-ordination: The Case of the EES', *Journal of European Public Policy*, 18(4): 485–503.

De la Porte, C. and K. Jacobsson (2012) 'Social Investment or Recommodification? Assessing the Employment Policies of the EU Member States', in N. Morel, B. Palier and J. Palme (eds) *Towards a Social Investment Welfare State? Ideas, Policies and Challenges*. Bristol: The Policy Press.

De la Porte, C. and D. Natali (2009) 'Participation Through the Lisbon Strategy: Comparing the European Employment Strategy and Pensions OMC', *Transfer: European Review of Labour and Research*, 15(1): 71–91.

De la Porte, C. and D. Natali (2014) 'Altered Europeanization of Pension Reform Suring the *Great Recession*: Denmark and Italy Compared', in D. Martinsen and H. Vollard (eds), 'Implementing Social Europe in Times of Crisis', Special Issue, *West European Politics*, forthcoming.

De la Porte, C. and P. Pochet, (2012) 'Why and How (Still) Study the OMC?' *Journal of European Social Policy*, 22(2): 336–49.

De Larosiére, J. (2009) 'The High-level Group on Financial Supervision in the EU', Report, 25 February 2009, Brussels.

De Roose, S., D. Hodson, and J. Kuhlmann (2008) 'The Broad Economic Policy Guidelines: Before and After the Re-launch of the Lisbon Strategy', *Journal of Common Market Studies*, 46(4): 827–48.

De Ruiter, R. (2008) 'Developing Multilateral Surveillance Tools in the EU', *West European Politics*, 31(5): 896–914.

De Streel A. (2011) *La Nouvelle Gouvernance* Économique *Européenne: Description et Critique*. Namur: FUNDP – Cepess.

De Witte, B. (2012) 'International Treaty on the Euro and the EU Legal Order', paper delivered at the international conference on The Euro Crisis and the State of European Democracy, Florence, EUI, 22–3 November.

Degryse, C. (2012) 'The New European Economic Governance', Working paper 2012.14, Brussels: ETUI.

Dehousse, R. (2011) 'The "Community Method" at Sixty', in R. Dehousse (ed.), *The 'Community Method': Obstinate or Obsolete?*. New York: Palgrave Macmillan.

Delors Report (1989) 'Report on Economic and Monetary Union in the European Community'. Brussels: European Commission.

Delors, J. and A. Vitorino (2012) *La Zone Euro, Creuset de l'Union Européenne*. Paris: Notre Europe.

DG ECFIN (2012) 'Macroeconomic Imbalances – France', Occasional Papers 105, Brussels: European Commission.

Die Welt (2012) 'Deutsche Glauben Nicht Mehr an Europa', 17 September 2012.

Doumbia-Henry, C., and E. Gravel (2006) 'Free Trade Agreements and Labour Rights', *International Labour Review*, 145(3): 185–206.

Draghi, M. (2012) 'For a European Public Space: Remarks on Receiving the M100 Media Award 2012', 06 September 2012, Potsdam, European Central Bank, http://www.ecb.europa.eu/press/key/date/2012/html/sp120906.en.html, last accessed 11 September 2012.

Dunlop, C.A. and C.M. Radaelli (2013) 'Systematising Policy Learning: From Monolith to Dimensions', *Political Studies*, 61(3): 599–619.

Dyson, K. (2000) *The Politics of the Euro-Zone. Stability or Breakdown?*, Oxford. Oxford University Press.

Dyson, K. and K. Featherstone (1999) *The Road to Maastricht: Negotiating Economic Monetary Union*. Oxford: Oxford University Press.

Ebbinghaus. B. (2011) *The Varieties of Pension Governance: Pension Privatization in Europe*. Oxford: Oxford University Press.

Eichengreen, B. (1999) *Towards a New International Financial Architecture*. Washington DC: Institute for International Economics.

Eichengreen, B.J. (2007) *Global Imbalances and the Lessons of Bretton Woods*. Cambridge, MA: MIT Press.

Eichengreen, B.J. (2010) 'The Euro: Love it or Leave it?', NBER Working Paper, 13393.

Eichhorst, W., and A. Hemerijck (2010) 'Welfare and Employment: A European Dilemma?', in J. Alber and N. Gilbert (eds), *United in Diversity? Comparing Social Models in Europe and America*. Oxford: Oxford University Press.

Eichhorst, W., Kendzia, M.J., Knudsen, J.B. and Wahl-Brink, D. (2010) 'External Dimension of EU Social Policy', IZA Research Report No. 26, Based on a study conducted for the European Parliament, July.

Emmenegger, P., S. Häusermann, B. Palier, M. Seeleib-Kaiser, (2012) *The Age of Dualization: The Changing Face of Inequality in De-industrializing Societies*. Oxford: Oxford University Press.

Entman, M.R. (1993) 'Framing: Toward Clarification of a Fractured Paradigm', *Journal of Communication*, 43(4): 51–8.

Esping-Andersen, G. (2001) 'Comments', in G. Bertola, T. Boeri and G. Nicoletti (eds) (2001) *Welfare and Employment in a United Europe*. Cambridge MA: MIT Press.

Esping-Andersen, G. (2009) *The Incomplete Revolution: Adapting to Women's New Roles*. Cambridge: Polity.

Esping-Andersen, G., D. Gallie, A. Hemerijck, and J. Myles (2002) *Why We Need a New Welfare State*. Oxford: Oxford University Press.

Esposito, P. and P. Guerrieri (2014) 'Intra-European Imbalances, Competitiveness and External Trade: A Comparison between Italy and Germany', in S. Collignon and P. Esposito (eds), *Competitiveness in the European Economy*. London: Routledge.

European Central Bank (2012a) 'Euro Area Labour Markets and the Crisis. Structural Issues Report', October, http://www.ecb.int/pub/pdf/other/euroarea labourmarketsandthecrisis201210en.pdf, last accessed 31 July 2013.

European Central Bank (2012b) 'A Fiscal Compact for a Stronger Economic and Monetary Union', May 2012, ECB Monthly Bulletin.

European Commission (1999) 'White Paper on Modernisation of the Rules Implementing Articles 85 and 86 of the EC Treaty', Commission Programme No. 99/027, 28 April 1999, Brussels.

European Commission (2001) 'European Governance: A White Paper', COM (2002) 428 final, 25 July 2001, Brussels.

European Commission (2004) 'Notice on Cooperation Within the Network of Competition Authorities', OJ C 101, 27 April 2004, Brussels.

European Commission (2008a) 'The Application of State Aid Rules to Measures Taken in Relation to the Financial Institutions in the Context of the Current Global Financial Crisis', Communication from the Commission, OJ C270, 25 October 2008, Brussels.

European Commission (2008b) 'The Recapitalisation of Financial Institutions in the Current Financial Crisis: Limitation of the Aid to the Minimum Necessary and Safeguards Against Undue Distortions of Competition', Communication from the Commission, OJ C10, 15 January 2008, Brussels.

European Commission (2008c) 'A European Economic Recovery Plan, Communication from the Commission', COM(2008) 800 final, 26 November 2008, Brussels.

European Commission (2008d) 'BNP Paribas/Fortis', Regulation (EC) No 139/2004, Merger Procedure, Case No COMP / M.5384, Article 6(1) (b) in Conjunction with Article 6(2), 03 December 2008, Brussels.

European Commission (2008e) 'Proposal for a Directive of the European Parliament and of the Council on the Coordination of Laws, Regulations and Administrative Provisions Relating to Undertakings for Collective Investment in Transferable Securities (UCITS)', COM (2008) 458 final, 16 July 2008, Brussels.

European Commission (2009a) 'Communication from the Commission on the Treatment of Impaired Assets in the Community Banking Sector' OJ C72, 26 February 2009, Brussels.

European Commission (2009b) 'Communication from the Commission on the Return to Viability and the Assessment of Restructuring Measures in the Financial Sector in the Current Crisis Under the State Aid Rules', OJ C195, 19 August 2009, Brussels.

European Commission (2009c) 'Proposal for a Directive of the European Parliament and of the Council on Alternative Investment Fund Managers and Amending Directives 2004/39/EC and2009/ ... /EC', COM(2009) 207 final, 30 April 2009, Brussels.

European Commission (2010a) 'Proposal for a for a Directive of the European Parliament and of the Council Amending Directive 97/9/EC of the European Parliament and of the Council on Investor Compensation Schemes', COM(2010) 371 final, 12 April 2010, Brussels.

European Commission (2010b) 'Proposal for a Directive ... / ... /EU of the European Parliament and of the Council on Deposit Guarantee Schemes [recast]', COM(2010)368 final, 12 July 2010, Brussels.

European Commission (2010c) 'Commission Staff Working Document: Summary of the Impact Assessment. Accompanying Document to the Proposal for a Directive ... / ... /EU of the European Parliament and of the Council on Deposit

Guarantee Schemes (recast) and to the Report from the European Commission to the European Parliament and to the Council: Review of Directive 94/19/EC on Deposit Guarantee Schemes', SEC(2010) 834/2, Brussels.

European Commission (2010d) 'Commission Proposes Package to Boost Consumer Protection and Confidence in Financial Services', IP/10/918, 12 July 2010, Brussels.

European Commission (2010e) 'Communication from the Commission. Europe 2020: A Strategy for Smart, Sustainable and Inclusive Growth', COM (2010) 2020 final, 3 March 2010, Brussels.

European Commission (2010f) 'Proposal for a Council Decision of 27.4.2010 on Guidelines for the Employment Policies of the Member States – Part II of the Europe 2020 Integrated Guidelines', COM (2010) 193 final, 27 April 2010, Brussels.

European Commission (2010g) 'Communication from the Commission to the European Parliament, the Council, the European Economic and Social Committee and the Committee of the Regions, Annual Growth Survey: Advancing the EU's Comprehensive Response to the Crisis', COM(2011) 11 final, 12 January 2010, Brussels, http://ec.europa.eu/economy_finance/articles/eu_economic_situation/pdf/2011/com2011_11_en.pdf, last accessed 20 May 2013.

European Commission (2010h) .State of the Art. Overview of Concepts, Indicators and Methodologies Used for Analyzing the Social OMC. Deliverable 1 of the study 'Assessing the effectiveness and the impact of the Social OMC in preparation of the new cycle'. Brussels.

European Commission (2011a) 'Commission Communication on the Action Taken on Opinions and Resolutions Adopted by Parliament at the July 2011 Part-session: European Parliament Legislative Resolution on the Proposal for a Directive of the European Parliament and of the Council amending Directive 97/9/EC of the European Parliament and of the Council on Investor-compensation Schemes', European Parliament reference number A7–0167/2011 / P7-TA-PROV(2011)0313, 8 September 2011, Brussels.

European Commission (2011b) 'Commission Staff Working Paper Impact Assessment Vol. I. Accompanying the Document Proposal for a Regulation of the European Parliament and of the Council on Applying a Scheme of Generalised Tariff Preferences', SEC(2011) 536 final, 10 May 2011, Brussels.

European Commission (2012a) 'Fiscal Union', MEMO/12/483, 25 June 2012, Brussels.

European Commission (2012b) 'Alert Mechanism Report 2013', COM(2012) 751 final, 28 November 2012, Brussels.

European Commission (2012c) *Employment and Social Developments in Europe in 2011*. Luxembourg: Publications Office of the European Union.

European Commission (2012d) 'Communication from the Commission. Annual Growth Survey', COM (2012) 815 final, 23 November 2012, Brussels.

European Commission (2013a) *Industrial Relations in Europe 2012*. Luxembourg: Publications Office of the European Union.

European Commission (2013b) 'Communication from the Commission to the European Parliament, the Council, the European Economic and Social Committee and the Committee of the Regions. Towards Social Investment for Growth and Cohesion – Including Implementing the European Social Fund 2014–2020', COM(2013) 83 final, 20 February 2013, Brussels.

European Commission (2013c) http://ec.europa.eu/trade/, last accessed 5 May 2013.

European Commission (2013d) 'Beyond the Six Pack and Two Pack: Economic Governance Explained', Memo/13/318, 10 April 2013, Brussels, http://europa.eu/rapid/press-release_MEMO-13-318_en.htm, last accessed on 30 April 2013.

European Commission (2013e) 'Commission Takes Steps Under the Excessive Deficit Procedure', Memo, 29 May 2013, Brussels.

European Commission (2013f) Towards Social Investment for Growth and Cohesion – Including Implementing the European Social Fund 2014–2020, Brussels, 20.2.2013 COM(2013) 83 final.

European Council (1962) 'Regulation No 17: First Regulation implementing Articles 85 and 86 of the Treaty', OJ 058, 10 July 1962, Brussels.

European Council (2000) Lisbon European Council, Presidency Conclusions, 23–24 March.

European Council (2001) Stockholm European Council, Presidency Conclusions, 23–24 March.

European Council (2003) 'Council Regulation (EC) No 1/2003 on the Implementation of the Rules on Competition Laid down in Articles 81 and 82 of the Treaty', OJ L1, 3 January 2003, Brussels.

European Council (2005) 'Council Regulation (EC) No980/2005 of June 2005: Applying a Scheme of Generalised Tariff Preferences', Official Journal of the European Union, L169/1, 30 June 2005, Brussels.

European Parliament (2008a) 'Resolution of 23 September 2008 with recommendations to the Commission on hedge funds and private equity', 2007/2238(INI).

European Parliament (2008b) 'Resolution of 23 September 2008 with recommendation to the Commission on transparency of institutional investors', 2007/2239(INI).

European Parliament (2011) 'Amending Directive 97/9/EC on Investor Compensation Schemes (ICS): Safeguarding investors' interests by ensuring sound financing of ICS. Compilation of briefing notes', April, IP/A/ECON/NT/2010–15.

European Parliament and European Council (2011) 'Regulation (EU) No 1173/2011 of 16 November 2011, on the Effective Enforcement of Budgetary Surveillance in the Euro Area', Official Journal of the European Union, L306/1–7.

European Voice (2008a) 'EU Increases Deposit guarantees', 7 October.

European Voice (2008b) 'Commission presses for higher deposit guarantees', 15 October.

Eurostat (2012) News Release – Euro-Indicators, No. 101/2012, 02 July 2012, http://epp.eurostat.ec.europa.eu/statistics_explained/index.php/Unemployment_statistics#Further_Eurostat_information, last accessed on 22 July 2012.

Eurostat (2013), http://epp.eurostat.ec.europa.eu/portal/page/portal/eurostat/home/, last accessed on 20 May 2013.

Fabbrini, S. (2010) *Compound Democracies: Why the United States and Europe Are Becoming Similar*. Revised and updated edition. Oxford: Oxford University Press.

Fabbrini, S. (2012) 'After the Euro Crisis: The President of Europe. A New Paradigm for Increasing Legitimacy and Effectiveness in the EU', CEPS and EuropEos Commentary, 12, 1 June.

Fabbrini, S. (2013) 'The Outcome of Intergovernmentalism, the Euro Crisis and the Transformation of the European Union', in B. De Witte, A. Heritier and A. Trechsel (eds) *The Euro Crisis and the State of European Democracy*. Florence: European University Institute, Robert Schuman Centre for Advanced Studies.

Fajertag, G. and P. Pochet (2000) *Social Pacts in Europe – New Dynamics*. Brussels: ETUI.

Featherstone, K. and K. Dyson (1999) *The Road to Maastricht: Negotiating Economic and Monetary Union*. Oxford University Press.

Ferran, E. (2011) 'After the Crisis: The Regulation of Hedge Funds and Private Equity in the EU', *European Business Organization Law Review*, 12(3): 379–414.

Ferrera, M. (2005) *The Boundaries of Welfare. European Integration and the New Spatial Politics of Social Protection*. Oxford: Oxford University Press.

Ferrera, M., A. Hemerijck, and M. Rhodes (2000) 'The Future of Social Europe: Recasting Work and Welfare in the New Economy'. Report prepared for the Portuguese Presidency of the EU. Oeiras: Celta Editora.

Flassbeck, H. and C. Lapavitsas (2013). 'The Systemic Crisis of the Euro – True Causes and Effective Therapies', STUDIEN published by Rosa-Luxemburg-Stiftung, Berlin, May.

Foster, N. (2010) *EU Treaties and Legislation 2010–2011*. Oxford: Oxford University Press.

Fox, E.M. (1999) 'Antitrust Law on a Global Scale – Races up Down and Sideways', NYU Law School, Public Law Working Paper, 15 December.

Frankfurter Allgemeine Zeitung, various dates.

Freeman, R. (2006) 'Learning in Public Policy', in M. Moran, M. Rein and R.E. Goodin (eds) *Oxford Handbook of Public Policy*. Oxford: Oxford University Press.

Friends of Europe (2011) 'An 8-Point Strategy to Revitalize the EU', http://www.friendsofeurope.org, last accessed on 23 June 2013.

Future of Europe Group (2012) Final Report, 17 September 2012, http://www. auswaertiges-amt.de/cae/servlet/contentblob/626338/publicationFile/171838/ 120918-Abschlussbericht-Zukunftsgruppe.pdf, last accessed on 05 March 2014.

Gasiorek, M. (2010) 'Mid-term Evaluation of the EU's Generalised System of Preferences: Final Report', Centre for the Analysis of Regional Integration at Sussex, Report commissioned and financed by the Commission of the European Communities.

Gauer, C., D. Dalheimer, L. Kjolbye and E. de Smijter (2003) 'Regulation 1/2003: a modernised application of EC competition rules', Competition Policy Newsletter, No. 1, Spring.

Gebhard, C. (2011), 'Coherence', in C. Hill and M. Smith (eds) *International Relations and the European Union*. 2nd edition. Oxford: Oxford University Press.

Gerhardt, M. and K. Lannoo (2011) 'Options for Reforming Deposit Protection Schemes in the EU', Policy Brief, 4, European Credit Research Institute.

Goetschy, J. (2009) 'The Lisbon Strategy and Social Europe: Two Closely Linked Destinies' in M.J. Rodrigues (ed.), *Europe, Globalisation and the Lisbon Agenda*. Cheltenham: Edward Elgar.

Goetschy J. (2013) 'Crises Économiques et Europe Sociale : Quelles Rôles Pour l'UE' ? in J.L. De Meulemeester, J.C. Defraigne, D. Duez, and Y. Vanderborght (eds), *Les Modèles Sociaux en Europe. Quel Avenir Face à la Crise?* Bruxelles: Editions Bruylant.

Goetschy, J. and F Cochoy. (2009) 'La Construction de l'Europe Sociale: Créativité Institutionnelle Communautaire et Réalités Nationales', *Sociologie du Travail*, 51(4): 447–60.

Graziano, P. (2009) 'Bringing the Actors Back In. Europeanization and Domestic Policy Change: The Case of the European Employment Strategy in Italy and France', Working paper, Paris, PACTE – CNRS.

Gwiazda, A. (2011) 'The Europeanization of Flexicurity: The Lisbon Strategy's Impact on Employment Policies in Italy and Poland', *Journal of European Public Policy*, 18(4): 546–65.

Haas, E. (1968) *The Uniting of Europe*. 2nd edition. Stanford/CA: Stanford University Press.

Hacker, J. and P. Pierson (2010) 'Winner-Take-All-Politics. Public Policy, Political Organization, and the Precipitous Rise of Top Incomes in the United States', *Politics and Society*, 38(2): 152–204.

Hall, P. (1993) 'Policy Paradigms, Social Learning, and the State: The Case of Economic Policy Making in Britain', *Comparative Politics*, 25(3): 275–96.

Hall, P.A. and D. Soskice (2011) 'An Introduction to Varieties of Capitalism', in P.A. Hall and D. Soskice (eds), *Varieties of Capitalism. The Institutional Foundations of Comparative Advantage*. Oxford: Oxford University Press.

Hartlapp, M. (2009) 'Learning About Policy Learning. Reflections on the European Employment Strategy', European Integration Online Papers-Eiop, 13.

Häusermann, S. (2010) *The Politics of Welfare State Reform in Continental Europe: Modernization in Hard Times*. Cambridge: Cambridge University Press.

Heidenreich, M. and G. Bischoff (2008) 'The Open Method of Co-ordination: A Way to the Europeanization of Social and Employment Policies?', *Journal of Common Market Studies*, 46(3): 497–532.

Heidenreich, M. and J. Zeitlin (eds) (2009) *Changing European Employment and Welfare Regimes. The Influence of the Open Method of Coordination on National Reforms*. London: Routledge.

Heipertz, M. and A. Verdun (2010) *Ruling Europe: The Politics of the Stability and Growth Pact*. Cambridge: Cambridge University Press.

Helleiner, E. and S. Pagliari (2010) 'Between the Storms: Patterns in Global Financial Governance', in G. Underhill, J. Blom, and D. Mügge (eds), *Global Financial Governance Thirty Years On. From Reform to Crisis*. Cambridge: Cambridge University Press.

Hemerijck A. (2011) '21st Century Welfare Provision is More Than the "Social Insurance State": A Reply to Paul Pierson', University of Bremen: Centre for Social Policy Research (ZeS), ZeS-Arbeitspapier, 03/2011.

Hemerijck, A. (2013) *Changing Welfare States*. Oxford: Oxford University Press.

Hemerijck. A. and F. Vandenbroucke (2012) 'Social Investment and the Euro Crisis: The Necessity of a Unifying Concept', *Intereconomics. Review of European Economic Policy*, 47(4): 200–206.

Héritier, A. (2004) 'New Modes of Governance in Europe: Increasing Political Capacity and Policy Effectiveness?', in T.A. Börzel and R.A. Cichowski (eds), *The State of the European Union*. Oxford: Oxford University Press.

Héritier, A. and M. Rhodes (eds) (2010) *New Modes of Governance in Europe*. London: Palgrave Macmillan.

Hervey, T.K. (2008). 'The European Union's Governance of Health Care and the Welfare Modernization Agenda', *Regulation and Governance*, 2(1): 103–20.

Hillion, C. (2008) 'Tous Pour Un, Un Pour Tous! Coherence in the External Relations of the European Union', in Cremona, Marise, *Developments in EU External Relations Law*, Oxford: Oxford University Press, 10–36.

Hix, S. and K. Goetz (2000) 'Introduction: European Integration and National Political Systems', *West European Politics, Special Issue on Europeanized Politics? European Integration and National Political Systems*, 23(4): 1–26.

Hodson, D. and I. Maher (2004) 'Soft Law and Sanctions: Economic Policy Co-ordination and Reform of the Stability and Growth Pact', *Journal of European Public Policy*, 11(5): 798–813.

Hoffmeister, F. (2008) 'Inter□Pillar coherence in the European Union's civilian crisis management', in Steven Blockmans, *The European Union and Crisis Management – Policy and Legal Aspects*. The Hague: T.M.C. Asser Press, 157–180.

Hollman, H.M. and W.E. Kovacic (2011) 'The International Competition Network: Its Past, Current and Future Role', *Minnesota Journal of International Law*, 20(4): 274–323.

Hooghe, L. and G. Marks (2009) 'A Postfunctionalist Theory of European Integration: from Permissive Consensus to Constraining Dissensus', *British Journal of Political Science*, 39(1): 1–23.

Howarth, D. (2007) 'Making and Breaking the Rules: French Policy on EU "Gouvernement Économique"', *Journal of European Public Policy*, 14(7): 1061–78.

Hueglin, O.T. and A. Fenna (2006) *Comparative Federalism – A Systematic Inquiry*. Quebec City: Broadview Press Ltd.

Huybrechts A. and R. Peels (2009) 'Civil society and EU development policies in Africa and Latin America', in Orbie J. and Tortell L. (eds), *The European Union and the Social Dimension of Europeanization: How the EU Influences the World*. Oxon: Routledge.

Idema, T. and D.R. Kelemen (2006) 'New Modes of Governance, the Open Method of Co-ordination and other Fashionable Red Herring', *Perspectives on European Politics and Society* 7(1): 108–23.

Jabko, Nicolas (1999) 'In the Name of the Market: How the European Commission Paved the Way for Monetary Union', *Journal of European Public Policy*, 6(3): 475–95.

Jacobsson, K. and C. West (2009) 'Joining the European Employment Strategy: Europeanization of Labour Market Policy Making in the Baltic States', in M. Heidenreich and J. Zeitlin (eds), *Changing European Employment and Welfare Regimes. The Influence of the Open Method of Coordination on National Reforms*. London: Routledge.

Jæger, M. and J. Kvist (2003) 'Pressures on State Welfare in Post-industrial Societies: Is More or Less Better?', *Social Policy and Administration*, 37(6): 555–72.

Jaumotte, F. (2003) 'Female Labour Force Participation: Past Trends and Main Determinants in OECD Countries', OECD Working Paper 376, Economics Department.

Jepsen, M. and A. Serrano Pascual (2005) 'The European Social Model: An Exercise in De-construction', *Journal of European Social Policy*, 15(3): 231–45.

Johansson, K.M. and T. Raunio, (2001) 'Partisan Responses to Europe: Comparing Finnish and Swedish Political Parties', *European Journal of Political Research*, 39(2): 225–49.

Kazepov, Y. (2010) *Rescaling Social Policies: Towards Multilevel Governance in Europe*. Farnham: Ashgate.

Keohane, R. (1984) *After Hegemony: Cooperation and Discord in the World Political Economy*. Princeton: Princeton University Press.

Koo, R. (2002) *The Holy Grail of Macroeconomics. Lessons from Japan's Great Recession*. Singapore: Wiley and Sons.

Krellinger, V. (2012) 'The Making of a New Treaty: Six Rounds of Political Bargaining', Notre Europe, Policy Brief, 32, February.

Kroes, N. (2008) 'EU Competition Rules – Part of the Solution for Europe's Economy', Speech, European Competition Day, Paris, SPEECH/08/625, 18 November.

Kroes, N. (2009) 'How Can the EU Contribute to a More Prosperous Future?' Speech to the Conference on Competition Policy after the Credit Crunch, Chatham House, 26 June.

Kroes, N. (2010) 'Competition Policy and the Crisis – the Commission's Approach to Banking and Beyond', Competition Policy Newsletter, 1: 3–6.

Kröger, S. (2009a) 'The Effectiveness of Soft Governance in the Field of European Anti-poverty Policy: Operationalization and Empirical Evidence', *Journal of Comparative Policy Analysis: Research and Practice*, 11(2): 197–211.

Kröger, S. (2009b) 'The Open Method of Coordination: Underconceptualisation, Overdetermination, Depoliticisation and Beyond', European Integration online Papers (EIoP), 13(5): http://eiop.or.at/eiop/index.php/eiop/article/view/2009_005a, last accessed 30 June 2013.

Kvist, J. (2013), 'The Post-crisis European Social Model: Developing or Dismantling Social Investments?' *Journal of International and Comparative Social Policy*, 29(1): 91–107.

Ladrech, R. (2009) 'Europeanization and Political Parties', *Living Reviews in European Governance*, 4/1, http://europeangovernance.livingreviews.org/Articles/lreg-2009-1, last accessed on 20 September 2010.

Lavenex, S. (2004) 'EU External Governance in "Wider Europe"', *Journal of European Public Policy*, 11(4): 680–700.

Lavenex, S. and F. Schimmelfennig (2009) 'EU Rules Beyond EU Borders: Theorising External Governance in European Politics', *Journal of European Public Policy*, 16(6): 791–812.

Le Figaro (2012) 'Vingt ans après Maastricht, les Français doutent toujours', 16 September 2012, http://www.lefigaro.fr/politique/2012/09/16/01002-2012 0916ARTFIG00197-vingt-ans-apres-maastricht-les-francais-doutent-toujours. php, last accessed 23 September 2012.

Lefkofridi, Z. (2009) 'National Party Response to European Integration: A Theoretical Framework and Evidence from Greece (1974–2007)', PhD Thesis, University of Vienna.

Lefkofridi, Z. and S. Kritzinger (2008) 'Battles Fought in the EP Arena: Developments in National Parties' Euro-manifestos', *Austrian Journal of Political Science*, 37(3): 273–96.

Lehmkuhl, D. (2008) 'Cooperation and Hierarchy in EU Competition Policy', in I. Tömmel and A. Verdun (eds), *Innovative Governance in the European Union: The Politics of Multilevel Policymaking*. Boulder, CO: Lynne Rienner.

Leibfried, S. (2005) 'Social Policy', in H. Wallace, W. Wallace, and M. Pollack (eds), *Policy-Making in the European Union*. Oxford: Oxford University Press.

Leschke, J. (2012) 'Has the Economic Crisis Contributed to More Segmentation in Labour Market and Welfare Outcomes?', Working paper 2012.02, Brussels: ETUI.

Lewis, J. (2006) *Children, Changing Families and Welfare States*. Cheltenham: Edward Elgar.

Liddell-Hart, B.H. (1967) *Strategy*. London: Faber and Faber Ltd.

Lodge, M. (2007) 'Comparing Non-Hierarchical Governance in Action: the Open Method of Co-ordination in Pensions and Information Society', *Journal of Common Market Studies*, 45(2): 343–65.

Lopez-Santana, M. (2009) 'Having a Say and Acting: Assessing the Effectiveness of the European Employment Strategy as an Intra-governmental Coordinative Instrument', European Integration Online Papers-Eiop 13.

Lowe, P. (2009) 'State Aid Policy in the Context of the Financial Crisis' Competition Policy Newsletter, 2: 3–8.

Lundvall, B.-Å. and M. Tomlinson (2002) 'International Benchmarking as a Policy Learning Tool', in M.J. Rodrigues (ed.) *The New Knowledge Economy in Europe: A Strategy for International Competitiveness and Social Cohesion*. Cheltenham: Edward Elgar.

McDermott (2009) Draft AIFM Directive Constricts Hedge Funds, available at: http://www.mwe.com/publications, last accessed 6 April 2013.

Maduro, M.P. (2012) 'A New Governance for the European Union and the Euro: Democracy and Justice', Report, Brussels: European Parliament, Directorate General for Internal Policies.

Maher, I. (2002) 'Competition Law in the International Domain: Networks as a New Form of Governance', *Journal of Law and Society*, 29(1): 111–36.

Mahon, R. (2006) 'The OECD and the Work/Family Reconciliation Agenda: Competing Frames', in J.E. Lewis (ed.), *Children, Changing Families and Welfare States*. Cheltenham: Edward Elgar.

Mailand, M. (2008) 'The Uneven Impact of the European Employment Strategy on Member States Employment Policies: A Comparative Analysis', *Journal of European Social Policy*, 18(4): 353–65.

Mailand, M. (2009) 'North, South, East, West: The Implementation of the European Employment Strategy in Denmark, the UK, Spain, and Poland', in M. Heidenreich and J. Zeitlin (eds), *Changing European Employment and Welfare Regimes. The Influence of the Open Method of Coordination on National Reforms*. London: Routledge.

Mair, P. (2000) 'The Limited Impact of Europe on National Party Systems', *West European Politics*, 23(4): 27–51.

Mair, P. (2007) 'Political Opposition and the European Union', *Government and Opposition*, 42(1): 1–17.

Mair, P. and I. Van Biezen, (2001) 'Party Membership in Twenty European Democracies, 1980–2000', *Party Politics*, 7(1): 5–21.

Majone, G. (2005) *Dilemmas of European Integration. The Ambiguities and Pitfalls of Integration by Stealth*. Oxford, Oxford University Press.

March, J.G. (1991) 'Exploration and Exploitation in Organizational Learning', *Organization Science*, 2(1): 71–87.

March, J.G. and J.P. Olsen (1989) *Rediscovering Institutions: The Organizational Basis of Politics*. N.Y.: Free Press.

Martin, A. and G. Ross (2004) *Euros and Europeans: Monetary Integration and European Model of Society*. Cambridge: Cambridge University Press.

Martiniszyn, M. (2013) 'European Commission Against Gazprom: An Analysis of the Contentious Issues', Paper presented at the EUSA Conference, Baltimore, 8–10 May.

Marzinotto B., G. Wolff and M. Hallerberg (2012) *An Assessment of the European Semester, Study for the European Parliament*. Brussels: Bruegel.

Mattila, M. and T. Raunio (2012) 'Drifting Further Apart: National Parties and their Electorates on the EU Dimension', *West European Politics*, 35(3): 589–606.

Mearsheimer, J. (1990) 'Back to the Future: Instability in Europe After the Cold War', *International Security*, 15(1): 5–56.

Meunier, S. and K. Nikolaïdis (2011) 'The European Union as a Trade Power', in Christopher Hill and Michael Smith (eds), *International Relations and the European Union*. Oxford: Oxford University Press.

Moravcsik, A. (2007) 'The European Constitutional Settlement', in S. Meunier and K.R. McNamara (eds), *Making History: European Integration and Institutional Change at Fifty, The State of European Union*. Vol. 8, Oxford: Oxford University Press.

Morel, N., B. Palier, and J. Palme, (eds) (2012) *Towards a Social Investment State? Ideas, Policies and Challenges*. Bristol: The Policy Press.

Morgan, E. and L. McGowan (2013) 'Explaining Changes in European Union Cartel Enforcement: the Americanization Factor', unpublished paper.

Mosher, J.S. and D.M. Trubek (2003) 'Alternative Approaches to Governance in the EU: EU Social Policy and the European Employment Strategy', *Journal of Common Market Studies*, 41(1): 63–88.

Mügge, D. (2011) 'Limits of Legitimacy and the Primacy of Politics in Financial Governance', *Review of International Political Economy*, 18(1): 52–74.

Mügge, D. and B. Stellinga (2010) 'Absent Alternatives and Insider Interests in Postcrisis Financial Reform', *Der Moderne Staat: Zeitschrift für Public Policy, Recht und Management*, 3(2): 321–38.

Mundell, R.A. (1961) 'A Theory of Optimum Currency Areas', *American Economic Review*, 51(4): 657–65.

Niemann, A. and P. Schmitter (2009) 'Neofunctionalism', in A. Wiener and T. Diez (eds), *Theories of European Integration*. 2nd edition. Oxford: Oxford University Press, 45–66.

Nitsch, V. and M. Pisu (2008) 'Scalpel, Please! Dissecting the Euro's Effect on Trade', Zurich and Brussels: ETH Zurich and National Bank of Belgium.

Novitz, T. (2009) 'In Search of a Coherent Social Policy: EU Import and Export of ILO Standards', in J. Orbie and L. Tortell (eds), *The European Union and the Social Dimension of Europeanization: How the EU Influences the World*. Oxon: Routledge.

NRC Handelsblad, various dates.

OECD (2008) *Growing Unequal*. Paris: OECD.

OECD (2011) *Doing Better for Families*. Paris: OECD.

Orbie, J. and O. Babarinde (2008) 'The Social Dimension of Globalization and EU Development Policy: Promoting Core Labour Standards and Corporate Social Responsibility', *Journal of European Integration*, 30(3): 459–77.

Orbie, J. and L. Tortell, (2009) 'From the Social Clause to the Social Dimension of Globalization', in J. Orbie and L. Tortell (eds), *The European Union and the Social Dimension of Europeanization: How the EU Influences the World*. Oxon: Routledge.

Orbie, J., L. Tortell, R. Kissack, S. Gstoehl, J. Wouters and N. Hachez (2009) 'Journal of European Social Policy Symposium: The European Union's Global Social Role', *Journal of European Social Policy*, 19(2): 99–116.

Orloff, A. (2009) 'Gendering the Comparative Analysis of Welfare States: An Unfinished Agenda', *Sociological Theory*, 27(3): 317–43.

Orloff. A. (2010) 'Gender', in F.G. Castles, S. Leibfried, J. Lewis, H. Obinger and C. Pierson, *The Oxford Handbook of the Welfare States*. Oxford: Oxford University Press.

Ostrom, E. (1990) *Governing the Commons*. Cambridge: Cambridge University Press.

Padoa-Schioppa T. (1987) 'Efficiency, Stability and Equity: A Strategy for the Evolution of the Economic System of the European Community', II/49/87, Brussels: European Commission.

Panagariya, A. (2002) 'EU Preferential Trade Agreements and Developing Countries', *The World Economy*, 25(10): 1415–32.

Pennings, P. (2006) 'An Empirical Study of the Europeanization of National Party Manifestos, 1960–2003', *European Union Politics*, 7(2): 257–70.

Pierson, P. (2001) 'Coping With Permanent Austerity – Welfare State Restructuring in Affluent Societies', in P. Pierson (ed.), *The New Politics of the Welfare State*. Oxford: Oxford University Press.

Pierson, P. (2011) 'The Welfare State Over the Very Long Run', ZeS-Working Paper, 02/2011.

Piris, J.-C. (2012) *The Future of Europe: Towards a Two-Speed EU?* Cambridge: Cambridge University Press.

Pisani-Ferry, J. (2013) 'Gli Errori Compiuti Dalla Troika', Il Sole 24 Ore, 8 June 2013.

Pochet, P. (2010) 'What's Wrong with EU2020?', ETUI Policy Brief 2/2010, Brussels: ETUI.

Poguntke, Th., N. Aylott, E. Carter, R. Ladrech and K.R. Luther (2007) *The Europeanization of National Political Parties: Power and Organizational Adaptation*. London and New York: Routledge.

Posner, Elliot and Nicolas Véron (2010) 'The EU and Financial Regulation: Power Without Purpose?', *Journal of European Public Policy*, 17(3): 400–15.

Price, V. and D. Tewksbury (1997) 'News Values and Public Opinion: A Theoretical Account of Media Priming and Framing. In Advances in Persuasion', in G.A. Barnett and F. J. Boster (eds), *Progress in the Communication Sciences*, vol. 13. Greenwich CT: Ablex Publishing Corporation.

Puetter, U. (2006) *The Eurogroup: How a Secretive Circle of Finance Ministers Shape European Economic Governance*. Manchester: Manchester University Press.

Puetter, U. (2012) 'Europe's Deliberative Intergovernmentalism: the Role of the Council and European Council in EU Economic Governance', *Journal of European Public Policy*, 19(2): 161–78.

Quaglia, L. (2011) 'The "Old" and "New" Political Economy of Hedge Fund Regulation in the European Union', *West European Politics*, 34(4): 665–82.

Radaelli, C.M. (2003a) *The Open Method of Coordination: A New Governance Architecture for the European Union*. Stockholm: SIEPS (Swedish Institute for European Policy Studies).

Radaelli, C. (2003b) 'The Europeanization of Public Policy', in Featherstone, K. and C. Radaelli (eds), *The Politics of Europeanization*. Basingstoke: Palgrave.

Radaelli, C.M. (2008) 'Europeanization, Policy Learning, and New Modes of Governance', *Journal of Comparative Policy Analysis: Research and Practice*, 10(3): 239–54.

Reding, V. (2012a) 'A Vision for Post-crisis Europe: A Political Union', http://ec. europa.eu/commission_2010-2014/reding/eufuture/index_en.htm, last accessed on 3 March 2013.

Reding V. (2012b) 'Observations on the EU Charter of Fundamental Rights and the Future of the European Union', XXV Congress of FIDE (Fédération Internationale pour le Droit Européen), Tallinn, 31 May 2012, European Commission SPEECH 12/403.

Reding, V. (2012c) 'A New Deal for Europe', Deutsche Bank's 13th Women in European Business Conference, Frankfurt, 14 March 2012, European Commission SPEECH/12/184.

Reif, K-H, and H. Schmitt (1980) 'Nine Second-Order National Elections – A Conceptual Framework for the Analysis of European Election Results', *European Journal of Political Research*, 8(1): 3–44.

Reynolds, M., S. Macrory and M. Chowdhury (2009–10) 'EU Competition policy in the Financial Crisis: Extraordinary Measures', *Fordham International Law Journal*, 33(6): 1670–737.

Ricard-Nihoul, G. (2012) *Pour une Fédération Européenne d'États-nations – La Vision de Jacques Delors Revisitée*. Bruxelles: Larcier.

Riese, H. (2004) 'Money, Development and Economic Transformation. Selected Essays by Hajo Riese', in J. Hölscher and H. Tomann (eds), *Money, Development and Economic Transformation*. Basingstoke, UK and New York: Palgrave.

Rodrigues, M.J. (ed.) (2002) *A New Knowledge Economy for Europe*. Cheltenham: Edward Elgar.

Rodrigues, M.J. (ed.) (2009) *Europe, Globalization and the Lisbon Agenda.* Cheltenham: Edward Elgar.

Rodrigues, M.J. (2013) 'The Eurozone Crisis and the Transformation of the EU Economic Governance. From Internal Policies to External Action'. mimeo.

Rose, A.K. (1999) 'Does a Currency Union Boost International Trade?', http://faculty.haas.berkeley.edu/arose/CMR.pdf, last accessed on 31 July 2013.

Sabel, C. (1994) 'Learning by Monitoring: the Institutions of Economic Development, 1994', in N.J. Smelser and R. Swedberg (eds), *The Handbook of Economic Sociology.* Ithaca, Princeton University Press.

Sabel, C. and J. Zeitlin (2008) 'Learning from Difference: The New Architecture of Experimentalist Governance in the EU', *European Law Journal*, 14(3): 271–327.

Sabel, C. and J. Zeitlin (eds) (2010) *Experimentalist Governance in the European Union. Towards a New Architecture.* Oxford: Oxford University Press.

Santos, J. and S. Peristiani (2011) 'Why Do Central Banks Have Discount Windows?', Federal Reserve Bank of New York; http://libertystreeteconomics.newyorkfed.org/2011/03/why-do-central-banks-have-discount-windows.html, last accessed on 31 July 2013.

Schammo, P. (2012) 'EU Day-to-Day Supervision or Intervention-based Supervision: Which Way Forward for the European System of Financial Supervision?', *Oxford Journal of Legal Studies*, 32(4): 771–97.

Scharpf, F. (1999) *Governing in Europe: Effective and Democratic?* Oxford: Oxford University Press.

Scharpf, F. (2002) 'The European Social Model', *Journal of Common Market Studies*, 40(4): 645–70.

Scharpf, F. (2009) 'Europe's Neo-liberal Bias', in A. Hemerijck, B. Knapen, and E. van Doorne (eds), *Aftershocks. Economic Crisis and Institutional Choice.* Amsterdam: Amsterdam University Press.

Scharpf, F. (2011) 'Monetary Union, Fiscal Crisis and the Preemption of Democracy', Discussion Paper 11/11, Cologne: Max Planck Institute for the Study of Societies.

Schäuble, W. (2011) 'Why Austerity is the Only Cure for the Eurozone', *The Financial Times*, 5 September 2011.

Schelling, T.C. (1966) *Arms and Influence.* New Haven: Yale University Press.

Schimmelfennig, F. (2004), 'Liberal Intergovernmentalism', in A. Wiener and T. Diez (eds), *European Integration Theory.* Oxford: Oxford University Press.

Schimmelfennig, F. (2010), 'Europeanization Beyond the Member States', paper for Zeitschrift für Staats – und Europawissenschaften, http://www.eup.ethz.ch/people/schimmelfennig/publications/10_ZSE_Europeanization__manu script_.pdf, last accessed 5 November 2012.

Schmid, G. (2008) *Full Employment in Europe: Managing Labour Market Transition and Risks.* Cheltenham: Edward Elgar.

Schmidt, V.A. (2002) *The Futures of European Capitalism.* Oxford: Oxford University Press.

Schmitter, P.C. (1970) 'A Revised Theory of Regional Integration', *International Organization*, 24(4): 836–68.

Schmitter, P.C. (1996) 'Imagining the Future of the Euro-Polity with the Help of New Concepts', in G. Marks, F.W. Scharpf, P.C. Schmitter, W. Streeck (eds), *Governance in the European Union*. London: Sage.

Schmitter, P.C. (2000) *How to Democratize the European Union ... and Why Bother?* Lanham: Rowman and Littlefield.

Schmitter, P.C. (2012) 'European Disintegration? A Way Forward', *Journal of Democracy*, 23(4): 39–48.

Schneider, F.B. (2012) 'Human Rights Conditionality in the EU's Generalised System of Preferences: Legitimacy, Legality and Reform', Heft 3, ZEuS.

Senden, L. (2005) 'Soft Law, Self-regulation and Co-regulation in European Law: Where Do They Meet?', *Electronic Journal of Comparative Law*, 9(1), http://www.ejcl.org/, last accessed on 13 May 2013.

Sevenska Dagbladet, various dates.

Singer, D. (2007) *Regulating Capital. Setting Standards for the International Financial System*. Ithaca: Cornell University Press.

Sinn, H.-W. (2013) 'Austerity, Growth and Inflation. Remarks on the Eurozone's Unresolved Competitiveness Problem', Cesifo Working Paper, 4086, January.

Sinn, H.W. and T. Wollmershaeuser (2011) 'TARGET Loans, Current Account Balances and Capital Flows: The ECB's Rescue Facility', NBER Working Paper Series, 17626, http://www.nber.org/papers/w17626, last accessed on 31 July 2013.

Smismans, S. (2012) (ed.) *The European Union and Industrial Relations – New Procedures, New Context*. Manchester: Manchester University Press.

Smith, M.P. (1997) 'The Commission Made Me Do It. The European Commission as a Strategic Asset in Domestic Politics', in N. Nugent (ed.), *At the Heart of the Union. Studies of the European Commission*. London: Macmillan.

Standard Eurobarometer (2011) Public Opinion in the European Union (Aggregate Report) No. 76, http://ec.europa.eu/public_opinion/archives/eb/eb76/eb76_en.htm, last accessed 18 September 2012.

Standard Eurobarometer (2012) Public Opinion in the European Union (First results). No. 77, http://ec.europa.eu/public_opinion/archives/eb/eb77/eb77_en.htm, last accessed 18 September 2012.

Strache, H-Ch. (2010) 'Entwicklung Europas', FPÖ Press Conference, 24 June 2010, http://www.youtube.com/watch?v=C9cvjkeGAkg, last accessed 29 August 2012.

Streeck, W. (2011) 'The Crises of Democratic Capitalism' *New Left Review*, 71, Sept/Oct 2011: 5–29.

Süddeutsche Zeitung, various dates.

Tabb, W.K. (2012) *The Restructuring of Capitalism in Our Time*. New York: Columbia University Press.

Tarullo, D.K. (2000) 'Norms and Institutions in Global Competition Policy', *The American Journal of International Law*, 94(3): 478–504.

Temin, P. (1989) *Lessons from the Great Depression*. Cambridge: MIT Press.

The Guardian, various dates.

The Warwick Commission on International Financial Reform (ed.) (2009) *In Praise of Unlevel Playing Fields*. Coventry: University of Warwick.

Thomassen, J. and H. Schmitt (1999) 'Issue Congruence', in H. Schmitt and J. Thomassen (eds), *Political Representation and Legitimacy in the European Union*. Oxford: Oxford University Press.

Tranholm-Schwarz, B., P. Ohrlander, B. Zanettin, M. Campo and G. Siotis (2009) 'The Real Economy – Challenges for Competition Policy in Periods of Retrenchment', *Competition Policy Newsletter*, 1: 3–6.

Trubek, D.M. and L. Trubek (2005) 'Hard and Soft Law in the Construction of Social Europe: The Role of the Open Method of Coordination', *European Law Journal*, 11(3): 343–64.

Van der Eijk, C. and M.N. Franklin (2004) 'Potential for Contestation on European Matters at National Elections in Europe', in G. Marks, and M.R. Steenbergen (eds), *European Integration and Political Conflict*. Cambridge: Cambridge University Press.

Van Rompuy, H. (2012) 'Towards a Genuine Economic and Monetary Union', Report by the President of the European Council, EUCO 120/12, 26 June 2012, Brussels.

Van Waarden, F. and M. Drahos (2002) 'Courts and (Epistemic) Communities in the Convergence of Competition Policies', *Journal of European Public Policy*, 9(6): 913–34.

Vandenberghe, J. (2008) 'On Carrots and Sticks: The Social Dimension of EU Trade Policy', *European Foreign Affairs Review*, 13(4): 561–81

Vandenbroucke, F. (2012) 'Europe: The Social Challenge. Defining the Union's Social Objective is a Necessity Rather than a Luxury', OSE paper series, 11.

Vandenbroucke, F., A. Hemerijck, and B. Palier, (2011) 'The EU Needs a Social Investment Pact', OSE Paper Series, Opinion Paper 5.

Verdun, A. (2003) 'La Nécessité d'un "Gouvernement Économique" Dans Une UEM Asymétrique', *Politique européenne*, 10(2): 11–32. www.cairn.info/revue-politique-europeenne-2003-2-page-11.htm, last accessed on 31 July 2013.

Viebrock, E. and J. Clasen (2009) 'Flexicurity and Welfare Reform', *Socio-Economic Review* 7(2): 305–31.

Visser, J. (2013) 'Wage Bargaining Institutions – from Crisis to Crisis', European Economy, Economic Papers 488.

Vitols, S. (2001) 'Varieties of Corporate Governance: Comparing Germany and UK', in P.A. Hall and D. Soskice (eds), *Varieties of Capitalism. The Institutional Foundations of Comparative Advantage*. Oxford: Oxford University Press.

Volkskrant, various dates.

Von Schöppenthau, P. (1998). 'Social Clause: Effective Tool or Social Fig Leaf?', *European Retail Digest*, 20: 44–5.

Waller, S.W. (1999) 'An International Common Law of Antitrust', *New England Law Review*, 34(1): 163–71.

Warwick Commission on International Financial Reform (ed.) (2009) 'In Praise of Unlevel Playing Fields'. Coventry: University of Warwick.

Weishaupt, T. (2011) *From the Manpower Revolution to the Activation Paradigm: Explaining Institutional Continuity and Change in an Integrating Europe.* Amsterdam: Amsterdam University Press.

White, L. (2009) 'The Credit-Rating Agencies and the Sub-Prime Debacle', *Critical Review*, 21(2–3): 389–99.

Wigger, A and H. Buch-Hansen (2013) 'Explaining (Missing) Regulatory Paradigm Shifts: EU Competition Regulation in Times of Economic Crisis', *New Political Economy*, 19(1): 113–37.

Wigger, A. and A. Nölke (2007) 'Enhanced Roles of Private Actors in EU Business Regulation and the Erosion of Rhenish Capitalism: The Case of Antitrust Enforcement', *Journal of Common Market Studies*, 45(2): 487–13.

Wilks, S. (2005) 'Agency Escape: Decentralization or Dominance of the European Commission in the Modernization of Competition Policy?', *Governance*, 18(3): 431–52.

Wilks, S. (2009) 'The Impact of the Recession on Competition Policy: Amending the Economic Constitution', *International Journal of the Economics of Business*, 16(3): 269–88.

Will, M. and K. Maskus (2001) 'Core Labour Standards and Competitiveness: Implications for Global Trade Policy', *Review of International Economics*, 9(2): 317–28.

Wincott, D. (2001) 'Looking Forward or Harking Back? The Commission and the Reform of Governance in the European Union', *Journal of Common Market Studies*, 39(5): 897–911.

Witt, A. (2012) 'Public Policy Goals Under EU Competition Law – Now is the Time to Set the House in Order', *European Competition Journal*, 8(3): 443–71.

Woll, Cornelia (2012) 'Lobbying under Pressure: The Effect of Salience on European Union Hedge Fund Regulation', *Journal of Common Market Studies*, 51(3): 555–72.

World Trade Organisation (2013) 'Text of the July Package – The General Council's Post Cancún Decision', 1 August 2004, http://www.wto.org/english/tratop_e/dda_e/draft_text_gc_dg_31july04_e.htm, last accessed 30 June 2013.

Xiarchogiannopoulou, E. and D. Tsarouhas (forthcoming) 'The EU Actorness in the ILO and the Diffusion of Flexicurity: A Case of Emulation', in A. Orsini-Bled, *The Long-term Political Action of the EU With(in) International Organizations: A Framework for Analysis*. Farnham: Ashgate.

Yap, J. (2013) 'Beyond "Don't Be Evil": The European Union GSP+ Trade Preference Scheme and the Incentivisation of the Sri Lankan Garment Industry to Foster Human Rights', *European Law Journal*, 19(2): 283–301.

Yoshizawa H. (2011) 'How Does the ICN Accommodate its Increasing Diversity? Putting Benchmarking into Practice', GR:EEN-GEM Doctoral working paper series.

Zeitlin, J. (2010) 'Towards a Stronger OMC in a More Social Europe 2020: A New Governance Architecture for EU Policy Coordination', in E. Marlier and D. Natali (eds), *Europe 2020: Towards a More Social Europe?*. Brussels: Peter Lang.

Zeitlin, J. and M. Heidenreich (eds) (2009) *Changing European Employment and Welfare Regimes: The Influence of the Open Method of Coordination on National Reforms*. London: Routledge.

Zhou, W. and L. Guyvers (2011) 'Linking International Trade and Labour Standards: The Effectiveness of Sanctions Under the European Unions' GSP', *Journal of World Trade*, 45(1): 63–85.

Websites

http://ec.europa.eu/citizens-initiative/public/initiatives/ongoing, last accessed 08 May 2014.

http://ec.europa.eu/economy_finance/economic_governance/sgp/deficit/index_en.htm, last accessed 30 May 2013.

http://eiop.or.at/eiop/index.php/eiop/issue/view/30, last accessed 02 March 2013.

http://en.wikipedia.org/wiki/European_Fiscal_Compact, last accessed 31 July 2013.

http://www.faz.net/aktuell/wirtschaft/europas-schuldenkrise/vor-ezb-zinsentscheid-merkel-fuer-deutschland-muessten-zinsen-hoeher-sein-12161702.html, last accessed 31 July 2013.

http://www.faz.net/artikel/S30638/die-ergebnisse-des-gipfels-status-quo-und-stossgebete-30486686.html, last accessed 31 July 2013.

http://www.intereuro.eu, last accessed 23 June 2013.

http://www.nottinghamenterprise.com/gep/documents/seminars/2008/mauro-pisu.pdf, last accessed 31 July 2013.

http://www.welt.de/politik/deutschland/article109261951/Deutsche-glauben-nicht-mehr-an-Europa.html, last accessed 23 September 2012.

Index

women, labour market participation of 143, **144**, 146
Works Councils 129
World Trade Organisation (WTO) 36–7

Xiarchogiannopoulou, E. 201

Zeitlin, J. 45, 51
zone of indifference 13, **13**